The ClarisWorks Companion

Barrie Sosinsky

Hayden Books

The ClarisWorks Companion

Copyright © 1994 Hayden Books
A Division of Prentice Hall Computer Publishing

All rights reserved. Printed in the United States of America. No part of this book may be used or reproduced in any form or by any means, or stored in a database or retrieval system, without prior written permission of the publisher except in the case of brief quotations embodied in critical articles and reviews. Making copies of any part of this book for any purpose other than your own personal use is a violation of United States copyright laws. For information, address Hayden Books, 201 West 103rd Street, Indianapolis, IN 46290.

Library of Congress Catalog No.: 93-80886

ISBN: 1-56830-083-2

This book is sold as is, without warranty of any kind, either expressed or implied. While every precaution has been taken in the preparation of this book, the publisher and author assume no responsibility for errors or omissions. Neither is any liability assumed for damages resulting from the use of the information or instructions contained herein. It is further stated that the publisher and author are not responsible for any damage or loss to your data or your equipment that results directly or indirectly from your use of this book.

96 95 94   4 3 2 1

Interpretation of the printing code: the rightmost double-digit number is the year of the book's printing; the rightmost single-digit number the number of the book's printing. For example, a printing code of 94-1 shows that the first printing of the book occurred in 1994.

Trademark Acknowledgments: All products mentioned in this book are either trademarks of the companies referenced in this book, registered trademarks of the companies referenced in this book, or neither. We strongly advise that you investigate a particular product's name thoroughly before you use the name as your own.Credits

Dedication

This book is dedicated to Alexandra Zoie Sosinsky.

Credits

Publisher	David Rogelberg
Acquisitions Editor	Karen Whitehouse
Development Editor	Dave Ciskowski
Production Editor	Rosie Blankenship
Copy Editor	Kandy Arnold
Technical Reviewer	Hans Hansen
Usability Reviewer	Dana Hansen
Cover Designer	Karen Ruggles
Interior Designers	Barbara Webster Alyssa Yesh
Indexer	Johnna VanHoose
Production Team	Gary Adair, Brad Chinn, Kim Cofer, Meshell Dinn, Mark Enochs, Stephanie Gregory, Jenny Kucera, Beth Rago, Marc Shecter, Kris Simmons, Greg Simsic, Carol Stamile, Robert Wolf

Composed in Times

About the Author

Barrie Sosinsky

Barrie Sosinsky began his computer career with Macintosh computers in 1987 when he bought a Macintosh II to start a small business. That computer continues to do yeoman's duty today in his office. He has written for the Boston Computer Society, various publishers, and several industry trade magazines as a freelance writer.

He is the author or co-author of eight computer books on areas such as integrated software, desktop publishing, systems software, and database management systems, some of which have appeared in multiple editions. This book is his ninth. Additionally, he has written over 70 articles on Macintosh and IBM PC based topics.

For several years now, Barrie Sosinsky has consulted companies and organizations on their needs for Macintosh based software and hardware solutions. Killer Apps, his company, specializes in software that runs on both the Macintosh and Windows operating systems across a network concurrently. In the jargon, Killer Apps builds cross-platform workgroup solutions. Killer Apps, Inc. is located in the town of Newton, Massachusetts, for which the Fig Newton was named. He can be reached by voice mail at (617)244-8100 or fax at (617)244-9078. Readers wishing to communicate with him through the ether may do so at his online addresses: CompuServe: 72020,2311, America Online: BASman, and at AppleLink: KillerApps.

The author would also like to thank Pam Borys for her contributions to several chapters in this book, including chapters on Macintosh basics, word processing, spreadsheets, and on making environments work together. Her input in regard to her experience as a professional trainer was invaluable in terms of making this book more readable to a beginning audience.

Pam Borys is the Director of Training for the Boston Computer Society's Macintosh Users Group, and the principal of Step-by-Step Training in Woburn MA, an organization that specializes in servicing individual's and organization's training needs. Should you require professional training or documentation, she can be reached at (617)935-0141. Her addresses in the ether world are: CompuServe: 72377,2325; AppleLink: P.A.M.Borys, and through the Boston Computer Society's MAC BBS in Cambridge MA. You can also reach the BCS MAC's BBS through its gateway on the Berkeley BMUG BBS.

To Our Readers

Dear Friend,

I want to thank you on behalf of everyone at Hayden Books for choosing the *ClarisWorks Companion* to learn how to get the most out of ClarisWorks. It can be challenging to learn something new without the right book to help you. We have carefully crafted this book to make it as helpful as possible.

What our readers think of our books is important to our ability to better serve you in the future. If you have any comments, no matter how great or small, we'd appreciate you taking the time to send us a note. Of course, great book ideas are always welcomed.

David Rogelberg
Publisher, Hayden Books and Adobe Press

David Rogelberg
Hayden Books
201 West 103rd Street
Indianapolis, Indiana 46290
(317) 581-3718 voice
(317) 581-4669 fax

Electronic mail addresses:

America Online: Hayden Bks
AppleLink: hayden.books
CompuServe: 76350,3014
Internet: hayden@hayden.com

Acknowledgments

The author wishes to acknowledge the help of many people who helped make this project possible. Hayden Books commissioned this book, and they had a clear vision of the need for it in the marketplace. Karen Whitehouse as acquisition editor was instrumental in this regard. Thanks go also to David Rogelberg, the Publisher of Hayden Books.

Thanks go to the many people at Hayden Books who helped edit and produce the book. Dave Ciskowski served as the development editor, and shepherded the book through writing and production. Special thanks go to the layout, proofreading, and indexing staff.

Parts of this book were written by Pam Borys. Her contributions were mentioned in the section "About the Author." It was a pleasure to work with her on this book. Her insight into important issues for beginning Macintosh users was invaluable.

In researching the book's potential, examining important features of ClarisWorks, and getting product to work with, Ynes Anderson at Claris was particularly helpful. Ynes was very candid about the positioning and strategy that Claris employs with ClarisWorks in order to reach its intended audience. I am grateful for the time she spent with me.

Claris is always a quality organization to work with, with high professional standards. Their success in marketing ClarisWorks against an entrenched product (Microsoft Works for the Macintosh) attests to their good work. Having such a fine program to write about made my job as an author all the easier. I also wish to thank Claris for making their artwork available for the book's cover.

My thanks go out to my literary agent Matt Wagner, and to Waterside Productions. Matt negotiated a good and fair deal for all concerned, with minimal fuss and bother. Waterside smoothes my path as I work in the rough and tumble world of computer trade books.

Finally, I recognize that all work takes time away from my family. To my wife Carol and my daughter Alexandra my apologies for missed evenings and nights at home.

Contents at a Glance

	Introduction	xvii
1	Getting Started With ClarisWorks	1
2	Some Basics	19
3	Working With Text in the Word Processor	43
4	Calculating Results With a Spreadsheet	85
5	Organizing Information With a Database	125
6	Adding Graphics to Your Work	165
7	The Communications Environment	197
8	Making It All Work Together	219
9	Advanced Topics	237
	Index	265

Table of Contents

1 Getting Started with ClarisWorks   1
What Is ClarisWorks? 2
   Why Buy Integrated Software? 2
   Understanding Integrated Software 3
The Six Major Environments 5
Installing ClarisWorks 13
Summary 17

2 Some Basics   19
Working With Files 20
   Creating Files 20
   Saving a File 22
   Save vs. Save As 24
   Opening and Closing Files 24
   Moving Information With Cut, Copy, and Paste 25
   Quitting ClarisWorks 26
Understanding and Navigating Your Screen 26
   Resize, Arrange, and Select Windows to
      Conveniently Organize Onscreen Information 27
   Zooming In and Out 29
   Splitting Windows 31
   Selecting, Hiding, and Showing Tools 32
   Working With the Shortcuts Palette 32
   Creating Frames 35
How to Print and Fax 37
   Selecting an Output Device 37
   Printing the Pages You Want 38
   Printer Options 39
Getting Help 39
   The ClarisWorks Help System 39
   System 7 Balloon Help 41
Summary 42

3 Working With Text in the Word Processor — 43

- What is a Word Processor? 44
  - Creating and Editing Text 44
  - Text Frames 45
  - Selecting and Moving Text 46
  - Basic Editing 47
  - Using the Cut, Copy, and Paste Commands to Edit Text 47
  - Don't Forget Undo! 47
  - Checking Your Spelling 48
  - Finding the Right Word: Using the Thesaurus 52
  - Searching and Replacing 53
  - Learning to Format Text with Style 55
  - About Characters, Paragraphs, and Document Formats 55
  - Character Formatting: Changing Fonts and Sizes 56
  - Using Formatting to Add Emphasis 57
  - Putting It All Together: Defining Character Styles to Create Consistent Documents 58
  - Using Define Styles to Change the Default Font 59
  - Paragraph formatting: Changing Margins and Indents 60
  - Using Tabs Instead of the Spacebar 62
  - Making Bulleted or Numbered Lists 63
  - Changing Alignment 65
  - Customizing the Ruler 66
  - Copying the Ruler to Duplicate Tabs and Indents 67
  - Document Formatting: Page Margins and Numbering 67
  - Adding Footnotes 67
- Working With an Outline 69
  - Creating New Topics 70
  - Rearranging the Contents of Your Document in the Outline View 70
  - Choosing a Structure for Your Outline 71
  - Formatting the Topic Labels of Your Outline 71
  - Viewing an Outline as Text 72

Incorporating Graphics in Your Writing 72
   Text-Embedded Graphics 72
   Graphic Objects 73
Composing a Page 74
   Composing With Frames 75
   Creating Columns 75
   Adding Page Breaks and Column Breaks 76
   Adding Tables 76
   Changing the Dimensions
      of Table Rows and Columns 77
   Changing How Many Rows
      and Columns Display 78
   Hiding Row and Column Headings 78
   Formatting a Table: Using Borders or Lines 79
   Entering Text in a Spreadsheet Frame 81
   Working With Headers and Footers 82
   Adding Page Numbers, Dates,
      and Times to Your Pages 83
Summary 84

4 Calculating Results With a Spreadsheet   85

What Is a Spreadsheet? 86
Using a Worksheet 86
Creating a Worksheet 87
   Entering and Editing Data 88
   Working With Cell Contents 89
   Moving About in Your Spreadsheet 89
Formatting Your Spreadsheet Document 90
   Setting the Margins of Your Spreadsheet ... 90
   Formatting Cell Width and Row Height 91
   Selecting a Range of Cells 92
   Formatting Cells 93
   Adding Borders and Solid Lines 94
   Changing Cell Alignment 95
   Formatting Numeric Entries in Spreadsheets 95
   Using the Time and Date Formats 97
Using Formulas 97
   Relative and Absolute Cell References 98
   Copying Formulas With the Fill Down
      and Fill Right Commands 98

Simple Formulas: Adding a Range of Cells 98
Simple Formulas: Multiplying, Dividing,
  or Subtracting a Range of Cells 99
How ClarisWorks Solves Formulas 100
More Complex Formulas: Using Functions 100
ClarisWorks Functions 101
Formula Errors 104
Using Variables Correctly 106
Changing How a Spreadsheet
  Displays Onscreen 106
Protecting Your Spreadsheet 107
Rearranging the Worksheet 107
Using the Cut, Copy, and Paste Commands
  in a Spreadsheet 108
Inserting and Deleting Rows and Columns 109
Inserting and Deleting Cells 109
Sorting 110
Transposing Columns and Rows 111
Charting Your Data 112
Creating a Chart 112
The Elements of a Chart 113
The Chart Types 113
Changing Chart Types 116
Adding a Chart Title 117
Customizing the Chart Axes 117
Customizing the Series Options 118
Changing the Data Range in a Chart 119
Printing a Spreadsheet 121
Printing a Range of Cells 121
Inserting Page Breaks 122
Summary 122

5 Organizing Information With a Database — 125

What Is a Database? 126
About Records and Fields 127
Views of a Database 128
Defining Fields 132
Field Types 135
Data Entry Options 136
Adding, Modifying, and Deleting Fields 139

    Working With Data 141
        Browsing Data in a Database 141
        Entering Data by Creating or Modifying
            Records 143
        Finding and Selecting Records 144
        Organizing Records by Sorting 148
    Using Layouts 149
        Creating and Deleting Layouts 150
        Parts of a Layout 155
        Adding and Removing Fields 157
        Using Columns 160
        Removing Unwanted Space 161
    Importing and Exporting Data 161
    Summary 164

6   Adding Graphics to Your Work   165

    Understanding the Difference Between Painted
        Images and Drawn Objects 166
    Working in the Drawing Environment 168
        About Objects 169
        Object Elements 170
        Creating Objects Using the Drawing Tools 171
        Manipulating Objects 175
        Adding Colors, Patterns,
            and Gradients to Objects 183
    Adding Pages to a Drawing Document 187
    Working in the Painting Environment 188
        The Painting Modes 188
        Using the Painting Tool Panel 189
        Editing Images 191
        Adding Colors, Patterns, and Gradients 193
    Summary 195

7   The Communications Environment   197

    A Communications Overview 198
        Modem Terms 198
        Communications Software 199
    Getting Connected using ClarisWorks 200
        Creating a Communications Document 200
        Setting Communications Settings
            and Preferences 203
        Capturing Text 207

	Receiving Calls	208
	Automating Your Sessions	209
	Uploading and Downloading Files	212
	Null-Modem Connections	214
	Terminal Emulation	216
Summary		218

8 Making It All Work Together — 219

Composing Compound Documents With Frames 220
    Text Frames 221
    Linking Text Frames to Create Newsletters 222
    Graphics Frames 224
    Spreadsheet Frames
       (Using Tables and Charts in Reports) 225
    Linking Frames 226
    Creating Master Pages 226
Importing Files and Inserting a Document
   Within Another Document 227
Automating Custom Printed Output 229
    About Mail Merge 230
Printing Envelopes 231
    Printing Mailing Labels 233
    Selective Merges and Sequenced
       Labels and Letters 235
    Summary 235

9 Advanced Topics — 237

Setting Preferences Within ClarisWorks 238
Using Macros to Automate Repetitive Tasks 240
    What Is a Macro? 240
    Recording and Editing a Macro 242
    Assigning Macros to the Shortcuts Palette 245
    Testing Your Macro 246
    Macro Ideas 247
Linking Information With Publish & Subscribe 248
    How to Publish a Document 249
    How to Subscribe to a Document 251
Using QuickTime Movies in Your Documents 253
    Creating a QuickTime Movie 255
    Playing Movies 256

Setting Up a Slide Show 258
   Ordering and Slides 259
   Display Options 260
   Slide Layers 261
   Running a Slide Show 262
Summary 263

Index   **265**

Introduction

Why This Book Was Written

The success of ClarisWorks is due to its clean logical design, and its well thought out feature set. Claris used the experience gleaned from creating software like MacWrite Pro, MacPaint, MacDraw Pro, FileMaker Pro, Impact, and Resolve to produce an integrated program that gives you the features you need to get your work done. ClarisWorks is a favorite program for new Macintosh (and Windows) users, and a good place to start to learn the fundamentals. You can then move up to the more powerful programs just mentioned, since many of the menus, dialog boxes, and interface elements have been adopted from Claris' more advanced programs.

ClarisWorks is a leader in the class of integrated software, and continues to receive accolades from many notable personal computer magazines and industry evaluators, such as: Macworld, MacUser, Byte, and PC Magazine. In 1992 Claris shipped one million copies of ClarisWorks, a remarkable achievement in a category that has for so long been neglected.

This book is written for new Macintosh users, to get you up and running with ClarisWorks in the shortest possible time. It's also written for experienced Macintosh users, who want a quick introduction to ClarisWorks. This book contains more task oriented-material than you will find in the *ClarisWorks Getting Started* manual that comes with ClarisWorks, and is more accessible than the *ClarisWorks User's Guide*. Because this book is independently written, we tell you when some aspect of ClarisWorks is unsatisfactory, needs a workaround, or requires the help of outside software. We can also recommend other software to you when we think it serves an important need.

How to Read This Book

This book is not meant to be read cover-to-cover, although you can certainly do so if you wish. As much as possible, each chapter is self-contained. You don't have to read other chapters in order to understand the material found therein.

There is one exception to this rule, however. If you are a novice Macintosh user, you should read the introductory material in chapters 1 and 2 to make sure that you know enough of the fundamentals to continue. If you are experienced using the Macintosh, you should browse these chapters for new information, since much of those first two introductory chapters concentrates on features specific to ClarisWorks.

This book is "task-oriented"—that is, you will find enough background in the text to help you understand the task at hand without lots of extraneous detail. Reference is made in the book to more complete explanations to be found in other work. If you are looking for a specific task that you need to accomplish, check the Table of Contents at the front of the book. A "How-To" section appears at the beginning of each chapter that tells you what you will learn in that chapter. You can also check the Index at the back of the book for listings by subject matter.

The following is a capsuie summary of the contents of this book:

- ❖ Chapters 1 and 2 are introductions to the Macintosh and to ClarisWorks, respectively.
- ❖ Chapter 3 describes writing text in a word processor.
- ❖ Chapter 4 introduces doing calculations with spreadsheets.
- ❖ Chapter 5 explains how to organize, retrieve, and analyze information with databases.
- ❖ Chapter 6 introduces graphics, and working with pictures, drawings, and images in the drawing and painting environments.
- ❖ Chapter 7 teaches you to communicate with other computers, with other people using computers, and transfer information electronically.
- ❖ Chapter 8 describes tasks requiring more than one set of ClarisWorks tools.
- ❖ Finally, Chapter 9 describes some of the more advanced projects that you can undertake in ClarisWorks.

This book contains a few devices meant to help you learn about important aspects of ClarisWorks quickly, and to break up the wall of text on a page to help you read the material with better comprehension. You will see the following icons and sections in the pages to come:

Take the Caution icon seriously. A Caution icon is a warning of a feature that can cause you to lose time or valuable information. Fortunately, there aren't many of these to be found.

Caution
This icon indicates a procedure or process that can cause the user trouble.

Tips generally repay the reader with increased efficiency. Tips can be aimed at any level of reader, but must be useful to be included.

Tip
A Tip icon contains information that will make your use of ClarisWorks easier, faster, or more fun.

You can read a note, or bypass it, at your whim, and your understanding of the material will not be diminished. A Note is like an abbreviated Sidebar (see below).

Note
A Note icon draws your attention to material that is related to the discussion, but not an integral part of it.

A Shortcut describes a keystroke, speed key, or whatever you want to call it—a set of keys that you type from your keyboard to accomplish a task. Many times they are menu command equivalents, other times dialog box selections. Where the shortcut is mentioned and explained completely in the text for the first time, you will see the Shortcut icon appear there. Each shortcut is described once and only once in the text, where most appropriate.

Shortcut
A keystroke that starts a process.

> A Sidebar is a section that is specially set off from the main chapter text, either with a shaded border, or grayed background. You can safely browse or skip a Sidebar without suffering any loss of understanding future material. When the task described in the Sidebar becomes of interest to you, go back and read the Sidebar.
>
> These are sections that generally have more involved information in them than the average chapter section. If you can read and understand the information in a Sidebar, chances are that you have a good working knowledge of the chapter that they are in. Most Sidebars are found at the end of a logical unit, or more often at the end of a chapter.

If this book's done its job, then it should earn a place beside your computer to serve as a reference for ClarisWorks in the time to come. We want this book to have long term value to you.

Just One More Thing...

This book was written for you. Yes, you! Hayden Books and the authors know that you are busy out there living your lives and doing your jobs. This book was meant to get you up and running without wasting your time, and distill a very rich program down to its essentials. Let us know how you liked this book, what we should have kept out, what we should have included, and whether the *ClarisWorks Companion* met your needs. You can do this by contacting the publisher, Hayden Books, or the author at the electronic addresses listed previously. Your input will be most valuable in improving the next edition of this book, and other books Hayden will publish in the future.

Chapter 1
Getting Started with ClarisWorks

This chapter answers the question, "What is ClarisWorks?," and explains some of ClarisWorks's advantages. It provides examples of how to use ClarisWorks in your own daily work. This chapter should help you decide if ClarisWorks is for you.

In this chapter, you are given an overview of ClarisWorks and each of its components, or "environments." An environment is a set of related tools meant to be used for a common task, such as writing, drawing, calculating, organizing information, communicating, and so on.

You also will learn how to:

Use the different environments in ClarisWorks	1
Recognize each environment	2
Pick projects appropriate to each environment	5
Use compound documents to mix data types	12
Install ClarisWorks on your hard drive by using the Installer	13
Do a full installation with Easy Install	14
Do a custom installation of ClarisWorks file(s)	15

ClarisWorks is integrated software. You make an initial selection of a document type in ClarisWorks based on the kind of data you primarily intend to use in that project, but you are not limited to only that kind of information. You also can include other supported data types in your document. ClarisWorks changes your menu choices and tools whenever you select a different data type so that your work seems natural and unimpeded.

At the end of this chapter, you are instructed on how to install ClarisWorks on your Macintosh and how to register the software.

What Is ClarisWorks?

ClarisWorks is integrated software. Integrated software describes a single package of applications meant to satisfy most of your computing needs. ClarisWorks provides you with six distinct environments: communications, database, drawing, painting, spreadsheets, and word processing. You can use these environments (which other software vendors call modules) to create text, calculate values, chart results, create line art, make images or painted art, and connect to other computers or online services, respectively. For an average user, this represents 95 percent of all the tasks for which you use a computer.

Why Buy Integrated Software?

ClarisWorks includes the most commonly used features in each environment, leaving out features that are used less often. For example, the word processor cannot generate an index or table of contents. For more advanced features like these you would have to use Claris's MacWrite Pro, Microsoft Word, WordPerfect, Nisus, WriteNow, or some other, more powerful word processor. But unless you frequently need to generate indices or tables of content, why pay for those features?

Integrated software offers several advantages for beginners and experts alike. In ClarisWorks you get highly functional software in a small package at a good price. A collection of six full-featured programs might cost you $1000 and take months to learn. ClarisWorks can be purchased for a fraction of that price, is considerably easier to learn, and offers consistent operation between its environments.

Intrinsic to ClarisWorks is an upgrade path for beginners to Claris's more powerful applications, such as MacWrite Pro (word processor), Resolve (spreadsheet), FileMaker Pro (database), MacDraw Pro (painting), and ClarisImpact (drawing). For example, when you are in ClarisWorks's database environment, the dialog boxes and interface features you see are as similar to those in FileMaker Pro as Claris could make them.

Understanding Integrated Software

Typically integrated software programs are multiple applications bundled together with a common interface. That is, each distinct program requires a separate document, and there is little mixing of data types within a single document. While you might be able to cut and paste a graphic or spreadsheet into your word processor as an object, you couldn't edit that object with the full set of tools available in its native module. ClarisWorks is better integrated. Although ClarisWorks still requires that you define a document type, you can switch to another set of tools and embed other data types in your document. Most objects are editable.

For example, in the word processor you can click on the Spreadsheet tool and then click and drag a spreadsheet frame. The menu changes to the spreadsheet environment, and all of the tools and functions that you find in a spreadsheet application are now at your disposal. You then can create a full-functioning spreadsheet within your word processing document, without having to paste in the spreadsheet as a graphic or embed a spreadsheet object that requires the launch of a separate spreadsheet application to use it. You can even create charts and graphs directly in your word processing document because the spreadsheet frame has all the functionality of a spreadsheet document. Compare the menus and tools in figure 1.1 (a word processor document selected) with the same document in figure 1.2 (the same text with a spreadsheet frame selected).

> **Tip**
> ClarisWorks loads entirely into RAM or volatile memory. The advantage of this becomes apparent when you work on a PowerBook or compare ClarisWorks to other programs. Because ClarisWorks is small and contained in memory when running, there is little reading or writing to your hard disk drive during operation. This means that you get increased battery life from a laptop computer and faster performance. The faster your Macintosh, the faster ClarisWorks runs. Versions written for Apple Computer's PowerPC Macintosh are wicked fast indeed!

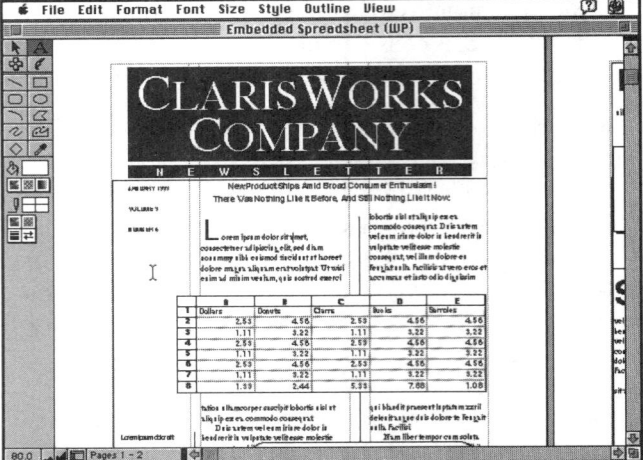

Figure 1.1. *A word processing document with text selected.*

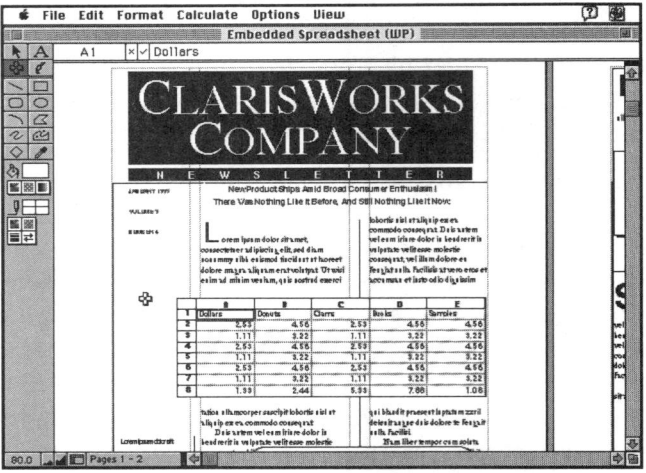

Figure 1.2. *The same document with a spreadsheet frame selected.*

In that same word processing document, you can add a painting frame or include drawn objects. Objects, frames, and text, for that matter, are layered (one above another) in your document and can be positioned and manipulated. You can have text wrap around objects or frames, just as professional magazines do. Combine ClarisWorks's multicolumn text support with autoflow to create sophisticated page-layout effects.

The net effect of this integration is that you work more quickly and easily in ClarisWorks than you do in other integrated packages. ClarisWorks's design presages the time to come when all applications will be small and work together simply to create a compound-document architecture. Apple's OpenDoc architecture represents a future expression of this trend. If you have used IBM PC and PC-compatible computers, you know Microsoft's Object Linking and Embedding (OLE) architecture represents a similar idea.

The Six Major Environments

In each ClarisWorks environment (document type) you observe a few unique window elements and a different set of menu commands. You can tell a document's type by reading the Title bar of the window. Each document type has the following characters in the title: word processing (WP); spreadsheet (SS); database (DB); drawing (DR); painting (PT); and communications (CM). In ClarisWorks 1.0 you will see a graphics window with (GR) in the title; the painting and drawing environments were not separated in the first version. Samples of each menu and title bar are shown in figure 1.3.

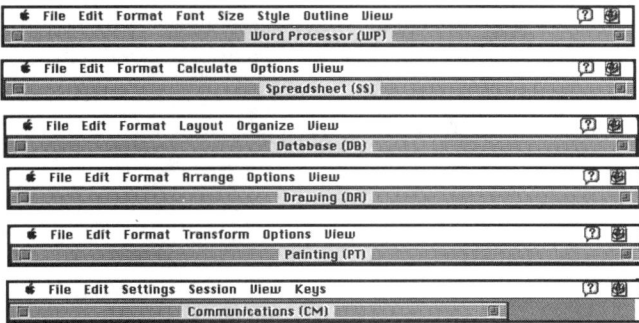

Figure 1.3. *The six document types' menu and title bars.*

The next section discusses how to create frames or objects for other data types and then embed them in your original document to create a compound document. Different menus and tools appear as you change from one data type to another, and the Title bar will not be decisive in telling you in which environment you are currently working.

> **Caution**
> You may be disconcerted to click somewhere accidentally and then watch your menus and tools change. You can avoid much confusion in ClarisWorks by learning which menus, tools, Shortcut palettes, and windows are associated with each environment.

> **Note**
> All ClarisWorks menu bars contain the Apple, File, Edit, Balloon (Help), and Application menus, as do almost all Macintosh applications. The Help and Application menus are new with System 7, and are not found in System 6. The View menu is also standard within ClarisWorks.

The word processing environment is used to create or edit written text. It is perhaps the environment you will spend the most time using. With the advent of computers, word processors enable you to apply sophisticated tools for formatting and automated editing. Projects you might do in a word processor include letters, reports, journals, free-form note-taking, and structured writing, such as outlines and formatted pages like those found in newsletters (see figure 1.1).

In the word processing environment you see the word processor-specific Format, Font, Size, and Style menus. Other elements that tip you off to the fact that you're working in the word processing environment are the appearance of a bar with icons for tabs, line spacing, and justification. Whether you see a toolbox or Shortcut palette depends on whether you chose to show those two elements by selecting them from the Preferences submenu (see the "Setting Preferences Within ClarisWorks" section of chapter 9, "Advanced Topics") or used the appropriate menu commands. Chapter 3, "Working With Text in the Word Processor," goes into much more detail introducing the functions of these word processor elements.

You use the spreadsheet environment to store and calculate numbers, and to analyze relationships. Using ClarisWorks's range of spreadsheet functions, you can think of a spreadsheet as a kind of super calculator. Typical spreadsheet projects are managing a budget, tracking checks in a checkbook, setting up tax categories, analyzing data, creating forecasts or predicting financial performance, and creating balance (profit and loss) statements or income statements for a business. As shown in figure 1.4, spreadsheets also can graph data.

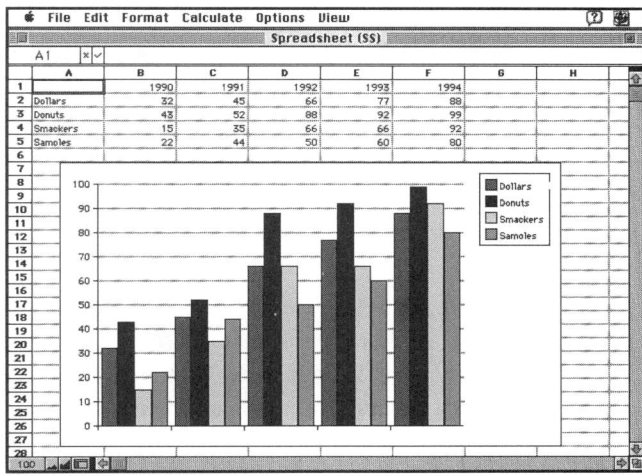

Figure 1.4. *A sample spreadsheet with its data graphed in a horizontal bar chart.*

Keeping with the spreadsheet environment for calculating purposes, you see the Format, Calculate, and Options menus. The Calculate menu is a dead giveaway for the spreadsheet environment. You also see a worksheet, in the form of a grid, in your work area. Each area where the rows and columns intersect is called a cell, and each cell can receive input data or contain data derived from a relationship or formula. Since the grid can be turned on and off, you cannot always count on seeing it displayed. However, the spreadsheet will always have an Entry bar with a Check and Cross box below the window title. A spreadsheet also can display a graph or chart. Chapter 4, "Calculating Results with a Spreadsheet," gives you more details about spreadsheets.

A database is where you collect and manage different pieces of information. Projects for which you use a database include address books, catalogs, bibliographies, sales tracking, inventory, and managing other list-based information. There is some overlap in utility between spreadsheets and databases. Typically spreadsheets are used for more calculation-intensive projects. Databases use a relationship that binds the data together into chunks or records— for example, addresses for multiple individuals.

The Layout and Organize menus are unique to the database environment. Another special feature of this environment is the appearance of the Database book icon that looks like a Rolodex in the Status panel, along with text indicating the number of records and the database's current condition.

Unlike the spreadsheet window, the database window is modal and looks different, depending upon whether you are in the design (Layout) or display (Browse) view. A sample database in the Browse mode is shown in figure 1.5. The database can be altered to look like an index card, data form, list, or any other kind of display. You can't always tell from the window that you are in the database environment. Since the Status panel isn't always shown, that isn't a reliable method either. Chapter 5, "Organizing Information With a Database," goes into more detail on the subject.

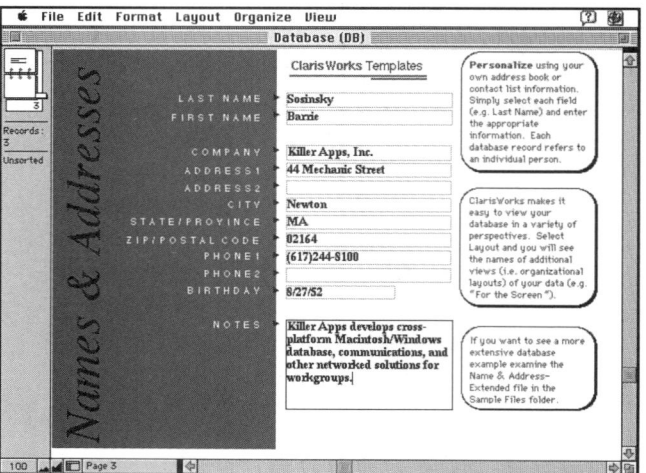

Figure 1.5. *A sample database viewed in the Browse mode.*

Drawing creates objects, based on lines and fills, that can be selected and manipulated in their entirety. Painting creates bitmapped images. Although you can create objects in a painting document, they lose their identity as objects and can be selected and manipulated as a mosaic of bits. Therefore, the simplest way to tell whether a graphic is a drawing or painting is to click or click and drag (or click-drag) on the object you see. When you see a set of black selection handles you have a drawn object(s). When a click-drag selects exactly the area you dragged, you have a painted object.

You use drawings to create line-art artwork, and to add elements to a page. Drawings typically, but not always, print better than paintings. Typical drawing projects would include design work, business forms, elements of a slide show, newsletters, charts, and other projects where artistic precision is required.

Figure 1.6. *A Drawing document.*

The Arrange menu is unique to the drawing environment (see figure 1.6). Most other elements of the drawing window are nearly identical to those found in the painting environment. The drawing toolbox is almost identical to the painting toolbox, except that it lacks the selection, paintbrush, spray can, and eraser tools.

Paintings are used for natural images or other graphics where showing texture is important. In a magnified view (available by clicking the Zoom tool, an icon of large mountains at the lower-right of the ClarisWorks window), drawings may be seen to be made up of a collection of spots called pixels, or picture elements. Paintings are not inferior to drawings; they are used to achieve a different effect. Typical painting projects are artwork, logos, simulations of photographs or natural images, textures, and so on.

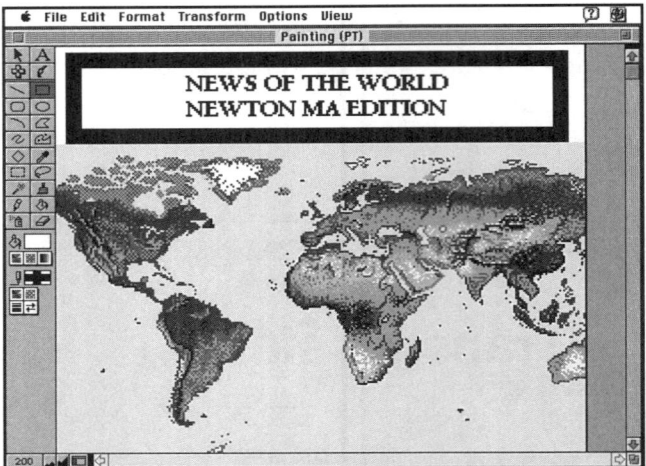

Figure 1.7. *The Painting environment looks similar to the Drawing environment.*

The Transform menu is unique to the painting environment (see figure 1.7). If the toolbox is showing, there are some unique painting tools to look for. They are the Eraser, the Brush, the Pencil, and the Selection tool. For more information about both the drawing and painting environments, see chapter 6, "Adding Graphics to Your Work."

The last environment is the communications environment. The communications environment is distinct from all of the others. You use the communications environment to connect to bulletin board systems (BBSes), online services, and to other computers. The range of tasks for which you might use the communications environment include receiving and sending electronic mail, finding information, and purchasing goods and services, to name just a few.

The communications environment has a Settings, Session, and Keys menu, all three of which are unique within ClarisWorks. Normally the window is horizontally split into two panes, one on top of the other. The top, or scrollback, pane shows you information that was recorded previously in your session, as shown in figure 1.8. You can choose to not show the scrollback pane. The bottom or Terminal working area contains an underline end-of-line marker, and is blank except for the characters you just typed or just received. A Clock icon with connection times also displays just above and at the upper left of the window in the Status area.

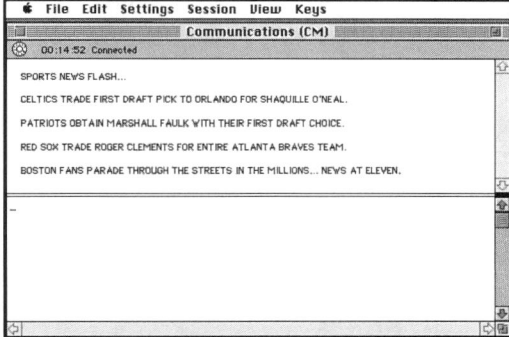

Figure 1.8. *Good news in a communication document.*

ANATOMY OF A COMPOUND DOCUMENT

A compound document is one that contains more than one data type (see figures 1.1 and 1.2). There are limitations as to which environments can be used with which documents. A summary of those limitations follows:

- ❖ Word processing. All environments are available except the database and communications environments.
- ❖ Spreadsheet. All environments are available except the database and communications environments.
- ❖ Database. All environments are available except the communications environment.
- ❖ Painting and Drawing. All environments are available except the database and communications environments.
- ❖ Communications. No other environment is available within a communications document.

If you want to place a data type in a document that doesn't support that environment (for example, drawings inside a communications document), you can still use the Copy and Paste commands from the Edit menu and transfer information through the Clipboard (see chapter 2). You will not, however, be able to modify the drawing with drawing-environment tools within that module.

To add another type of data to a document, select the tool for that data type and then click and drag a frame. The menus and tools change. You can fill that frame as you desire. For environments that create objects, such as the drawing module, you simply select a drawing shape tool and then click on and drag the resulting drawn object. Text, spreadsheets, and paintings are added as frames by first clicking the Text (the A), the Spreadsheet (the Cross), or the Paint (the Paint Brush) tool. Frames are objects, and they can be manipulated as such. For example, you can alter whether a frame is above or below another frame or the document work area. The next chapter explains in full how to create frames. For a fuller discussion of compound documents see chapter 8, "Making It All Work Together."

Installing ClarisWorks

Installing ClarisWorks 2 is easy when you use the Apple Installer program. Before you proceed with the installation, there are only a few things of which you need to be aware.

ClarisWorks has the following minimum requirements:

- ❖ A compatible Macintosh. You must have a Mac Plus or later. You cannot use ClarisWorks 2 on a Mac 128K or a Mac 512K computer.
- ❖ System 6.0.5 or above. To identify the version of your system software, select the About This Macintosh or About the Finder command from the top of the Apple menu while on the Macintosh desktop.
- ❖ 2M of memory (RAM) for System 7, or 1M of RAM for System 6. These are the minimum amounts of memory necessary to load these two system software versions. So if you are up and running in either system version, you are all set.
- ❖ 3.1M of free disk space.

To begin installation, restart your computer and turn off the system extensions. Some extensions that check for code-writing activity common to viruses (SAM, Virex, and others) can interrupt the installation process and hang your system during installation. Also, if you have a PowerBook with an installed internal modem, the installer cannot overwrite your modem extensions if they are active.

To turn off all extensions, do the following:

1. Quit all of your open applications. You should see the Macintosh desktop, and be in the Finder.
2. Select the Restart command from the Special menu. After closing all files and applications your Macintosh will shut down and then turn itself back on.
3. Hold the Shift key while your Macintosh starts up. Holding the Shift key disables all system extensions. Once you see the dialog box that says "Welcome to the Macintosh. Extensions Off," you can release the Shift key.

Note
ClarisWorks requires the use of a hard disk drive for successful installation and usage.

> **Tip**
>
> Double-click on the Read Me file icon and read the document. It contains information that was not available when the manual was printed. It documents known conflicts, bugs, problems, and special features. To print the file, choose the Print command from the File menu, make your selections in the Print dialog box, and click the OK button. See the "How to Print and Fax" section of chapter 2 for more information on printing.

The Installer program copies files from the installation disks to your hard disk drive by placing files in the appropriate places.

Before installing ClarisWorks, lock each installation master disk. Slide the small tab in the upper-right corner so that you can see through the hole it covers. Locking the disks prevents them from being accidentally altered and allows the installation to proceed.

The Installer can install ClarisWorks on different hard disk drives. The best results are obtained when you install ClarisWorks on your startup hard disk. You can do a full installation by using the Easy Install option, or install specific components through a custom installation. The Installer is smart enough to know which components are required for your system software, and to replace old outdated components. In almost all instances, people use the Easy Install option.

You can use the Easy Install option to install all the components of ClarisWorks onto your hard disk.

To begin an Easy Installation, insert Disk 1 into your Macintosh. Double-click on the Disk 1 icon to open its window and reveal the Installer icon on your desktop. Double-click on the Installer icon, and follow the instructions; when the main Installer screen displays, as shown in figure 1.9, click on the Easy Install button to install ClarisWorks on your startup disk.

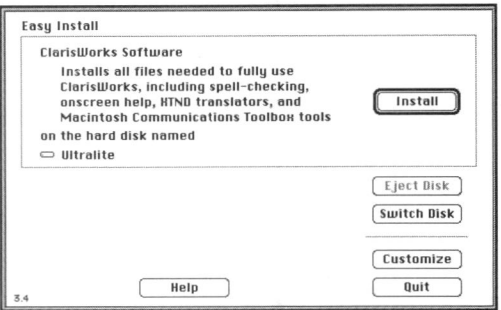

Figure 1.9. *The Installer screen.*

As it goes through the installation progress, the Installer will ask you for the other program disks. When it's done, the Installer will ask you to restart the Macintosh. Click on the Restart button to do so; when your Macintosh restarts, you'll have ClarisWorks ready to run!

To install ClarisWorks on another (non-startup) hard disk, click on the Switch Disk button in the Installer dialog box. This will switch between mounted volumes on your desktop. When you've selected the hard disk where you want to install ClarisWorks, click on the Install button.

You also can perform a custom installation by using the Installer to install just the components you want. A custom installation is most useful in situations like PowerBook installations where you want to conserve limited disk space by not installing template files, dictionaries, and so on.

To install ClarisWorks using the Customize feature:

1. Click on the Customize button in the Installer dialog box (figure 1.9). The custom installation dialog box (figure 1.10) appears.

Caution
Installing ClarisWorks on a non-startup hard disk drive will not result in a working copy of ClarisWorks when you start up from the other drive. Essential system files, such as translators, dictionaries, the help system, and others, are only copied to the active System folder of your startup drive during installation.

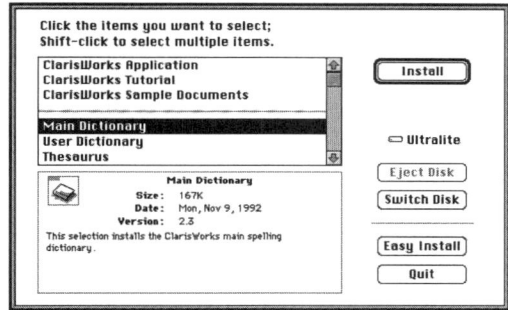

Figure 1.10. *The Custom Install dialog box.*

2. Select the item(s) to install from the scrolling list.

   As you select each item, a description of the file's size, version, and purpose appears below the list. Select multiple items to install by holding down the Shift key and clicking on the items.

3. Click the Install button or press the Return or the Enter key.

The installation then proceeds as before for the Easy Install option.

The Installer is smart enough to replace older files with newer files, to recognize your system configuration, and to check for adequate free space on your hard disk. If your attempt at installation fails for any reason, restart your computer, turn off your extensions, and begin the installation process again.

> **Tip**
> Installing ClarisWorks on non-startup disk drives and custom installations are not recommended procedures for beginning Macintosh users.

Once your software is installed, you should personalize and register it, a procedure that starts when you first launch the program. Registering your software qualifies you for Claris technical support should you encounter problems. To personalize ClarisWorks 2, begin by launching ClarisWorks. The program icon will be found in the ClarisWorks folder, which the Installer places at the top level of your disk drive. Double-click on the ClarisWorks icon (figure 1.11) to launch the program.

Figure 1.11. *The ClarisWorks program icon.*

The first time you launch the program the personalization screen shown in figure 1.12 displays and stays on your screen until you enter the required information. Once personalized, when the program flashes the personalization screen briefly each time the program loads.

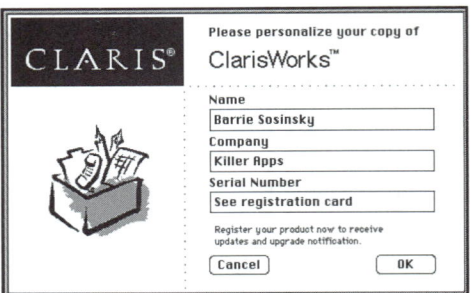

Figure 1.12. *The ClarisWorks personalization screen.*

Type your name and (optionally) company into the boxes provided. Select the text "See registration card" in the Serial Number text box and replace it with the registration number found on the registration card packed in the software box. Then, if you need to call Claris, the registration number is easily found. Click the OK button to complete the personalization and to launch the application for the first time.

You will find a registration card in the software box. Be sure to fill it out and send it to Claris so that you are fully registered.

Summary

In this chapter you learned that ClarisWorks is integrated software. Integrated software is a collection of programs used for your most common tasks. ClarisWorks creates a working interface for these programs that actually lets you create and work with different data types in the same document, a feature called compound-document architecture. ClarisWorks has some important advantages for new Macintosh users, PowerBook users, and experienced users who want a small, fast program that offers a lot of functionality, or "bang" for the buck.

ClarisWorks contains six different tool sets, called environments: word processing, spreadsheet, database, drawing, painting, and communications. Each environment creates its own document type and has its own special purpose. Sample projects were given in this chapter for each type. Depending on the environment, you can add additional data types to your document as frames or objects. When you work with those added data types, your menus and tools change to give you the full range of the environment appropriate to that data type. A discussion of how to recognize which environment you are working is included in this chapter.

ClarisWorks is best installed on your computer by using the Apple Installer utility found on Disk 1. Claris recommends that you first turn off all system extensions before performing an installation, and then do a full installation on your startup hard disk drive.

Chapter 2, "Some Basics," gives information for new Macintosh users and information about ClarisWorks that is common to all environments. If you are a novice, read on. For more experienced Macintosh users, browse the chapter before proceeding to chapter 4, "Working with Text in the Word Processor."

Tip
Claris sends notification of special offers and upgrade promotions to registered users. With ClarisWorks slated for future upgrades, it's smart to register.

Chapter 2
Some Basics

This chapter provides new ClarisWorks users with information about the screen elements of ClarisWorks and step-by-step instructions on how to create, save, open, and close files. You'll also find useful information on printing and faxing your files.

Beginning Macintosh users will find the overview of moving information with the cut, copy, and paste commands and the step-by-step procedures for saving your work especially useful. We'll also introduce you to the on-line help systems designed to give you help when you're using ClarisWorks.

Below are some of the how-to topics covered in this chapter:

How to create a file 20
How to save a file the first time 22
How to save a file inside of a
    folder on a different disk 23
How to close a file without saving
    changes 25
How to zoom in or out by
    a custom factor 30
How to split a window vertically 31
How to split a window horizontally 32
How to modify the Shortcuts palette ...34
How to create a frame
    in an open file 35
How to scale a frame 36
How to specify the exact
    measurements of a frame. 36
How to use the Object Size
    command 36
How to select a printer from
    the Chooser 37
How to print 38
How to use the ClarisWorks
    Help system 40
How to access Balloon Help
    information 41

Working With Files

ClarisWorks uses the Macintosh's operating system to work with files. A disk can contain applications, folders, and files. A folder may contain applications and multiple files and file types. How you organize your hard disk is up to you and should reflect how you use your computer. For more information on hard disks and file management, refer back to your Macintosh documentation or to some of the books mentioned in the introduction.

Files have a treelike structure, with the contents of folders located at the top of the tree. You can visualize the filing system as being the trunk of the tree, with folders and their contents being limbs and branches. This concept will help you understand how to navigate through the contents of your disk.

Creating Files

With ClarisWorks, you can create the following kinds of documents:

- ❖ Word processing documents, in which you can create and format text
- ❖ Spreadsheets, in which you can enter numbers, formulas, perform calculations, and create charts
- ❖ Databases, in which you can organize and store information
- ❖ Draw files, in which you can create objects with drawing tools
- ❖ Paint files, in which you can create objects with painting tools
- ❖ Telecommunications, with which you can exchange files with other computers

To create a file, follow these steps:

1. Open ClarisWorks by double-clicking on the ClarisWorks icon or single-clicking on the ClarisWorks icon, pulling down the File menu and choosing the Open command. The ClarisWorks icon is shown in figure 2.1.

Figure 2.1. *The ClarisWorks icon.*

Your computer loads ClarisWorks into RAM and then displays the New Document dialog box, as shown in figure 2.2.

2. Click on the radio button of the type of file you wish to create.

   You can also press the arrow keys or the Tab key to select a different radio button.

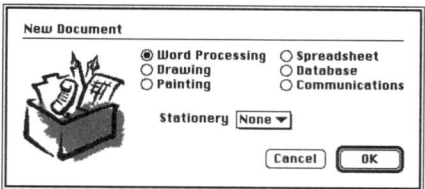

Figure 2.2. *The New Document dialog box.*

3. Click on the OK button or press the Return or Enter key.

   ClarisWorks displays the appropriate menu bar and an untitled file, as shown in figure 2.3.

Figure 2.3. *An untitled word processing document.*

To create a new file when you are already in ClarisWorks, follow these steps:

1. Pull down the File menu and choose the New command.

   The New Document dialog box displays, as shown above in figure 2.3.

2. Click on the radio button of the type of file you wish to create.

3. Click on the OK button or press the Return or Enter key.

   ClarisWorks displays the appropriate menu bar and an untitled file.

Depending on the type of document you create, you will see Untitled 1 (WP) for a word processing document, Untitled 1 (SS) for a spreadsheet document, Untitled 1 (DR) for a draw document, Untitled 1 (PT) for a paint document, Untitled 1 (DB) for a database document, and Untitled 1 (CM) for a telecommunications document.

Saving a File

When you enter information in a file, the information is stored in random-access memory (RAM). RAM is temporary (or volatile), and everything stored in RAM is permanently lost when the computer is turned off or crashes. You must save your files to a disk if later you want to retrieve their contents.

You should save your work at least every 15 minutes. Be sure to save at major interruptions—when the phone rings, a co-worker starts to speak with you, or when changing to a different environment in a file. Computers do freeze up or crash occasionally, and it's better to lose 15 minutes rather than hours worth of work. Anything saved to disk will be there when your computer is turned on again.

To save a file the first time, follow these steps:

1. Pull down the File menu and choose the Save As command.

   The Save As dialog box displays, as shown in figure 2.4.

2. Type in the name of the file. You can use up to 16 characters and spaces.

3. Click on the Save button or press the Return or Enter key.

   The name of the file appears in the Title bar, as shown in figure 2.5.

Unless you specify otherwise, all saved files will reside in the ClarisWorks folder.

> **Shortcut**
> To create a new file, press Command-N.

> **Shortcut**
> To save your work, press Command-S.

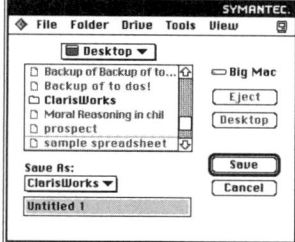

Figure 2.4. *The Save As dialog box.*

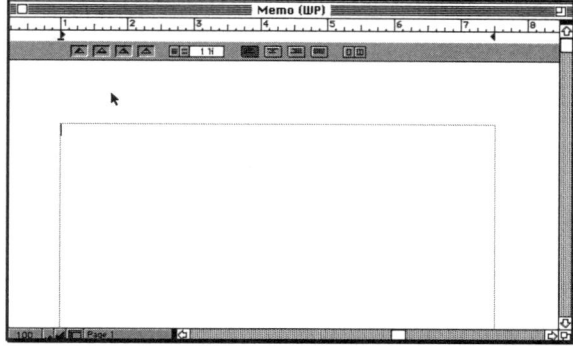

Figure 2.5. *Saved file.*

To save a file inside of a folder on a different disk, follow these steps:

1. In the Save As dialog box, click on the Desktop button (System 7) or the Disk button (System 6).

    The name and icon of the drive change and the contents of the scroll box change, as shown in figure 2.6.

2. Click on the disk to which you want to save your file and click on the OK button or press the Return or the Enter key. Or, simply double-click on the disk name.

    You have selected the disk, now select the location to which you want to save the file.

3. Scroll through the list until you locate the appropriate folder and click on the OK button or press the Return or Enter key. Or, double-click on the folder name to open it.

    The contents of the folder display in the scrollable area. You may save your file here or navigate through additional layers of folders.

Tip

If you think you've lost a file, check the ClarisWorks folder. If you still can't find it, pull down the File menu in the Finder and choose the Find File command. Type part of the file name and click on the OK button to search for the file.

Chapter 2 • Some Basics

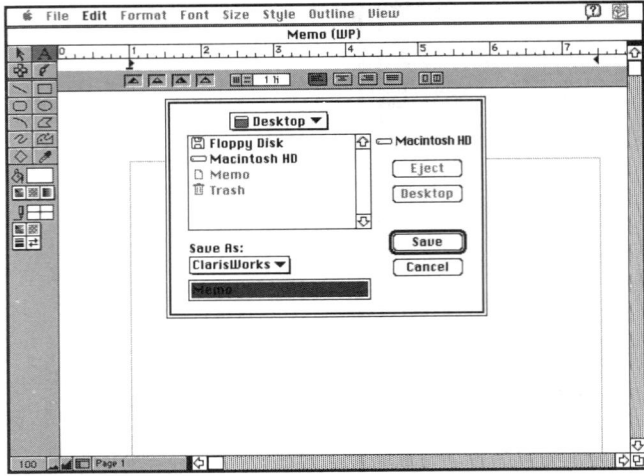

Figure 2.6. *Save As box at the Desktop level.*

4. Click on the Save button or press the Return or Enter key.

Save vs. Save As

The Save and Save As commands both record your work to a disk. The two commands have different uses:

❖ Use the Save command to record changes to a file that has already been named.

❖ Use the Save As command to make a copy or a backup of an existing file. When you use Save As, your original file is closed and a new file displays onscreen.

Opening and Closing Files

When you want to work on a file, you must first open it. Your computer loads a file into RAM so that you are able to make changes. When you finish making changes to a file, you can close it. Closing a file removes the file from RAM but leaves ClarisWorks open so you can continue to work.

To open a file within a folder, follow these steps:

1. Pull down the File menu and choose the Open command.

   The Open dialog box displays, as shown in figure 2.7. Note the similarities between the Open and the Save As dialog boxes.

> **Tip**
> Use the Save As command to eliminate retyping frequently used files such as letters, memos, and reports. You can then make any changes you need to without altering the original file.

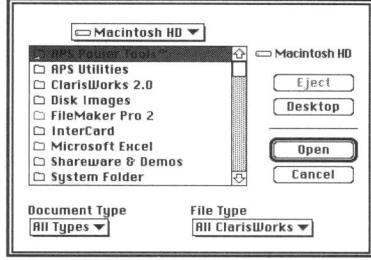

Figure 2.7. *The Open dialog box.*

2. If needed, click on the Drive button and select the appropriate disk drive.

   The contents of the scrolling list change when you select a different disk.

3. Scroll through the contents of the list, select the folder containing the file you want to open, then click on the Open button.

   The contents of the folder display on the screen.

4. Select the file you want to open by clicking on its name and then clicking the Open button.

   ClarisWorks displays the selected file onscreen.

To close a file without saving any changes, pull down the File menu and choose the Close command. If you have made changes, ClarisWorks prompts you to save your file before closing. Click on the No button to close the file without saving the changes.

Moving Information With Cut, Copy, and Paste

The easiest way to copy or move information from one file to another or from one part of a file to another part is to use the Cut, Copy, and Paste commands on the Edit menu. Before you cut or copy information, you must first select part of your file.

When you cut information, it is removed from the area where you selected it and is transferred to the Clipboard for temporary storage. The Clipboard can hold only one selection; when you use the Cut or Copy commands, the Clipboard deletes the previous information. Since the Clipboard is part of the Macintosh operating system, it is common to all

Shortcut
Press Command-O to open a file.

Shortcut
Click on the close box at the top of your window or press Command-W.

Tip
To close all windows at the same time, hold down the Option key when you click on the close box.

Macintosh applications. For example, you can copy text from Microsoft Word and paste it into ClarisWorks. You can use the Clipboard to transfer graphics, text, and spreadsheet information.

When you copy information, it is duplicated from the area where you selected it and is transferred to the Clipboard for temporary storage.

When you use the Paste command, the contents of the Clipboard are transferred to the selected area. You may paste the same information repeatedly.

To view the contents of the Clipboard, pull down the Edit menu and select the Show Clipboard command.

Quitting ClarisWorks

When you quit ClarisWorks, all open files are closed, the menu bar no longer displays, and the program is no longer listed under the Application menu. To quit, pull down the File menu and choose the Quit command, or press Command-Q. The Quit command is common to all Macintosh applications. ClarisWorks prompts you to save changes to any files for which there are unsaved changes.

Allocating more RAM to ClarisWorks might help it work faster. To allocate more RAM to ClarisWorks, quit ClarisWorks. Select the ClarisWorks icon and pull down the File menu and choose the Get Info command. Type a number larger than the one in the Suggested Size box. How much to increase the amount depends on the amount of RAM in your Macintosh. In general, increase the Suggested Size amount by around ten percent.

Understanding and Navigating Your Screen

The ClarisWorks program generates a slightly different screen for each of its different environments. For detailed information on screen information for specific environments, refer to the appropriate chapter in this book. Figure 2.8 shows the elements of a word processing window.

Shortcut
Press Command-X to Cut, Command-C to Copy, and Command-V to Paste.

Tip
Use Cut and Paste to move the contents of a frame from one file to another.

Shortcut
Press Command-Q to quit ClarisWorks.

Caution
Getting out-of-memory messages? Pull down the Application menu for a list of all open applications and quit any unnecessary programs.

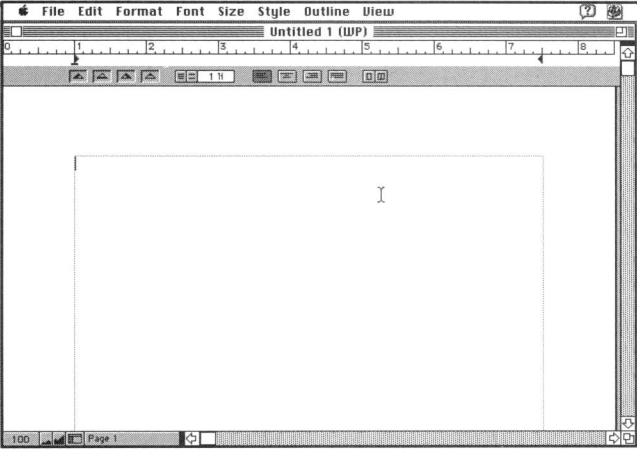

Figure 2.8. *The elements of a ClarisWorks window.*

Resize, Arrange, and Select Windows to Conveniently Organize Onscreen Information

When you're sitting in front of a computer, remember that you're the one in charge. Resize, arrange, and select the information you work with so you can work efficiently. Figure 2.9 illustrates the screen elements that enable you to resize and zoom.

Figure 2.9. *The Resize and Zoom options.*

A window is a rectangular area of your computer screen that contains information. You can change the size of a window by:

- ❖ Clicking on the Zoom box to the right of the Title bar
- ❖ Dragging on the Resize box in the lower-right corner of the window
- ❖ Using the Zoom controls in the lower-left corner

Just as you can have more than one piece of paper on the top of a desk, you can have multiple windows on your electronic desktop. You can resize these windows to help you work more conveniently with the information contained in each window.

To view more than one open file at a time, arrange them with the Tile command. To tile windows, pull down the View menu and choose the Tile Windows command. The windows of all open ClarisWorks files are reduced in size and brought into view, as shown in figure 2.10. You can scroll in each window, which makes tiling useful when you need to copy information from one file to another.

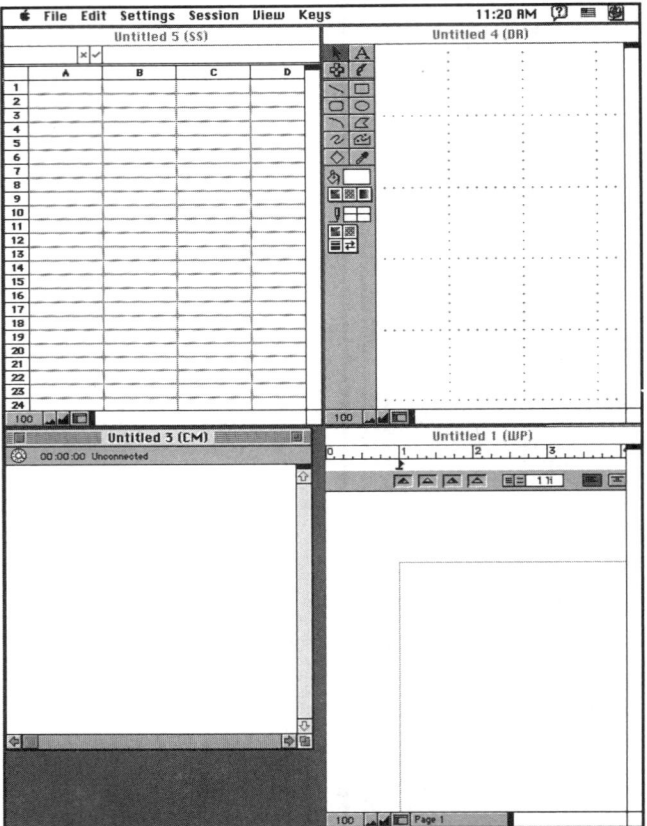

Figure 2.10. *Tiled windows.*

To stack the files so that you can view a larger area of a window, use the Stack Windows command. To stack windows, pull down the View menu and choose the Stack Windows command. The Title bars of all open ClarisWorks files are stacked so that you can identify each open file, as shown in figure 2.11.

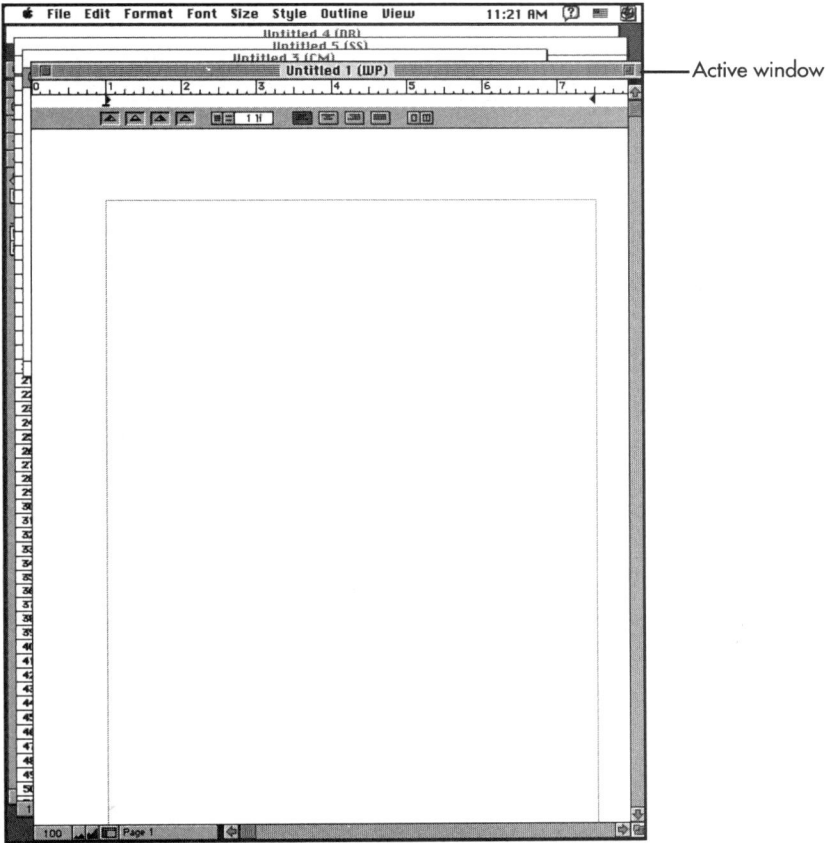

Figure 2.11. *Stacked windows with callouts for active window.*

To select a window, click on the window or its Title bar, or select its title from the View menu. When you bring a file forward, it becomes the active window. The active window is identified by stripes in the Title bar, as shown in figure 2.11.

Zooming In and Out

With ClarisWorks, you can zoom in and out of your screen to magnify or reduce the images on it. Zooming in is a useful way of previewing pages before you print. Zooming out lets you work on draw or paint images with more detail.

To zoom in or out, click on the Zoom controls on the bottom left of your screen. Each time you click on the Zoom Out control, your screen grows smaller by 50 percent. Clicking the Zoom In control magnifies the images on your screen. You can magnify images by 3200 percent or reduce them to 3.3 percent of their original size. Figure 2.12 shows a window reduced by using the Zoom command.

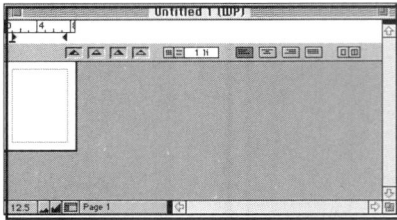

Figure 2.12. *A Window reduced by using the Zoom Out command.*

To zoom in or out by a custom factor, follow these steps:

1. Click on the box on the left side of the Zoom controls and hold down the mouse button.

    A list of sizes displays, as shown in figure 2.13.

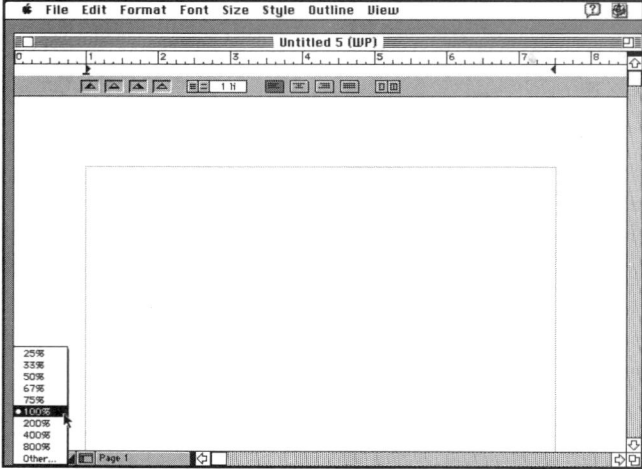

Figure 2.13. *The Pop-up Zoom menu.*

2. Select Other from the pop-up menu.

   The View Scale dialog box displays, as shown in figure 2.14.

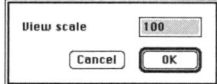

Figure 2.14. *The View Scale dialog box.*

3. Type a number between 3.3 and 3200 and click on the OK button or press the Return or Enter key.

   Any number under 100 reduces the window; any number over 100 magnifies it.

Splitting Windows

When you work on a large file—one that is longer or wider than your screen—you have to do a lot of scrolling, unless you split the window of the current file. Splitting a window lets you look at two parts of your file simultaneously. Refer to figure 2.8 for the Pane controls.

To split a window vertically, follow these steps:

1. Drag the Pane control to the right.

   A double line divides your window into two side-by-side parts, as shown in figure 2.15. You may scroll within both parts of the window.

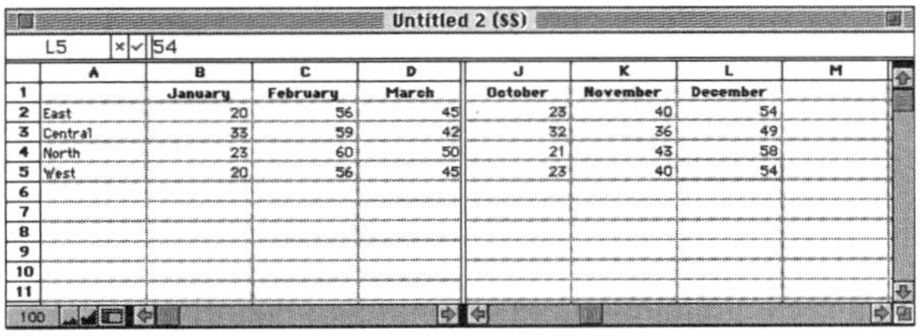

Figure 2.15. *A vertically split window.*

To restore the window, drag the Pane control until the left pane disappears.

> **Tip**
> Split vertical windows are especially helpful when working in spreadsheets.

To split a window horizontally, follow these steps:

1. Pull down the View menu and choose the Show Tools command.

   The Tool palette displays.

2. Drag down the Pane control.

   A double line divides your window into two horizontal parts, as shown in figure 2.16. You may scroll within both parts of the window.

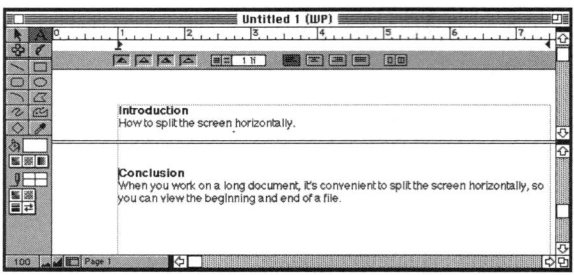

Figure 2.16. *A horizontally split window.*

To restore the window, drag the Pane control back to the palette until the top pane disappears.

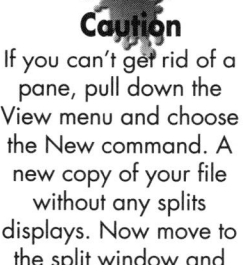

Caution
If you can't get rid of a pane, pull down the View menu and choose the New command. A new copy of your file without any splits displays. Now move to the split window and close it.

Selecting, Hiding, and Showing Tools

Although you can enter text or numbers in a spreadsheet or word processing files without using the Tools panel, you need these tools to draw or paint and to add colors and patterns. With the Tools panel you also can add various types of data (spreadsheet, drawing, painting, or text) in the same file.

To show the Tools panel, pull down the View menu and select the Show Tools command. Figure 2.17 illustrates the uses of each of the tools on the Tools panel.

Working With the Shortcuts Palette

ClarisWorks provides you with several ways to make your work more efficient. The Shortcuts submenu under the File menu contains commands for the Shortcuts palette and macros, as shown in figure 2.19. (For more information on macros, see chapter 8, "Making It All Work Together.")

Tools panel —

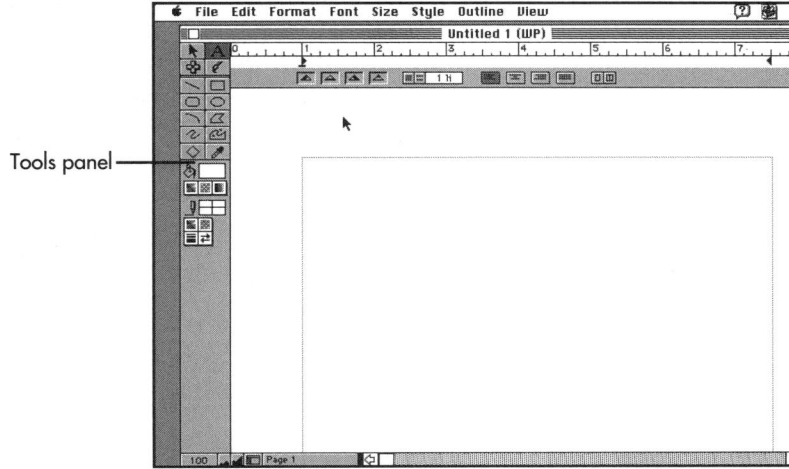

Figure 2.17. *The Tools panel.*

Figure 2.18. *The Show/Hide tools control.*

Shortcut
Click on the Show/Hide tools control at the bottom left of your screen, as shown in figure 2.18.

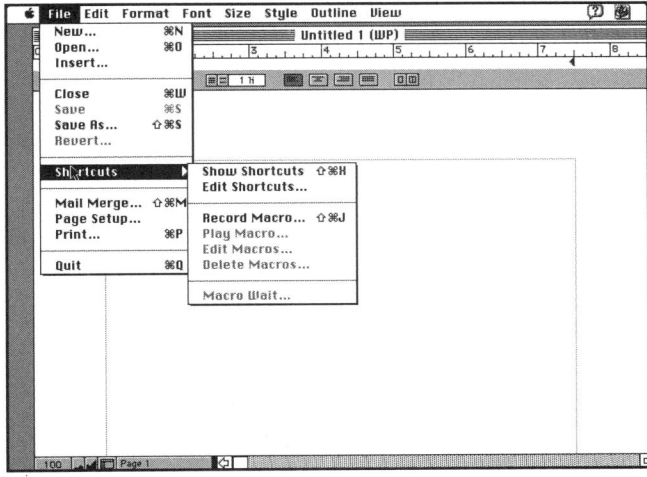

Figure 2.19. *The Shortcuts submenu.*

The Shortcuts palette displays a useful collection of buttons that help you perform tasks, such as opening, closing, and printing files; adding or removing bold, italic, and underling styles; or cutting, copying, and pasting. You can also customize the Shortcuts palette by adding or removing buttons.

To display the Shortcuts palette, pull down the Edit menu and choose the Show Shortcuts command from the Shortcuts submenu. Figure 2.20 shows the Shortcuts palette.

Figure 2.20. *The Shortcuts palette.*

To reduce the amount of space the Shortcuts palette takes up on your screen, click on the box in the upper-right corner. Figure 2.21 shows a minimized Shortcuts palette. To restore it to full size, click again in the upper-right box.

Figure 2.21. *The Minimized Shortcuts palette.*

To modify the Shortcuts palette, follow these steps:

1. Pull down the File menu and select the Edit Shortcuts command from the Shortcuts submenu.

    The Edit Shortcuts dialog box displays, as shown in figure 2.22.

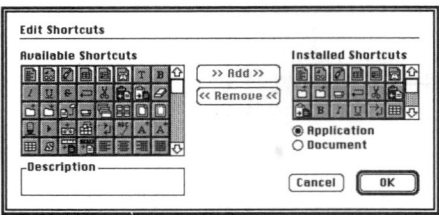

Figure 2.22. *The Edit Shortcuts dialog box.*

> **Shortcut**
> To display the Shortcuts palette, press Command-Shift-X.

2. To add a button, click on the button on the right side that you would like to add and then click on the Add button.

or

3. To remove a button, click on the button on the right side which you would like to remove and then click on the Remove button.

4. Click on the OK button to close the Edit Shortcuts dialog box.

The shortcuts palette reflects your changes.

Creating Frames

ClarisWorks gives you the capability to create compound document files. A compound file combines more than one type of information (text, spreadsheet, drawing, painting) in the same file. When you want to insert an object that is different from the document you are using, you create a frame to determine its size and placement.

To create a frame in an open file, follow these steps:

1. Click on a button that describes the type of document environment on the top of the Tools panel, as shown in figure 2.23.

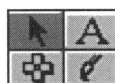

Figure 2.23. *The environment tools on the Tools panel.*

2. In the window, hold down the mouse button and drag an area in the shape of a rectangle.

The cursor displays as an icon of the document type that you drag into the area of the frame.

To move a frame, follow these steps:

1. Click on the Arrow tool on the Tools panel.

Black "handles" display on the frame's corners, enabling you to reshape the frame by dragging on any of its handles.

2. Press down the mouse button in the middle of the frame and drag it to a new location.

Once you create a frame, you may need to scale it so that it fits correctly on the page. One way you can do this is to scale the frame. This is very effective for graphics.

> **Tip**
> Use the Edit Shortcuts dialog box to identify the shortcut buttons.

> **Tip**
> To view the contents of the Shortcuts palette by name, pull down the Edit menu and choose the Preferences command. In the Preferences dialog box, click on Palettes and Show Names.

To scale a frame, follow these steps:

1. Click on the frame.

   The black handles display on the frame's corners.

2. Pull down the Option menu and choose the Scale Frame command.

   The Scale Frame dialog box displays, as shown in figure 2.24.

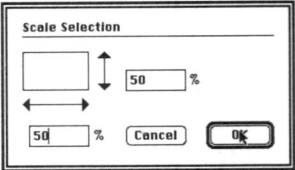

Figure 2.24. *The Scale Selection dialog box.*

3. Type the amounts you want to scale by in the horizontal and vertical text boxes.

4. Click on the OK button or press the Return or Enter key.

   The frame will be scaled according to your specifications.

When creating a newsletter or brochure where the layout has to be accurate, you probably will want to specify the exact measurements of a frame.

To use the Object Size command, follow these steps:

1. Click on the frame.

   The black handles display on the frame's corners.

2. Pull down the Option menu and choose the Object Size command.

   The Object Size dialog box displays as shown in figure 2.25.

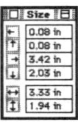

Figure 2.25. *The Object Size dialog box.*

3. Type the measurements for the object from the left, top, right, and bottom margins into the text boxes. You also can specify the object's width and height.

4. Press the Return key.

   The frame will be placed and resized according to your specifications.

How to Print and Fax

To print, you'll require a printer connected to your Macintosh computer and the appropriate printer driver (instructions to your computer about the printer) in your computer. To send a file by fax, you'll need an internal or external fax modem connected to both your computer and a telephone line. For instructions on faxing, refer to your fax modem documentation. (See chapter 7 "The Communications Environment" for more information on ClarisWorks' telecommunications features.)

Selecting an Output Device

The first step in printing is to identify the printer that will print your file. It's possible for your computer to be connected to more than one printer. If this is the case with your computer, you need to choose the printer you want to use. You make this selection by using the Chooser desk accessory.

To select a printer from the Chooser, follow these steps:

1. Turn on the printer, if it is not already on.
2. Pull down the Apple menu and select the Chooser.

   The Chooser window displays, as shown in figure 2.26.

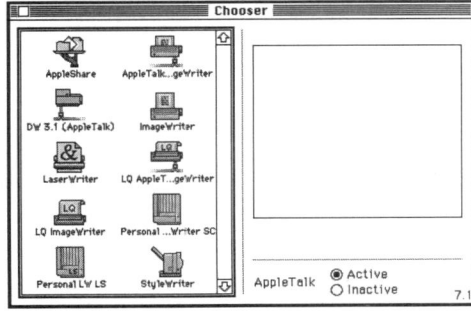

Figure 2.26. *The Chooser desk accessory.*

Caution

If you are going to print from a printer that is not attached to your computer, make sure that the computer you're printing from has ClarisWorks and that the same fonts that you're using are installed.

Caution

Always save your files before you print in case your computer freezes and you are forced to restart your computer.

Note

Place the date and time in the footer of your file so you'll be able to tell when it was printed.

> **Note**
>
> Laser printers and printers connected over a network require that AppleTalk be turned on. Other printers such as stand-alone StyleWriters and ImageWriters require that AppleTalk be turned off.

> **Tip**
>
> If you have problems printing, select the printer from the Chooser. If you still have problems, turn the printer on and off again. Don't forget to check the cables to be sure they are firmly attached.

3. Click on the icon of the printer you want to use.

   The name of the printer displays in the scrolling window to the right. If a name does not display, check to see if the printer is turned on.

4. Close the Chooser by clicking its Close box or pressing Command-W.

5. Pull down the File menu, and select the Page Setup command

6. Click on the OK button or press the Return or Enter key.

   By opening and closing the printer settings in Page Setup, you verify the printer information in ClarisWorks. This step is important even though you don't feel like you're doing anything.

The Print Monitor (see figure 2.27) is part of your Macintosh's system software. Whenever you print, the Print Monitor keeps track of the status of your printing job. You can view the Print Monitor by choosing it from the Application menu at the top right of your screen.

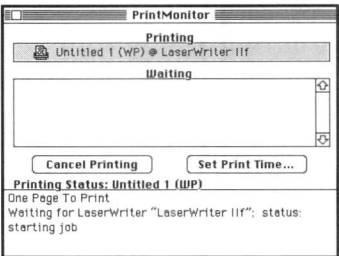

Figure 2.27. *The Print Monitor.*

Printing the Pages You Want

You can print all or part of a file. To print, follow these steps:

1. Pull down the File menu and choose the Print command.

   The Print dialog box displays, as shown in figure 2.28.

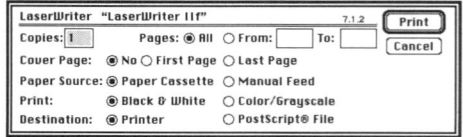

Figure 2.28. *The LaserWriter Print dialog box.*

2. Type the number of copies you want in the Copies box.

   Since your computer sends information to your printer page by page, if you are printing six copies of a 10-page file, you'll get six copies of page 1, six copies of page 2, and so forth. You will have to do the collating.

3. To print only a part of your file, type the appropriate page numbers in the From and To text boxes.

   To print only page 9, you would type 9 in the From box and 9 in the To box.

4. Click on the OK button or press the Return or Enter key.

Printer Options

Depending on the printer selected in the Chooser, you have several printing options available to you from the Print dialog box or by pressing the Option button and opening the Page Setup dialog box. Refer to your printer's documentation for more information.

Getting Help

With ClarisWorks and System 7, you have access to two excellent online, context-sensitive help systems. The ClarisWorks Help System contains information that describes various features and assists you in using them. System 7's Balloon Help offers context-sensitive information that helps you identify screen elements and the purpose of the items in the Tools palette.

The ClarisWorks Help System

You have access to ClarisWorks Help as long as it is installed on your computer. If you do not see the ClarisWorks Help System in the ClarisWorks folder, as shown in figure 2.29, you will need to install it using the Installer program. (See chapter 1, "Getting Started with ClarisWorks.")

The ClarisWorks Help System is a collection of cards with information on how to use various features.

Shortcut
To print, press Command-P.

Tip
To cancel printing, press Command-.
(Command-period).

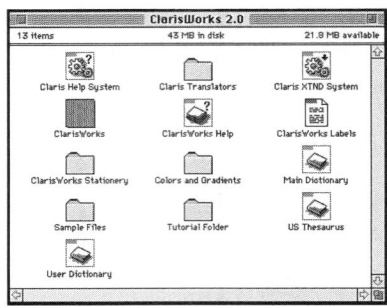

Figure 2.29. *The ClarisWorks folder.*

To use the ClarisWorks Help System, follow these steps:

1. Pull down the Apple menu and select the Help command, or press Command-?.

    A Help window related to the environment that you are currently working in displays. For example, if you are working in a spreadsheet frame, ClarisWorks displays a Help window with information on spreadsheets.

2. To find out how to navigate the help system, click on the Question Mark button on the upper-right side of the screen (see figure 2.30).

    The Navigation Overview card displays.

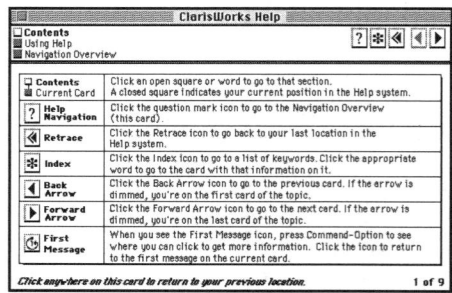

Figure 2.30. *The ClarisWorks Navigation Overview card.*

3. Click on the * (asterisk) button to view the contents of the help system in alphabetical order.

    The alphabetical index displays, as shown in figure 2.31. To find a topic, click on a letter. ClarisWorks will display a window listing the topics that begin with that letter.

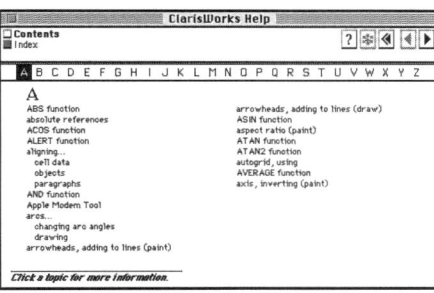

Figure 2.31. *The ClarisWorks Help System alphabetical index.*

> **Tip**
> Use the Help key on an extended keyboard to access the ClarisWorks Help System.

System 7 Balloon Help

Balloon Help is a System 7 feature. When you click on an area of your screen for which there is Balloon Help, it offers short, informative text in small balloons, much like the ones you see in comic books.

Balloon Help slows down your machine, so you should use it to get information and then turn it off.

To obtain access to Balloon Help information, open the Help menu—the second menu from the right edge of the menu bar, with a balloon icon—and select the Show Balloons icon. As you position the mouse pointer above various elements of ClarisWorks (or other programs, for that matter), balloons will apperar, with useful information about the element (see figure 2.32).

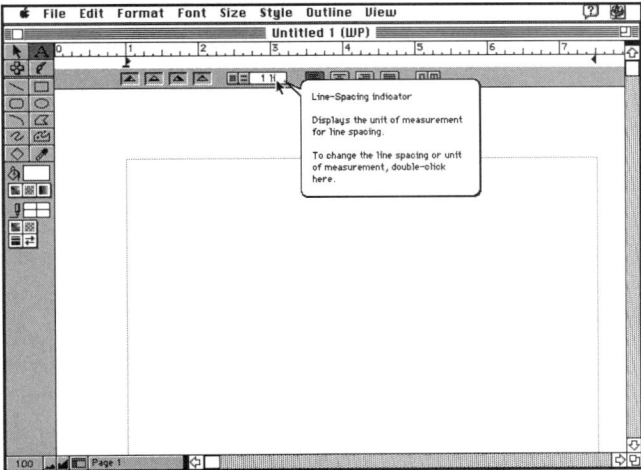

Figure 2.32. *Balloon Help.*

To turn Balloon Help off, click on the Balloon Help icon on the upper-right corner of the menu bar and choose the Hide Balloons command.

Summary

The basic skills of opening, closing, saving, and printing ClarisWorks files are crucial to effectively use ClarisWorks. The Cut, Copy, and Paste commands are especially useful, and can make working with ClarisWorks much simpler. And, ClarisWorks provides a Help System and Balloon Help for those times when you're stumped by the program.

Chapter 3
Working With Text in the Word Processor

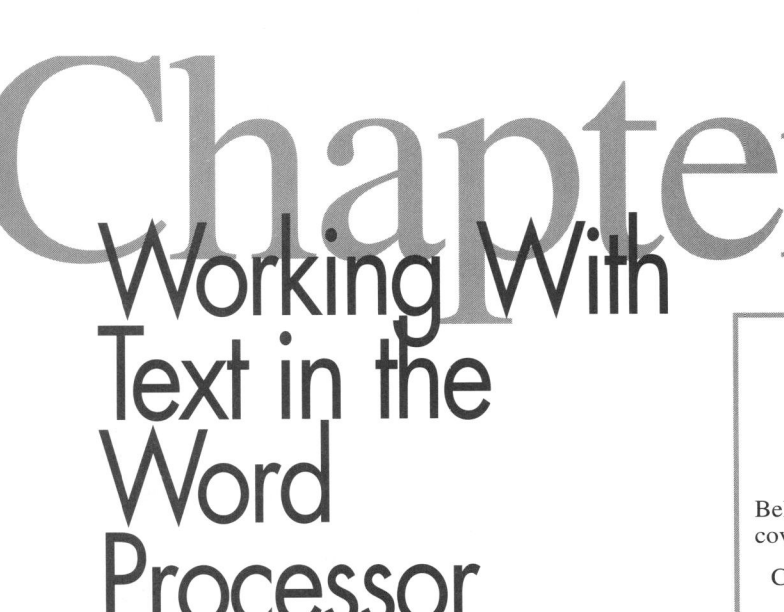

In this chapter, you'll find both the basics of word processing in ClarisWorks and time-saving tips that help you create good-looking documents by formatting text; finding synonyms; inserting page breaks; creating custom styles; setting margins and tabs; creating bulleted lists; and inserting footnotes, headers, and footers. You also will learn how to make use of ClarisWorks' integrated software to insert a spreadsheet frame or graphic into a word processing document.

Below are some of the how-to topics covered in this chapter:

Create a word processing document	44
Check spelling on all or part of a document	48
Find text	53
Change words and invisible characters	55
Create a custom style from a selection	58
Create a simple bulleted or numbered list	63
View invisible characters like tabs and spaces	65
Customize the Ruler	66
Insert a numbered footnote	68
Copy and paste a graphic from another document or application	72
Create a graphics frame in a text document	73
Work with snaking columns	75
Work with tables	76
Insert a page or column break	76
Work with headers or footers in a document	82
Add page numbers, dates, and times to a header or footer	83

Word processing applications, like the one in ClarisWorks, represent the most common use of the computer. While other environments in ClarisWorks, such as database and spreadsheet, also allow you to work with text, the word processing environment provides you with the most control over the appearance of your text.

If you don't know where to begin with ClarisWorks, read this chapter.

What is a Word Processor?

A word processor is a computer program (or application) designed to capture text entered from a keyboard. Your word processor borrows some principles from the typewriter, such as tabs, margins, and line spacing. Those of you who learned how to type on a typewriter and have not yet worked on a computer will need to change some habits. With a computer, it is not necessary to hit the Return key to begin a new line. Your word processor calculates the amount of text that can fit on one line and then begins a new line. This feature is called *text wrap*.

On a typewriter, each character has the same width— for example, the letter "i" is given as much space on the page as the letter "m." This is referred to as *monospacing*. You inserted two spaces after every period to help break the page into readable chunks. The computer, for the most part, uses *proportionally spaced* fonts to produce very readable and professional-looking text. Since the text is already very readable, you need only insert one space after any mark of punctuation. While this might seem arbitrary, this is what professional typesetters have been doing for years. If you are creating text for a brochure or newsletter, you will find that those extra spaces look out of place. Remember: only one space after a period.

Creating and Editing Text

As you work in ClarisWorks, you will create word processing documents and word processing frames in other documents. Editing encompasses changes made to the meaning of the text, such as replacing one word with another or copying and pasting passages of text.

To create a word processing document, follow these steps:

1. Launch ClarisWorks by double-clicking on the ClarisWorks icon or single-clicking on the ClarisWorks icon and pulling

down the File menu and choosing the Open command.

Your computer loads ClarisWorks into RAM and then displays the New Document dialog box, as shown in figure 3.1.

By default, word processing is already selected.

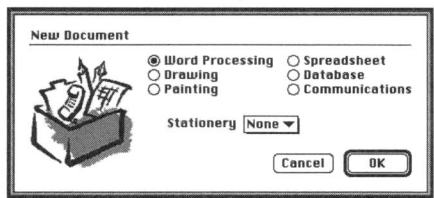

Figure 3.1. *The New Document dialog box.*

2. Click on the OK button, or press the Return or the Enter key.

ClarisWorks displays the appropriate menu bar and an untitled file, as shown in figure 3.2.

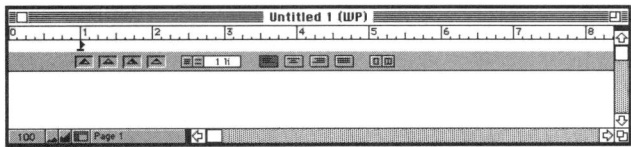

Figure 3.2. *An untitled word processing document.*

Text Frames

Because ClarisWorks gives you the opportunity to work in various environments, such as spreadsheets, drawings, and paintings, you can add text to other types of documents besides word processing documents. To create text in another document type, you must create a *text frame* and indicate its size and placement on the page. Once you have created a text frame, any text entered will wrap based on the dimensions of the frame. You can resize the frame at any time and perform all of the functions you might use in ClarisWorks' word processing environment. When you click on a frame, the menu bar changes to provide you with the appropriate commands.

To create a text frame in another type of document, follow these steps:

1. In an open file, pull down the View menu and select Show Tools, if necessary.

   The Tools panel displays, as shown in figure 3.3.

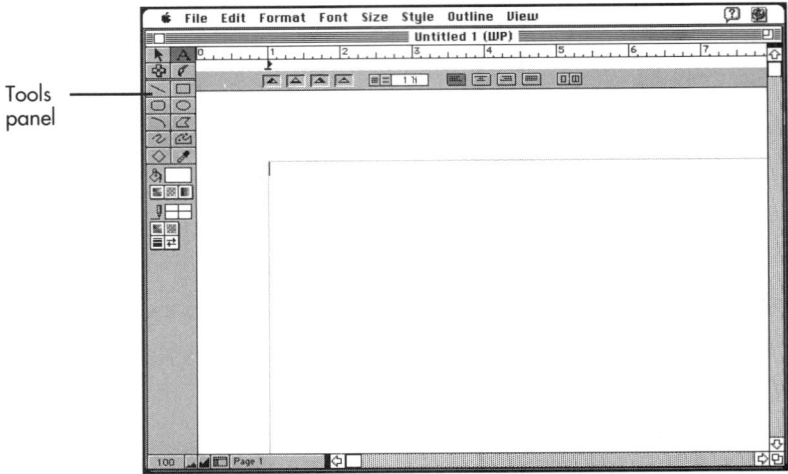

Figure 3.3. *The Tools panel.*

2. Click on the Text tool (the A) on the Tools panel.

   The Text tool puts you in the word processing environment. The I-beam or text-insertion cursor displays.

3. Click in the frame to create the text frame.

   An outline of the text frame displays. You may enter text or drag the frame to another position on the page.

Selecting and Moving Text

Before you can make any changes to existing text, you must first highlight it or select it by using the mouse or the keyboard. Below are several techniques that will enable you to select all or part of your document.

Table 3.1. *Techniques for selecting text in ClarisWorks Works*

To select a single word	Double-click on the word.
To select a line	Click on the line three times.
To select a paragraph	Click somewhere in the paragraph four times.
To select a large portion of text	Place the cursor at the beginning of the selection, hold down the Shift key, scroll to the end of the selection and click the mouse button.
To select the entire document	Pull down the Edit menu and choose Select All, or press Command-A.

Basic Editing

Editing or changing the contents of a word processing document is easy in ClarisWorks. Editing does not change the appearance of your document. The most basic way to change existing text is to use the Backspace or the Delete key to erase the text, and then retype the correct text.

If you don't use the Backspace or the Delete key, you must first select the text you want to change. When the text is selected, you can type right over it to replace the selected text with the text you type.

Using the Cut, Copy, and Paste Commands to Edit Text

One of the more powerful ways to edit text in ClarisWorks is to duplicate text with the Copy and Paste commands. You can move text by using the Cut and Paste commands. For a more complete treatment of the Cut, Copy, and Paste commands, refer to chapter 2, "Some Basics."

Don't Forget Undo!

From time to time, you may make a mistake. Even if you select the entire contents of a document and delete it, you can recover it—if you don't panic. Don't do anything else to the document. Pull down the Edit menu

Tip

If you did not act in time to use the Undo command, close your document and don't save any changes.

Shortcut

To undo your last action, press Command-Z.

Caution

Be sure to select Undo immediately. Even if you hit the Spacebar by accident, it's too late to use Undo.

and select Undo. ClarisWorks reverses your *last* action, restoring the deleted text to the screen.

Checking Your Spelling

As you enter and edit text, you may make some spelling errors. The Spelling Checker in ClarisWorks is flexible: you can add words to create a custom dictionary, use keyboard shortcuts to speed up the process, and check the entire document or only a selected portion of it. These options are listed on the Spelling submenu under the Edit menu, as shown in figure 3.4.

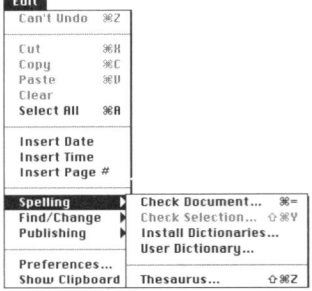

Figure 3.4. *The Spelling submenu.*

When you use the spelling checker, the computer compares the contents of your document to a list of words and offers possible alternatives. You must remember that your computer does not understand the context that words are used in and will not flag words that are correctly spelled but improperly used. If you had intended to type "disk drive" and instead typed "dish drivel," the spelling checker would not detect any errors, to your embarrassment and everyone else's amusement. It's your responsibility to proof all documents you pass on to other people.

You may need to install a dictionary before you begin to check the spelling in your document, if:

❖ You are using the spelling checker for the first time since you installed ClarisWorks.

❖ You just used another dictionary, such as the thesaurus.

❖ You want to use a specific dictionary such as the User dictionary or dictionaries of specific terms that you purchased elsewhere.

To install a dictionary, follow these steps:

1. Pull down the Edit menu, then select Install Dictionaries from the Spelling submenu.

   The Install Dictionaries dialog box displays, as shown in figure 3.5.

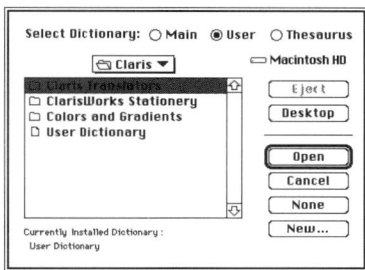

Figure 3.5. *The Install Dictionaries dialog box.*

2. Select the type of dictionary to install by clicking on a radio button. The Main dictionary is supplied by Claris, the User dictionary is composed of all the words you have added in previous spelling-checking sessions. The Thesaurus dictionary contains lists of synonyms to provide you with other word choices. The Thesaurus is not used to check spelling.

3. Click on the OK button, or press the Return or Enter key. You are now ready to begin checking your spelling.

Now that you have selected a dictionary, you are ready to check the spelling in the current document.

To check spelling on all or part of a document, follow these steps:

1. Pull down the Edit menu, then select Check Document or Check Selection from the Spelling submenu. The Check Selection command will be dimmed unless you have text selected in your document. The Spelling dialog box displays, as shown in figure 3.6.

   As ClarisWorks detects each spelling error, you need to decide whether to correct the word, leave it as it is, or add it to your dictionary.

2. To correct the spelling, click on any of the suggestions in the list box. If the correct word is not listed, retype it in the highlighted text box. Or, to leave the word spelled as is, click on the Skip button.

Shortcut
To check the spelling of the entire document, use the Command-= keystroke.

Shortcut
To check the spelling of a selected area, press Command-Shift-Y.

Shortcut
To select a spelling from a list of alternatives, use the keyboard shortcut listed to the left of the entry in the Spelling dialog box.

Caution
The Spelling command does not detect repeated words, such as the "the."

3. Click on the OK button, or press the Return or Enter key. ClarisWorks corrects the word and highlights the next possible error.
4. To view a word in context, click on the lever on the bottom right side of the Spelling dialog box. The Spelling dialog box expands to provide you with information about how the word is used in the document, as shown in figure 3.6.
5. Click on the OK button, or press the Return or Enter key. ClarisWorks corrects the word and highlights the next possible error.
6. When you have finished the spelling checking procedure, click on the Done button to return to your document.

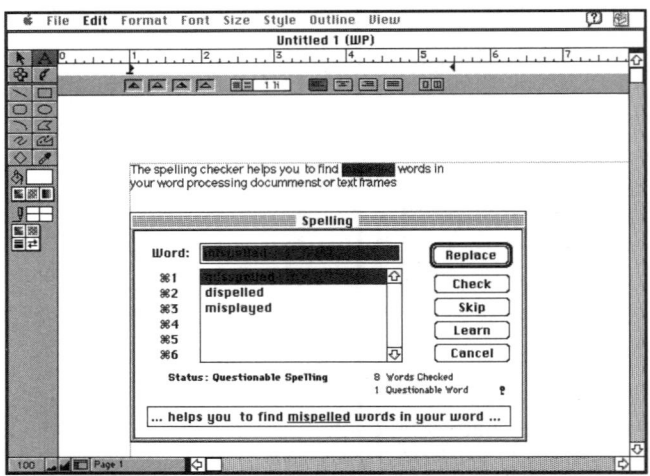

Figure 3.6. *The Spelling dialog box.*

Frequently used words such as names, cities, or product names repeatedly show up as misspelled words in the Spelling dialog box. To prevent this from happening, create a User dictionary. ClarisWorks refers to this dictionary and the default dictionary each time you use the Spelling command.

To add words to the dictionary, follow these steps:

1. When ClarisWorks detects a possibly misspelled word, click on the Learn button. ClarisWorks adds the word to the User dictionary and continues to check the spelling of the document.
2. Continue to check for spelling errors.
3. Click on the Done button to return to your document.

You can edit the User dictionary and remove words that you have added in previous spelling-checking sessions. It's a good idea to review the contents of the User dictionary from to time in case misspelled words have inadvertently been added to the dictionary.

To remove words from the User dictionary, follow these steps:

1. Pull down the Edit menu and choose User dictionary from the Spelling submenu. The User dictionary dialog box displays, as shown in figure 3.7.

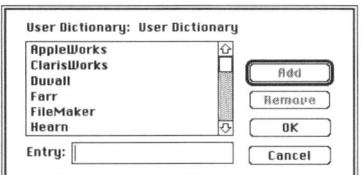

Figure 3.7. *The User dictionary dialog box.*

2. Scroll through the contents of the dictionary to locate the words you want to delete.
3. Click on each word you want to delete, then click on the Delete button, or press the Return or the Enter key.
4. Click on the Cancel button to restore a deleted word. The Cancel alert box displays to verify this command.
5. Click on the OK button to leave the word(s) in the dictionary. Click on the Cancel button to return to the User Dictionary dialog box.
6. To restore the word to the dictionary, click on the Add button.
7. When you are finished, click on the Done button to return to your document.

Tip

To add a lot of words at one time to the user dictionary, create a document filled with frequently used terms and names. Then check the spelling of the entire document and add each word to the dictionary. Save this file and share it with friends and co-workers.

Caution

Clicking on the Cancel button will undo all the changes you have made while editing the User dictionary.

Be sure to proofread your document!

Finding the Right Word: Using the Thesaurus

The ClarisWorks thesaurus is a dictionary of synonyms, or words that have the same meaning. A thesaurus does not check spelling or provide definitions. If you are working in ClarisWorks and struggling to find just the right word, use the thesaurus.

To find a list of synonyms, follow these steps:

1. Select a word in your document.
2. Pull down the Edit menu and choose Thesaurus from the Spelling submenu, or press Command-Shift-Z . If the word you select is not in the thesaurus, you will see the following dialog box, as shown in figure 3.8.

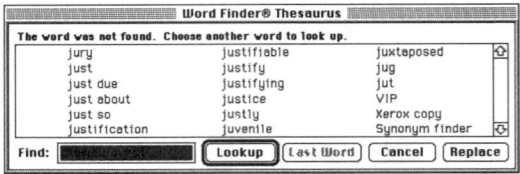

Figure 3.8. *The WordFinder dialog box with error message.*

If the word you select is in the thesaurus, you will see the following dialog box, as shown in figure 3.9.

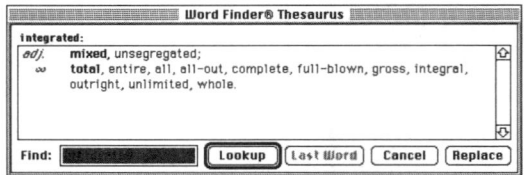

Figure 3.9. *The WordFinder Thesaurus dialog box.*

3. Scroll through the list of alternate words, make a selection, then click on the Change button. ClarisWorks replaces the selected word in your document with the word you selected from the WordFinder Thesaurus dialog box.
4. Click on the OK button, or press the Return or Enter key to return to your document.

Shortcut
To display the WordFinder Thesaurus dialog box, use Command-Shift-Z.

Shortcut
To close the dialog box, press the Command-. (period) keystroke. Command-. can be used to stop a process like printing or as a substitute for clicking on a Cancel button in most dialog boxes.

To continue to find synonyms for other words without closing the WordFinder Thesaurus dialog box, follow these steps:

1. In the WordFinder dialog box, type a word in the Find text box.
2. Click on the Lookup button. ClarisWorks displays a list of synonyms.
3. Click on the OK button, or press the Return or Enter key to return to your document.

Searching and Replacing

One of the advantages of using a word processor is the capability to quickly search the contents of your document.

To find text, follow these steps:

1. Pull down the Edit menu and select the Find/Change command from the Find/Change submenu. The Find/Change dialog box displays, as shown in figure 3.10.

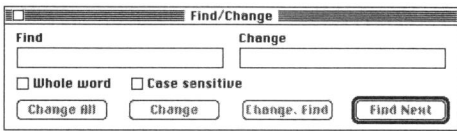

Figure 3.10. *The Find/Change dialog box.*

2. In the Find text box, type the word or words you want to locate. You can ask ClarisWorks to match the capitalization and to match whole words only. By matching whole words, you eliminate false finds. For example, typing "news" could also result in finds for "newspaper," and "newsreel" if the search was not restricted to matching whole words only.
3. Click on the Find button to begin the search. ClarisWorks locates the next instance of the contents of the Find text box.
4. Click on the Find Again button to locate the next instance.
5. Click on the Close box, or press Command-W to close the Find/Change dialog box.

ClarisWorks' Find/Change command provides you with the capability to replace a word or phrase with another and to correct some

Shortcut
To display the Find/Change dialog box, press Command-F.

Tip
Use the Find/Change command to move quickly to a specific place in your document.

typographical errors. Use the Change text box in the Find/Change dialog box to specify how you want to modify the contents of the Find text box and make changes instantaneously.

To replace text, follow these steps:

1. Pull down the Edit menu and select the Find/Change command from the Find/Change submenu, or press Command-F.
2. In the Find text box, type the word or words you want to locate.
3. In the Change text box, type the word or words that will replace the contents of the Find text box.
4. Click on the Find button to begin the search. ClarisWorks locates the next instance of the contents of the Find text box.
5. Click on the Find Again button to locate the next instance.
6. To replace all instances of the Find text box, click on the Change All button.

   ClarisWorks displays an alert warning you that you will not be able to undo the results, as shown in figure 3.11.

> **Caution**
> Clicking on the Cancel button will undo all the changes you have made while editing the User dictionary.

> **Tip**
> Use the Find/Change command to save typing time. For example, type an abbreviation such as CW in the text. Type CW in the Find text box and ClarisWorks in the Change text box.

> **Caution**
> Before using the Change All option, save your document. Then, if the Change All option did not turn out as you expected, you can close your document without saving changes.

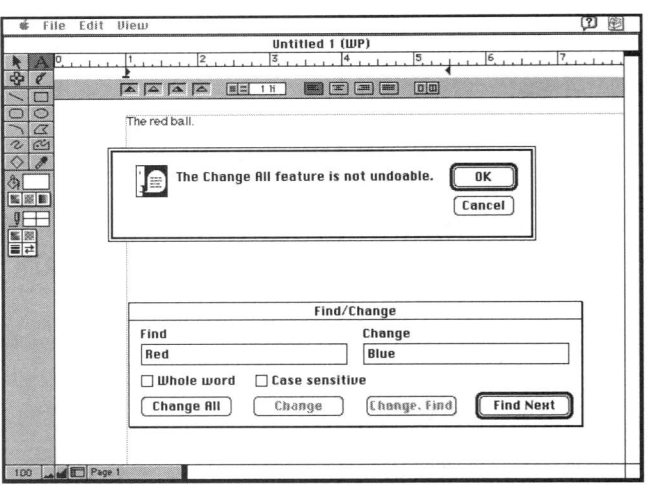

Figure 3.11. *The Change All feature alert.*

7. Click on the OK button to replace all instances or on the Find Next button to continue changing one instance at a time.

8. Click on the Close box, or press Command-W, to close the Find/Change dialog box.

Use the Find/Change command to detect and correct mechanical errors such as spaces before commas and to replace double spaces with tabs.

To replace hidden or invisible characters such as page breaks, tabs, and spaces, type the following in either the Find or the Change text boxes:

> **Tip**
> Use the Find/Change command to change all double spaces to single spaces.

Table 3.2. *Invisible character equivalents*

To find or replace this...	Type this...
Backslash	\\
Date	\d
Hard return	\p
Line break	\n
Nonbreaking space	Option-Spacebar
Page break or column break	\c
Space	Spacebar
Tab	\t
Time	\h

Learning to Format Text with Style

Formatting, unlike editing, only changes the way text looks. Formatting includes setting margins and tabs, choosing a font, selecting a font size, and applying bold, italic, underline, and other text styles.

Formatting with a word processor like the one in ClarisWorks involves selecting the text you want to change and then choosing the appropriate command. Most formatting commands are located on the Format menu, as shown in figure 3.12.

About Characters, Paragraphs, and Document Formats

There are three major types of formatting: Character, Paragraph, and Document. Character formatting is applied to the characters entered from the keyboard. Character formatting includes changing fonts, font size, and font appearance (by applying bold, italic, and underline styles), to name a few examples.

Paragraph formatting changes the way text flows on a page. Paragraph formatting includes margins, indents, tabs, the amount of space between lines and paragraphs, and text alignment.

Document formatting is used to set the margins for the entire document, to specify the starting page number, and to determine how margins display onscreen.

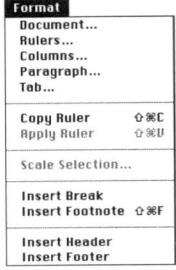

Figure 3.12. *The Format menu.*

Character Formatting: Changing Fonts and Sizes

As you type in ClarisWorks, your text displays in 12-point Helvetica. You may want to change the font and size to create a document that communicates a different mood.

When you use character formatting, let form follow function. A traditional font such as Times or Helvetica is suitable for a resume. For ease of reading or faxing, a more open font such as Palatino is a good choice.

Consider who will be reading your document and how they will be using it. If you are creating a menu for use in a candlelit restaurant, don't use a small font size and italics—the diners may develop a headache before they decide what to order! In general, body text should be between 10 and 14 points. Fonts and line spacing are measured in points. 72 points equal one inch, so a 12-point font is roughly one-sixth of an inch high.

Character formatting commands are located in several places in ClarisWorks. A listing of available fonts appears under the Font menu.

To change the font of any text, select the text you want to change and make a selection from the Font menu.

A list of font sizes displays on the Font menu. To change the size of any selected text, make a selection from the Font menu.

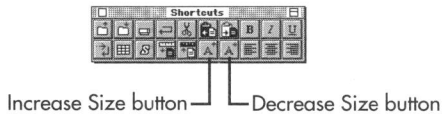

Figure 3.13. *The Increase Size and Decrease Size buttons.*

Using Formatting to Add Emphasis

Adding formatting to your text to adds emphasis to certain words or phrases. For example, you can italicize book or magazine titles and use bold for headlines. Formatting options are listed on the Style menu, as shown in figure 3.14.

Figure 3.14. *The Style menu.*

To change the style attributes of selected text, make one or more selections from the Style menu. Or, to add or remove bold, italic, or underline style attributes, click on the Bold, Italic, or Underline buttons in the Shortcut palette, as shown in Figure 3.13.

It's easy to change fonts and to add style attributes. Create one hideous document with various combinations of formatting. Once you have the urge to over-format out of your system, you will be more content to use attributes like underlining with restraint and taste.

> **Tip**
> To specify a custom size, select Other from the Font menu or press Command-Shift-O and type a whole number between 4 and 255. To increase or decrease the font size, click on the Increase Size or Decrease Size buttons in the Shortcuts palette, as shown in figure 3.13.

> **Shortcut**
> To add or remove bold, italic or underline style attributes, use the Command-B, Command-I, or Command-U keystrokes, respectively.

> **Tip**
> To develop an appreciation of good design and effective formatting, collect junk mail for a couple of weeks. Sort through it and divide it into three piles: Great, so-so, and ugly. Look at each pile and decide what they have in common. Try to replicate some of the good designs by using ClarisWorks. Consider keeping a file folder of excellent design ideas.

Putting It All Together: Defining Character Styles to Create Consistent Documents

With ClarisWorks, you can define custom styles and append them to your document. ClarisWorks styles contain only character formatting. This book, for instance, uses various styles for the text, captions, and headings. The real power of styles is the capability to update easily the formatting applied throughout a document. If you have applied a defined style throughout your document, and decide that you don't like the way it looks, you then can edit the style and reapply the style at each occurrence. ClarisWorks reformats each selection.

You can either create a style from an example or build a style right in the Define Style dialog box.

To create a custom style from a selection, follow these steps:

1. Format the text the way you want it.
2. Select the text whose attributes you want to duplicate.
3. Pull down the Style menu and choose Define Styles.

    The Define Style dialog box displays with a styles description of the current selection, as shown in figure 3.15.

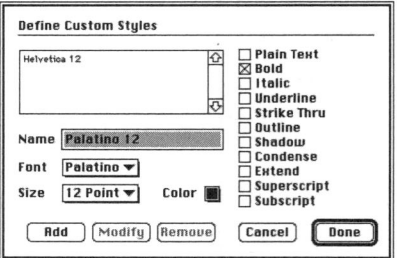

Figure 3.15. *The Define Custom Styles dialog box with descriptions of a current selection.*

4. Type a name for the style in the Name text box.
5. Click on the Add button to add the style to your document.
6. Click on the Done button, or press the Return or the Enter key to close the dialog box. When you pull down the Style menu, you will see your new style at the bottom.

Building styles right from the Define Custom Styles dialog box is a more advanced technique, but one that allows you to create all your styles before you type even one word.

To create a custom style in the Define Custom Styles dialog box, follow these steps:

1. Pull down the Style menu and choose Define Styles. The Define Style dialog box displays, as shown in figure 3.15.
2. Select a font from the pop-up list.
3. Select a font size from the pop-up list.
4. Type a name for the style in the text box.
5. Click on the Add button to add each style to your document.
6. Click on the Done button, or press the Return or Enter key to close the dialog box.

To modify a custom style, follow these steps:

1. Pull down the Style menu and choose Define Styles.

    The Define Custom Styles dialog box displays, as shown in figure 3.15.
2. Select a style from the list box.
3. Make any changes to the font, size, or attributes.
4. Click on the Modify button.
5. Click on the Done button, or press the Return or Enter key to close the dialog box.

Apply custom character styles to any part of a line, sentence, or document by selecting text, pulling down the Style menu, and selecting a style.

Using Define Styles to Change the Default Font

To change the font used automatically by ClarisWorks in a specific word processing document, you need to redefine the style for plain text.

To change the default font for a specific word processing document, follow these steps:

1. Pull down the Style menu and choose Define Styles. The Define Custom Styles dialog box displays, as shown in figure 3.15.

Shortcut
To apply a custom style to a selection, use the keystroke shortcut that appears next to its name on the Style menu.

> **Tip**
>
> If you need to use the same styles in many documents, create a document that has these styles. Using the Save As command, give it a name like Book Template and choose the Stationery file type from the pop-up list. Whenever you open a Stationery document, ClarisWorks displays an Untitled document with the contents and style characteristics of the original.

2. Pull down the font list in the dialog box and select a new font.
3. Specify a new font size, if desired.
4. Click only on Plain Text in the upper-right corner. You may not select any other styling features.
5. Delete the name Helvetica 12 and do not type over it.
6. Click on the Add button, then click on the OK button.

ClarisWorks updates the definition of Plain Text and closes the Define Custom Styles dialog box. All subsequent text typed into this word processing document has the attributes of the newly defined Plain Text.

Paragraph formatting: Changing Margins and Indents

A paragraph is a group of characters and may be of any length. The length of a paragraph is determined by how much text is entered before the Return or the Enter key is pressed.

The initial page margins are determined by the entries in the Format Document dialog box. Local changes to margins are made on the Ruler or in the Format Paragraph dialog box. Changes made using either of these techniques affect only the area selected.

To change the margins of a paragraph by using the Ruler, follow these steps:

1. Click in the text of the paragraph. The insertion point, or I-beam cursor, blinks where you clicked.
2. Click on either the left-pointing or right-pointing triangle on the Ruler. The left-pointing triangle determines how much the text is indented from the left. The right-pointing triangle determines how much the text is indented from the right.
3. Hold down the mouse button and drag either triangle to a new position on the Ruler, then release it.

To change the margins of a paragraph by using the Paragraph dialog box, follow these steps:

1. Click in the text of the paragraph. The insertion point, or I-beam cursor, blinks where you clicked, as mentioned above.
2. Pull down the Format menu and choose Paragraph. The Paragraph dialog box displays, as shown in figure 3.16.

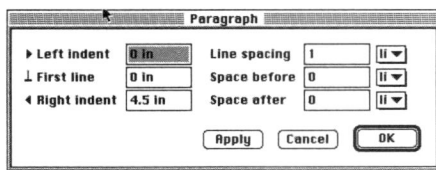

Figure 3.16. *The Paragraph dialog box.*

3. Type how much you want to indent the text from the left or the right.
4. Click on the OK button, or press the Return or Enter key. The paragraph shifts position to reflect the measurements entered the dialog box.

Several styles of writing call for the first line of a paragraph to be indented. Indents achieved by pressing down the Spacebar are uneven. You can specify the indentation of the first line by using either the Ruler or the Paragraph dialog box.

To change the first-line indentation of a paragraph using the Ruler, follow these steps:

1. Click in the text of the paragraph.

   The insertion point, or the I-beam cursor, blinks where you clicked.
2. Click on the line below the left-margin symbol on the Ruler. The first-line indentation marker is shaped like an upside-down T, as shown in figure 3.17.

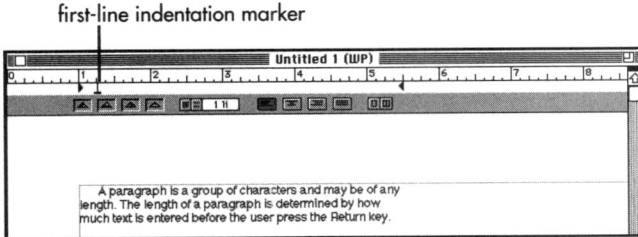

Figure 3.17. *The Ruler with an indented first line.*

3. Holding down the mouse, drag the first-line indent marker to a new position on the Ruler. The paragraph reflows to reflect the new indentation.

> **Tip**
> Even though the procedures using the Paragraph dialog box appear longer, they take less time, since you can navigate quickly through the dialog box with the Tab key and end the task by pressing the Return or Enter key.

To change the first-line indentation of a paragraph by using the Paragraph dialog box, follow these steps:

1. Click in the text of the paragraph. The insertion point or the I-beam cursor blinks where you clicked.
2. Pull down the Format menu and choose Paragraph. The Paragraph dialog box displays, as shown in figure 3.16.
3. In the First Line text box, type in the amount of indentation you want.
4. Click on the OK button, or press the Return or Enter key. The paragraph shifts position to reflect the measurements entered the dialog box.

Using Tabs Instead of the Spacebar

Using spaces to create the illusion of evenly indented text often produces text that looks lined up onscreen. Reality sets in, however, when you look at the printed page. Unless you are using a monospaced font like Courier, your text margins will waver. The only feasible way to create text that lines up is by using tabs.

ClarisWorks comes with four kinds of tabs:

- ❖ The left tab: Specifies where tabbed text should begin. This is the most commonly used tab.
- ❖ The center tab: Specifies a center point for tabbed text. This tab is useful for centering headlines in newsletters.
- ❖ The right tab: Specifies where the tabbed text should end. This tab is rarely used, but can be employed for page numbers in tables of contents and interesting layouts.
- ❖ The decimal tab: Specifies that the tabbed text should align at decimal points or other custom symbols. This tab is wonderful for aligning columns of figures that have been typed in a word processing frame.

You can access these tabs by clicking on their icons on the Ruler, as shown in figure 3.18.

Setting a tab is a two-step process. First, you must insert a tab in the text. Then select the kind of tab you want and drag it to a position on the Ruler. By default, ClarisWorks' automatic tab stops are set at every one-half inch. You may set different kinds of tabs in the same line, as shown in figure 3.19 below. ClarisWorks continues to display the same tab settings for each new line until you change them. When you change the tab settings in a new line, the previous settings remain unchanged unless you select the text and then manually make the changes.

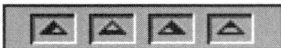

Figure 3.18. *Tab icons on the Ruler.*

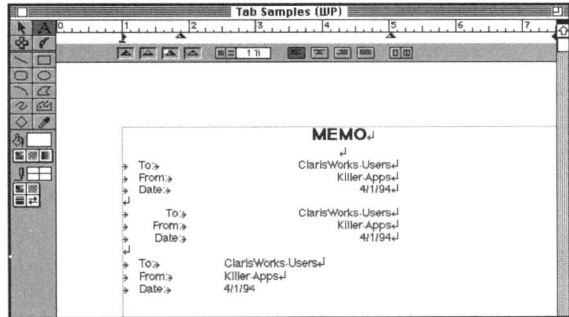

Figure 3.19. *Memo with various tab settings.*

To remove a tab, drag the icon off the Ruler.

You must insert a tab by pressing the Tab key in the text for ClarisWorks to recognize a tab setting on the Ruler. Be sure to use the Show Invisibles option in the Preferences dialog box when working with tabs. Tabs appear onscreen as small arrows but do not print.

Your documents will be easier to work with if you don't use excessive tabs. This is a good habit to develop, especially if you work in desktop publishing programs such as Aldus PageMaker or QuarkXPress. Most programs are similar in their approach to tabs; if you learn how to use them in ClarisWorks, you'll be able to use them in most Macintosh and Windows applications.

Making Bulleted or Numbered Lists

By using the first-line-indent control and tabs, you can create bulleted or numbered lists with indented text.

To create a simple bulleted or numbered list, follow these steps:

1. Type Option-8 to create a bullet, or type a number such as 1.

2. Press the Tab key.

   If you have the Show Invisibles option turned on in the Preferences dialog box, you will see an arrow when you press the Tab key.

3. Type the text following the bullet or number.

4. Click on the left-tab icon and drag it to a position on the Ruler (such as to 0.25 inches).

   ClarisWorks adjusts the positioning of your text on the screen, as shown in figure 3.20.

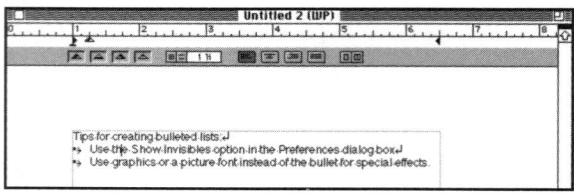

Figure 3.20. *Single-line bulleted text.*

5. Continue to type each new line, inserting the bullet or a number, the tab, and the text.

To create a multiple-line bulleted or numbered list, follow these steps:

1. Type Option-8 to create a bullet, or type a number such as 1.

2. Type the text of the bullet.

3. Hold down the Option key and drag the left-margin indent on the Ruler without moving the first-line indent control. Bulleted text reflows, as shown in figure 3.21.

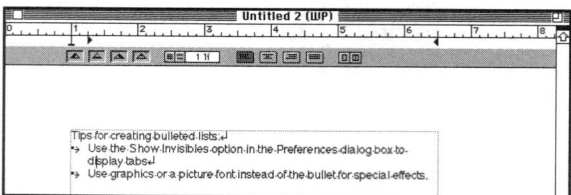

Figure 3.21. *Multiple-line bulleted text.*

4. Continue to type each new line, inserting the bullet or a number, the tab, and the text.

Changing Alignment

Alignment determines the shape of text. For example, centered text has ragged edges on both sides. Left-aligned text begins each line on the left side but leaves the right side ragged. Right-aligned text creates a visual line on the right side while the left side is uneven. Text that stretches evenly across a page has been justified (like the text in this paragraph). Figure 3.22 shows examples of each type of alignment.

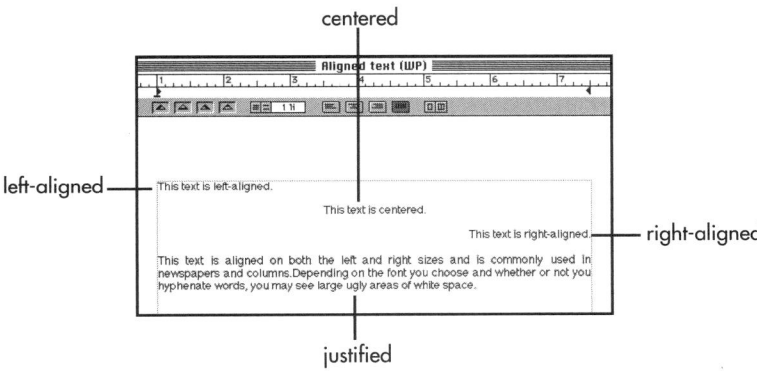

Figure 3.22. *Examples of left-aligned, centered, right-aligned, and justified text.*

You can change the text alignment by clicking on the alignment buttons on the Ruler, as shown in figure 3.22, or by pressing the Align Left, Align Center, or Align Right buttons on the Shortcuts palette, as shown in figure 3.13.

Working with formatting is easier when you can see the placement and number of non-printing characters such as spaces and tabs.

To view invisible characters such as spaces and tabs, follow these steps:

1. Pull down the Edit menu and choose Preferences. The Preferences dialog box displays, as shown in figure 3.23. Or, press the Show Invisibles button on the Shortcuts palette, as shown in figure 3.13.
2. Click on the Show Invisibles checkbox.
3. Click on the OK button, or press the Enter or Return key to close the dialog box. Invisible characters such as line breaks, spaces, and tabs display onscreen. They will not print.

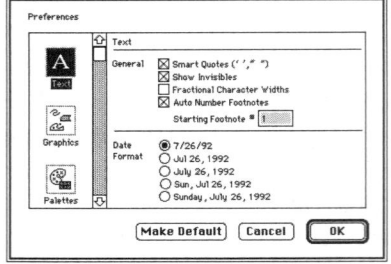

Figure 3.23. *The Preferences dialog box.*

Customizing the Ruler

As a default, ClarisWorks displays a ruler that uses inches. You can display a ruler that uses other systems of measurements, including points, picas, centimeters, or millimeters. You also have the option to determine how the Ruler is divided and whether you want a graphics ruler that displays both vertically and horizontally.

To customize the Ruler, follow these steps:

1. Pull down the Format menu and choose the Rulers command. The Rulers dialog box displays, as shown in figure 3.24.

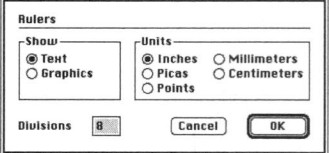

Figure 3.24. *The Rulers dialog box.*

2. Select the type of measurement, division, and type of ruler (text or graphics).
3. Click on the OK button or press the Return or Enter key.

   ClarisWorks displays the Ruler with the characteristics you specify in the dialog box.

Copying the Ruler to Duplicate Tabs and Indents

You can easily duplicate paragraph formatting created elsewhere in a document.

To copy the settings of a ruler to another location, follow these steps:

1. Click in the text of the paragraph you want to copy.
2. Pull down the Format menu and choose the Copy Ruler command, or press Command-Shift-C.
3. Click in the text of the paragraph you want to format.
4. Pull down the Edit menu and choose the Apply Ruler command, or press Command-Shift-V.

   The paragraph takes on the formatting characteristics of the original paragraph and the text is unchanged.

Document Formatting: Page Margins and Numbering

Document formatting applies to the entire document. By using the Document command on the Format menu, you can specify the overall margins of a document, how many pages to view onscreen, whether to show margins and pages, and the starting page number for a document. Figure 3.25 displays the Document dialog box.

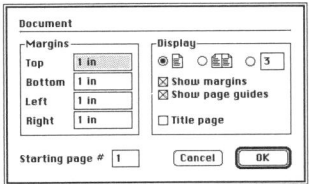

Figure 3.25. *The Document dialog box.*

Adding Footnotes

With ClarisWorks, you easily can add footnotes to a word processing document. You can specify whether the footnotes are automatically numbered, are set off by a custom character, and what the starting number of the footnotes should be.

To insert a numbered footnote, follow these steps:

1. Click where you want the footnote to appear.
2. Pull down the Format menu and choose Insert Footnote, or press Command-Shift-F.

   ClarisWorks displays the footnote number and the insertion point blinks below, in the Footnote panel under the footnote separator line, as shown in figure 3.26.

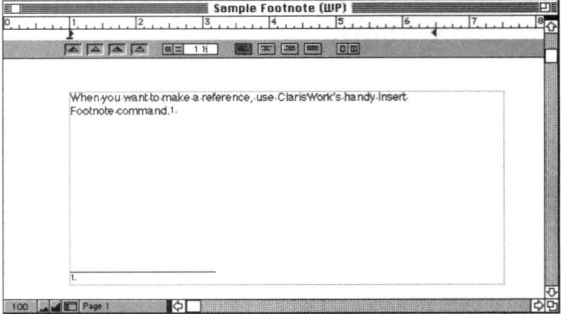

Figure 3.26. *The Footnote panel.*

3. Type the text of the footnote in the Footnote panel.
4. Press the Enter or the Return key. ClarisWorks moves the insertion point back to the document. You are ready to resume typing.

If you insert text in or delete text from a document, ClarisWorks automatically updates footnote reference numbers.

To use a custom mark instead of numbers, you must first disable the auto-numbering option in the Preferences dialog box.

To specify a custom footnote symbol, follow these steps:

1. Pull down the Edit menu and select the Preferences command.

   The Preferences dialog box displays, as shown in figure 3.27.

2. Clicking on the Auto Number Footnotes checkbox clears the "x" from it.
3. Click on the OK button, or press the Return or Enter key. The Preferences dialog box closes.

Shortcut
To create a footnote, press Command-Shift-F.

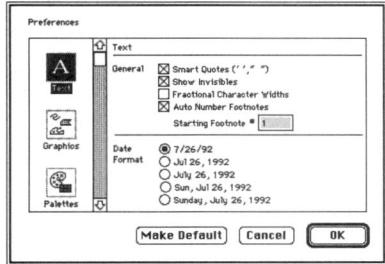

Figure 3.27. *The Preferences dialog box.*

4. Click in the text to indicate where the footnote reference should be.
5. Pull down the Format menu and choose Insert Footnote. The Mark With dialog box displays, as shown in figure 3.28.

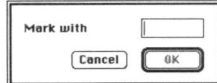

Figure 3.28. *The Mark With dialog box.*

6. Type a symbol character, such as "†" or "*."
7. Click on the OK button, or press the Return or the Enter key. ClarisWorks displays the footnote symbol and the insertion point blinks below in the Footnote panel under the footnote separator line.
8. Type the text of the footnote into the Footnote panel.
9. Press the Enter or the Return key. ClarisWorks moves the insertion point back to the document. You are ready to resume typing.

Working With an Outline

You can use the commands on the Outline menu to help you write a report, produce overheads, organize information effectively, or create convenient check lists. To create a new document as an outline or view an existing document as an outline, create the document and select the Outline View command from the Outline menu.

ClarisWorks' outlining commands are powerful and allow you a great deal of flexibility in both editing and formatting your outline. The contents of the Outline menu are displayed in figure 3.29.

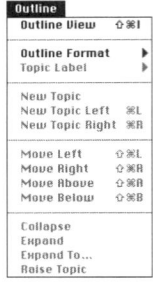

Figure 3.29. *The Outline menu.*

Once the Outline View command is selected, you can add new topics, promote and demote topics, expand and collapse topics so that you can view more or less of your outline onscreen, and even create custom formats. The commands on the Outline menu are descriptive, so we'll cover just a few of the most important ones here.

> **Shortcut**
> Press Command-Shift-I to view your document in Outline View.

Creating New Topics

While you are viewing your document in Outline View, you can create new topics by choosing the New Topic command from the Outline menu. Next, type the text of the new topic.

> **Shortcut**
> To create a new topic, press the Return key.

Rearranging the Contents of Your Document in the Outline View

Even if you don't like to work with outlines, you'll love the flexibility they provide when moving text around in any word processing document. Select the Outline View command from the Outline menu, or press Command-Shift-I. Click on the diamond in front of the body of text you wish to move and drag it to its new location. When you do this, all of the text that belongs to that topic heading moves with it. This method of reordering text is much faster than cutting, scrolling, and pasting large bodies of text to new locations. Since you are moving entire topics, you don't have to worry about possibly corrupting previously applied formatting. Outline formatting applies to a document only when it is in Outline View.

When you return to the normal word processing view, your pre-existing formatting is unchanged.

You also can use the Move Left, Move Right, and Raise commands to change the level of importance of a selected topic.

Choosing a Structure for Your Outline

You can choose a variety of number formats or outline styles for your outline. The Outline Format command, shown in figure 3.30, allows you to create an outline that follows a specific format such as legal, bulleted list, checklist, and so forth. When you make a selection from the Outline Format, ClarisWorks instantly updates your outline. You don't have to add the bullets or checkboxes; ClarisWorks does it all for you. If none of the predefined formats are to your liking, you can build and edit a custom format by selecting Custom Format from the bottom of the Outline Format submenu.

Shortcut
Use Shift-Command-L or Shift-Command-R to move topics to the left or to the right.

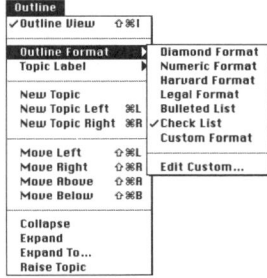

Figure 3.30. *The Outline Format submenu.*

The Check List option is handy for making to-do lists. If you click on a checkbox, ClarisWorks adds or removes a check mark.

Formatting the Topic Labels of Your Outline

Whether you use your outline to organize your thoughts, create a to-do list, or compose a presentation, you will probably want to change the formatting of your outline. Several formats are available to you from the Topic Label submenu, which is shown in figure 3.31. You can select from Roman numerals, letters, numbers, and symbols, such as diamonds or bullets.

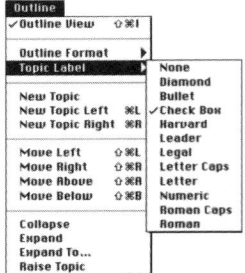

Figure 3.31. *The Topic Label submenu.*

Viewing an Outline as Text

To exit the Outline View, reselect the Outline View command from the Outline menu, or press Command-Shift-I, and the document returns to the word processing view.

Incorporating Graphics in Your Writing

Because of ClarisWorks' integrated software, it's easy to incorporate graphics into a word processing document. You can:

- ❖ Copy and paste a graphic.
- ❖ Create a drawing or painting graphics frame.

See chapter 6, "Adding Graphics to Your Work," for information on graphics.

Text-Embedded Graphics

To copy and paste a graphic from another document or application, follow these steps:

1. Copy the graphic in the original document by selecting it and choosing Copy from the Edit menu. The graphic is then placed on the Clipboard, a temporary storage area in the computer's random-access memory.

2. Open the new ClarisWorks document and place your insertion point where the graphic should go.
3. Pull down the Edit menu and choose Paste. The graphic appears at the insertion point. This graphic cannot be edited in the Graphics layer, and you will need to position it by using the alignment controls, spaces, or tabs.

You can delete a graphic by selecting it and pressing the Delete key.

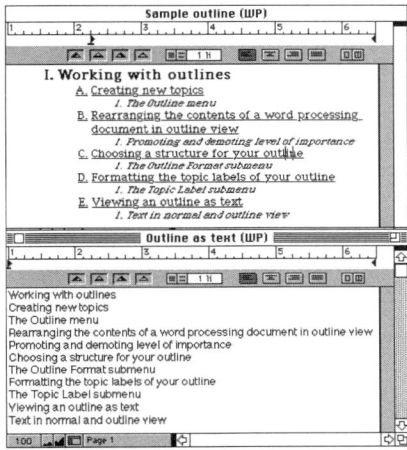

Figure 3.32. *A document in Outline View and Normal word processing view.*

Graphic Objects

The more powerful way to insert a graphic is to create a graphics frame. This enables you to use the graphics tools to edit or to add colors and borders, and it easily can be dragged to a new position in the document.

To create a graphics frame in a text document, follow these steps:

1. Pull down the View menu and choose Show Tools. The Tools panel displays.
2. Click on the Graphics tool. The text pointer changes to a graphics (paintbrush) pointer.

3. In the window, hold down the mouse button and drag a rectangular-shaped area. This creates the frame, as shown in figure 3.33.

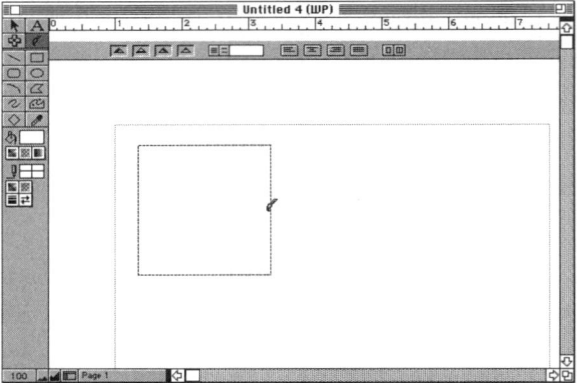

Figure 3.33. *A graphics frame.*

4. Create a graphic by using the available tools or paste a graphic into the frame.
5. Click outside the graphic frame to resume word processing tasks.

Composing a Page

When you work in ClarisWorks, you easily can design a page with various attributes. For instance, you can combine columns, tables, headers, footers, page numbers, and page breaks in one document.

There are no rules to tell you how to design your page, other than the natural inclination to make the various kinds of information presented as accessible and readable as possible.

For more information on creating complex pages, refer to the "Composing Compound Documents with Frames" section in chapter 8 where I discuss ways that ClarisWorks' several capabilities can be combined to create complex documents.

Composing With Frames

One effective way of putting a complex document together is to divide the pages into different types of frames—spreadsheet, graphics, and so on. By drawing and moving each frame, you can design attractive, informative documents that have the best functions of major software applications.

Creating Columns

With ClarisWorks, you'll find it easy to create snaking, or newspaper-style, columns. A snaking column starts at the top of the page and when it reaches the bottom, continues at the top of the page in the next or the adjacent column.

To create snaking columns, click on the Increase Columns control tool on the far right of the Ruler, as shown in figure 3.34. Each time you click this button, ClarisWorks adds a column.

Figure 3.34. *The Increase Column and Decrease Column controls.*

To reduce the number of columns, click on the Decrease Columns control tool on the far right of the Ruler, as shown in figure 3.34. Each time you click on this button, ClarisWorks deletes a column and reflows the text.

All columns added from the Ruler have the same width. You can specify how many columns you want and the set size of each one by using the Columns command.

To resize columns individually, follow these steps:

1. Pull down the Format menu and choose the Columns command. The Columns dialog box displays, as shown in figure 3.35.
2. Click on the Variable Width radio button. A pop-up list that shows each column displays.
3. Scroll to the number of the column you wish to resize. The Column Width box displays the number of the column you selected.

4. Type the size of the column you want in the box to the right.
5. Click on the OK button, or press the Return or Enter key.

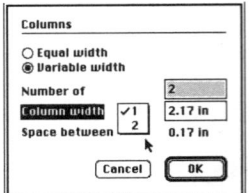

Figure 3.35. *The Columns dialog box.*

Adding Page Breaks and Column Breaks

As you type, ClarisWorks wraps your text to the next line and automatically computes where a page ends. To specify where you want a page or column to end, you need to insert a manual break.

To insert a manual break, follow these steps:

1. Click to indicate where the page should end.
2. Pull down the Format menu and choose Insert Break. ClarisWorks inserts the page break and changes the display on the screen.

Adding Tables

Sometimes it's easier to convey information presented in table form. Unlike Microsoft Word, which has a table tool, ClarisWorks offers a spreadsheet frame to create tables. Tables are created using the spreadsheet tool.

To create a table using a spreadsheet frame, follow these steps:

1. Pull down the View menu and choose Show Tools. The Tools panel displays, as shown in figure 3.36.
2. Click on the Spreadsheet tool. The text pointer changes to a spreadsheet pointer.
3. In the window, hold down the mouse button and drag an area in the shape of a rectangle. This creates the frame, as shown in figure 3.36.

Shortcut
To create a page break, press the Enter (not the Return) key. When you press the Return key, ClarisWorks creates a new paragraph.

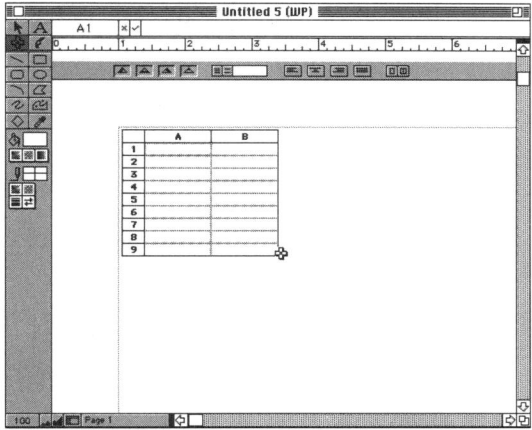

Figure 3.36. *A spreadsheet frame/table.*

Changing the Dimensions of Table Rows and Columns

You will need to change the width or height of the columns or rows so that your table will effectively present the information it contains. For more information about spreadsheets, see chapter 4, "Calculating Results With a Spreadsheet."

To change the width or height of columns or rows with the mouse, follow these steps:

1. Position the cursor over the border between a column heading or a row heading. The resize cursor displays in the form of a double-headed arrow, as shown in figure 3.37.

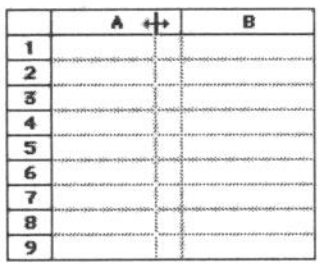

Figure 3.37. *The spreadsheet column and row resize cursor.*

2. Drag the column or row to the desired width or height. ClarisWorks resizes the columns and rows.

Changing How Many Rows and Columns Display

As you work with a table, you will need to change the number of rows and columns that display on your screen. To change the number of rows and columns, follow these steps:

1. Pull down the View menu and choose Show Tools. The Tools panel displays.
2. Click on the arrow-shaped Pointer tool on the Tools panel. The text pointer changes an arrow cursor.
3. Click on the table. Black handles appear on its corners.
4. Click on a handle and drag the table to the desired size.

Hiding Row and Column Headings

If you are using a spreadsheet frame to create a table, you may want to suppress the row and number headings so that the reader will focus on the information in the table.

To suppress the row and column headings, follow these steps:

1. Pull down the View menu and choose Show Tools.
2. Click on the Spreadsheet tool. The text pointer changes shape and the menus change.
3. Click anywhere on the table.
4. Pull down the Options menu and choose Display. The Display dialog box appears, as shown in figure 3.38.

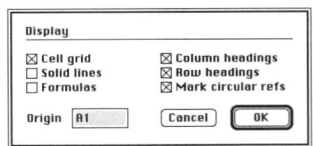

Figure 3.38. *The Display dialog box.*

5. Click on Column Headings and Row Headings. The checkboxes are cleared.
6. Click on the OK button, or press the Return or Enter key. ClarisWorks displays the table without row and column headings, as shown in figure 3.39.

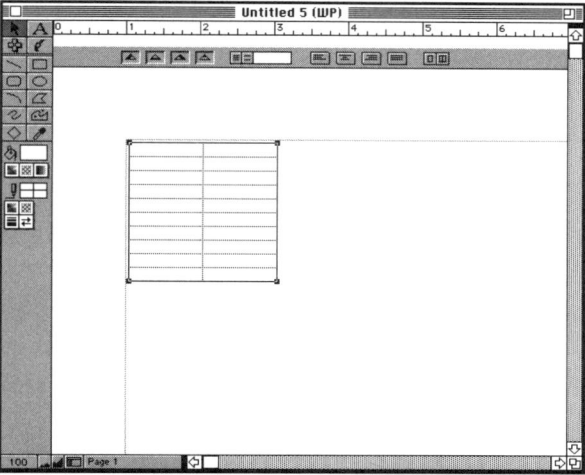

Figure 3.39. *A table without row or column headings.*

Formatting a Table: Using Borders or Lines

With ClarisWorks, you can add lines of the same weight to the entire spreadsheet frame or apply borders to all or part of a selected area.

To add lines, follow these steps:

1. Pull down the View menu and choose Show Tools.
2. Click on the Spreadsheet tool. The text pointer changes shape and the menus change.
3. Click anywhere on the table.
4. Pull down the Options menu and choose Display. The Display dialog box appears, as shown in figure 3.38.
5. Click on Solid Lines to add borders to all the cells. An X displays in the checkbox.
6. Click on the OK button, or press the Return or Enter key. ClarisWorks displays the table with lines, as shown in figure 3.40.

Caution

When you hide the row and column headings, you will not be able to resize the column width or height with the mouse. To change the column width or height, you need to use the Column Width command from the Format menu.

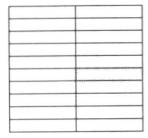

Figure 3.40. *A table with lines.*

If you don't want to use lines, you can apply borders selectively to all or part of a selected area in a spreadsheet frame.

To apply a border to a selected area of a spreadsheet frame, follow these steps:

1. Pull down the View menu and choose Show Tools.
2. Click on the Spreadsheet tool. The text pointer changes shape and the menus change.
3. Select an area of the table.
4. Pull down the Format menu and choose the Borders command. The Border dialog box displays, as shown in figure 3.41.

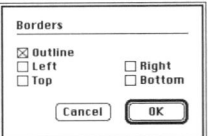

Figure 3.41. *The Borders dialog box.*

5. Click on the areas where you would like to apply a border.
6. Click on the OK button, or press the Return or Enter key. ClarisWorks displays the table with borders, as shown in figure 3.42.

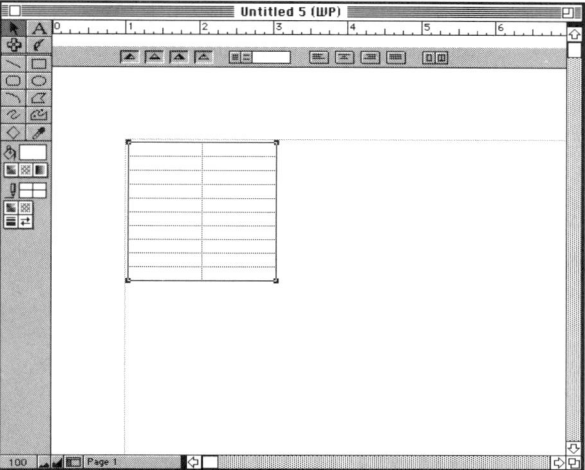

Figure 3.42. *A table with borders.*

Entering Text in a Spreadsheet Frame

As you begin typing in your table, you notice that the font varies from the word processing environment. ClarisWorks' default font for the spreadsheet environment is 9-point Geneva. To change the default font in the spreadsheet environment, enter your preferences in the Default Font dialog box, located on the Options menu. Figure 3.43 shows the Default Font dialog box below.

> **Tip**
> If you want to add more pizzazz to your table, use the painting environment to create shapes filled with colors and patterns that can be positioned behind the table.

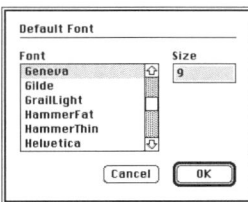

Figure 3.43. *The Default Font dialog box.*

Typing in a spreadsheet frame differs from typing in a word processor. In a spreadsheet frame the text area is divided into cells, and you need to move from one cell to another.

To enter text in a spreadsheet frame, follow these steps:

1. Click on the Spreadsheet tool. The top of the screen displays the Entry bar. You are ready to enter information.
2. Click on the cell in which you want to enter information. A border displays around the selected cell to indicate that it is active.
3. Type your information into the selected cell. What you type displays in the Entry bar, as shown in figure 3.44.

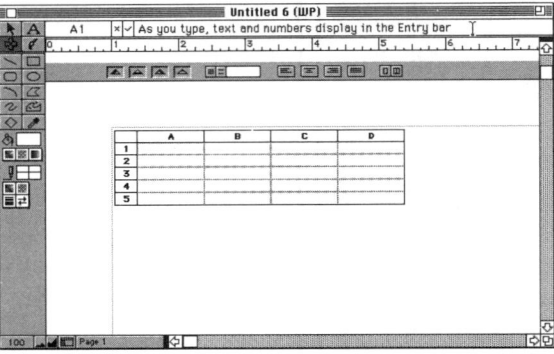

Figure 3.44. *The Entry bar.*

4. When you have finished typing, do one of the following:
    - Press the Right Arrow or Tab key to move to the right.
    - Press the Left Arrow or Shift-Tab keys to move to the left.
    - Press the Down Arrow or Return key to move down one cell.
    - Press the Up Arrow or Shift-Return key to move up one cell.

> **Tip**
> You can easily reposition a table by selecting it with the Pointer tool and then dragging it to a new location.

Working With Headers and Footers

Adding headers and footers to a document enables you to repeat information such as page numbers, addresses, or content facts at a specified location at the top or bottom of your document.

To insert a header or footer in a document, follow these steps:

1. Pull down the Format menu and choose either the Insert Header or the Insert Footer command. The insertion point moves either to the top or the bottom of the page, respectively. You are ready to type in or paste in the information.
2. Type in or paste in the appropriate information. You can use text or graphics in headers and footers.
3. Position the contents of the header or footer by using the Ruler.
4. Click in the main area of the page when you are finished.

Adding Page Numbers, Dates, and Times to Your Pages

To add page numbers, dates, and times to an existing header or footer, follow these steps:

1. Scroll to the top or the bottom of the page and click in the header or the footer.
2. Pull down the Edit menu, and select Insert Date, Insert Time, or Insert # (page number).
3. Position and format the header or footer information.
4. Click in the main area of the page when you are finished. Figure 3.45 shows a document with a header and footer.

Tip
Adding automatically updating page numbers, dates, and times to a header or footer makes it easy to identify the latest version of a document.

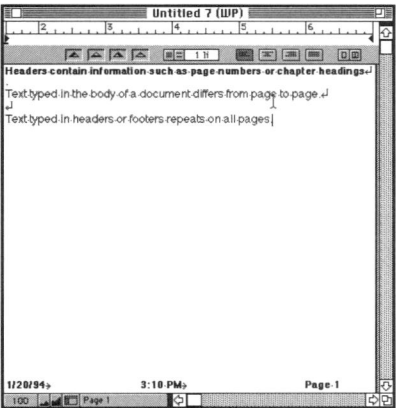

Figure 3.45. *A document with a header and a footer.*

Summary

In ClarisWorks' word processing environment, you can create memos, presentations, checklists, and long documents. These documents can incorporate information from the spreadsheet, the drawing, or the painting environments.

Documents can be viewed and edited as outlines or displayed in snaking columns. You can format the text of a word processing document or a word processing frame by selecting fonts, sizes, and styles (font attributes). You also can organize information in tables and add headers and footers that include page numbers, as well as time and date information.

In the next chapter, you'll learn how to use ClarisWorks' spreadsheet environment. Using spreadsheet tools, you can use formulas to calculate the relationships between numbers. You can also build charts to communicate the information in a worksheet visually. Everything that you can do in a spreadsheet can be done in the spreadsheet frame that you learned to insert into a word processing document. You also can add text frames to your spreadsheet document and make use of all the functionality of the word processing environment.

Chapter 4
Calculating Results With a Spreadsheet

In this chapter, you'll discover how you can employ ClarisWorks's spreadsheet environment to store information, perform calculations, and create charts to display the results of your calculations or data visually. You'll learn how to create spreadsheet documents and to recognize and use the various screen and menu elements. You also will learn the best ways to move around in a worksheet.

Below are some of the how-to topics covered in this chapter:

How to create a spreadsheet	87
How to enter information into a spreadsheet	88
How to move around in a spreadsheet	89
How to set the margins of a spreadsheet	90
How to change cell width and row height	91
How to format cell contents	93
How to add borders and lines	94
How to apply number formatting	95
How to use formulas	97
How to use the Fill Right and Fill Down commands	98
How to create formulas	98
How to use functions	100
How to design an effective spreadsheet	104
How to change how a spreadsheet displays onscreen	106
How to rearrange the contents of your spreadsheet	107
How to sort information	110
How to transpose columns and rows	111
How to create a chart	112
How to edit and enhance a chart	116
How to create a check register	119
How to print a spreadsheet	121

Spreadsheet applications, like the one in ClarisWorks, represent an effective use of the computer's capability to perform calculations rapidly. With ClarisWorks's integrated environments, you can include text and graphics frames to build attractive reports, without leaving your spreadsheet document.

What Is a Spreadsheet?

Accountants and bookkeepers use spreadsheets to capture information over a period of time. They then apply formulas to calculate the meaning of the data. A spreadsheet organizes information by horizontal rows and vertical columns that intersect to create individual *cells*. Each cell has a specific location, or address, and contains specific information. Figure 4.1 shows a new spreadsheet document.

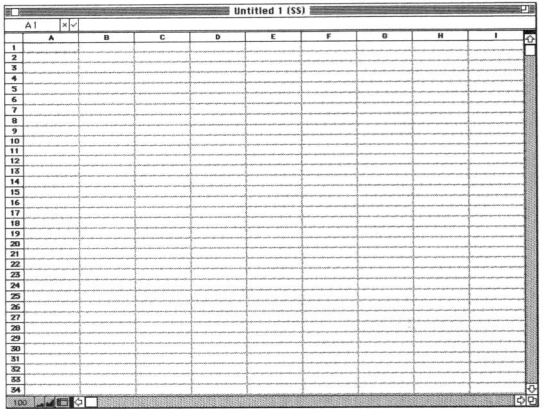

Figure 4.1. *A spreadsheet document.*

Using a Worksheet

A worksheet is the basic document type of a spreadsheet program. You can use a worksheet for many purposes, including inventories, electronic check registers, payroll reports, sales reports, budgets, and lists.

Creating a Worksheet

To work in ClarisWorks's spreadsheet environment, you must either create a spreadsheet document or a spreadsheet frame within another spreadsheet document or document type.

To create a spreadsheet document, follow these steps:

1. Launch ClarisWorks by double-clicking on the ClarisWorks icon or by single-clicking on the ClarisWorks icon and pulling down the File menu and choosing the Open command, or press the Command-O keystroke. Your computer loads ClarisWorks into RAM and then displays the New Document dialog box.
2. Click on the Spreadsheet radio button to select the document type, as shown in figure 4.2.
3. Click on the OK button, or press the Return or the Enter key.

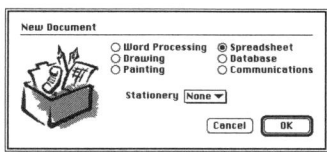

Figure 4.2. *The New Document dialog box.*

4. Click on the OK button, or press the Return or the Enter key. ClarisWorks displays the appropriate menu bar and an untitled worksheet, as shown in figure 4.1.

To create a spreadsheet frame in an existing document, follow these steps:

1. Pull down the View menu and choose the Show Tools command. The Tools panel displays, as shown in figure 4.3.

Figure 4.3. *The Tools panel.*

2. Click on the cross-shaped Spreadsheet tool. The text pointer changes to a spreadsheet pointer.

3. In the window, hold down the mouse button and drag an area in the shape of a rectangle. This creates a spreadsheet frame, as shown in figure 4.4.

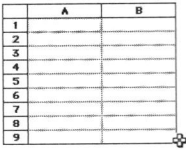

Figure 4.4. *A spreadsheet frame in a word processing document.*

Entering and Editing Data

To enter information into a cell, you must first select the cell and then type the information into the cell. As you type, the information displays in the Entry bar at the top of your window rather than the cell itself, as shown in figure 4.5. If you have not used spreadsheets before, this may seem awkward at first. Many times, however, we don't want to see what's really in the cell; we're more interested in seeing the results of a formula. The Entry bar provides plenty of room for viewing formulas.

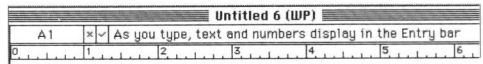

Figure 4.5. *The Entry bar.*

To enter information into a spreadsheet frame, follow these steps:

1. Click on the Spreadsheet tool. The top of the screen displays the Entry bar, as shown in figure 4.5.
2. Click on the cell in which you want to enter information. A border displays around the selected cell to indicate that it is active. You are ready to enter information.
3. Type the information for the selected cell. What you type displays in the Entry bar.
4. Click on the Accept button (the check mark symbol) on the Entry bar, shown in figure 4.5, to confirm that the information is correct. The contents of the Entry bar display in the cell.

To edit or change information in a cell, follow these steps:

1. Click on the cell you want to edit. A border displays around the selected cell to indicate that it is active and its contents display in the Entry bar.

> **Tip**
> ClarisWorks can open many spreadsheet formats. The SYLK format is commonly used to transfer spreadsheets between different programs, and may be right for you. ClarisWorks 2.1 adds a filter that can open Excel 4.0 spreadsheets; if you also use Excel, you may want to upgrade to ClarisWorks 2.1.

2. Move the cursor up to the Entry bar. The cursor changes from the cross-shaped spreadsheet cursor to the I-beam or text-insertion cursor.
3. Click in the Entry bar.
4. Edit the contents of the Entry bar as you would normally entered text.
5. If you make a mistake, click on the X-shaped Cancel button (to the left of the check mark), shown in figure 4.5, to return the contents of the cell to what they were before you changed them.
6. Click on the check mark on the Entry bar to confirm that the information is correct.

Working With Cell Contents

The cell is the basic element of a spreadsheet. Cells can contain text, numbers, and graphics. ClarisWorks recognizes text and numeric entries. If you want to begin a label with a number, you must enclose the number in quotation marks, for example `"1995"` `Sales`. Cell contents can be copied, cut, and pasted.

You also can format text and numbers in several ways. If a cell entry exceeds the width of a cell, and the adjacent cell is empty, ClarisWorks spills the contents into the empty cell(s). If, however, the adjacent cells have entries, ClarisWorks clips the entry visually—but all the data remains intact.

Moving About in Your Spreadsheet

Moving around in a worksheet differs from moving around in a word processor, painting, or drawing document, or in a database. In a worksheet, you need to move from cell to cell. You can use the mouse to click in each cell; although, you'll probably find that moving around a spreadsheet can be done quickly from the keyboard.

Arrow or cursor keys, located to the right of the Spacebar, can be pressed to move in the direction indicated on the key. For instance, pressing the upward pointing arrow moves you up one cell.

Table 4.1 describes a variety of keyboard shortcuts you can use to move around in your worksheet.

Table 4.1. *Keyboard shortcuts for moving around a spreadsheet*

To move...	...press this:
Right	Right Arrow or Tab key
Left	Left Arrow or Shift-Tab keystroke
Down	Down Arrow or Return key
Up	Up Arrow or Shift-Return keystroke

Formatting Your Spreadsheet Document

With ClarisWorks, you have a set of powerful tools that you can use to format or tailor the appearance of your spreadsheet. Most of the formatting commands are located on the Format menu.

Setting the Margins of Your Spreadsheet

When you're using a spreadsheet, you may want to change the orientation of your page so that you can fit more columns on a page.

To change the orientation of your document, follow these steps:

1. Pull down the File menu and choose the Page Setup command. The Page Setup dialog box displays, as shown in figure 4.6.

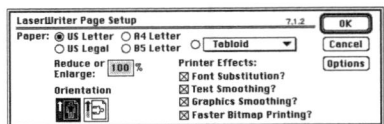

Figure 4.6. *The Page Setup dialog box.*

2. Click on the icon of the sideways page.
3. Click on the OK button or press the Return or the Enter key.

You may also need to change your spreadsheet's margins to help fit more information onto the page.

To change the margins of your document, follow these steps:

1. Pull down the Format menu and choose the Document command. The Document dialog box displays, as shown in figure 4.7.

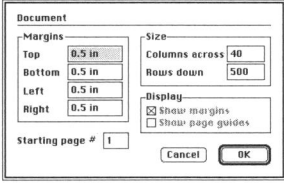

Figure 4.7. *The Document dialog box.*

2. Type the appropriate margins into the text boxes.
3. Click on the OK button or press the Return or the Enter key.

You also can specify how many columns and rows your document contains by entering these values into the Size area of the Document dialog box.

Formatting Cell Width and Row Height

As you work with a particular spreadsheet, you may find that wider columns or higher rows improve your worksheet's readability. You can alter row height and column width by using menu commands and mouse techniques.

To change the column width or the row height by using the mouse, follow these steps:

1. Position the cursor over the border between a column heading or a row heading. The resize cursor displays in the form of a double-headed arrow, as shown in figure 4.8.

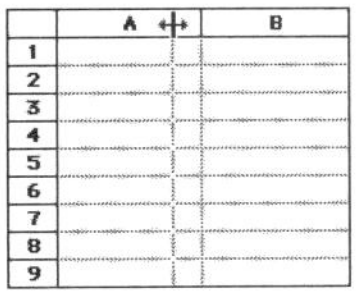

Figure 4.8. *The resize cursor.*

2. Drag the column or row to the desired width or height. ClarisWorks resizes the columns and rows.

To change the column width or the row height by using the menu bar, follow these steps:

1. Pull down the Format menu and select the Column Width or Row Height command. The Row Height or Column Width dialog box displays, as shown in figures 4.9 and 4.10.

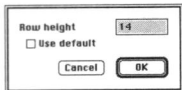

Figure 4.9. *The Row Height dialog box.*

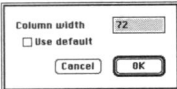

Figure 4.10. *The Column Width dialog box.*

2. Type a number into the value box to change the width. The default column width of 72 points equals one inch. The default row height of 14 points roughly equals one-fifth of an inch.
3. Click on the OK button or press the Return or the Enter key.

Selecting a Range of Cells

A range of cells is a group of contiguous cells. When you select a range, the first cell of the range appears lighter while the rest of the range is darker, as shown in figure 4.11.

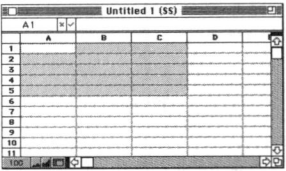

Figure 4.11. *A selected range of cells.*

Select a range of cells when you want to apply formatting to more than one cell at a time.

Formatting Cells

The Format menu provides you with many options for formatting the contents of selected cells.

You can choose to format text in cells in several ways:

- ❖ By changing the font.
- ❖ By changing the font size.
- ❖ By applying bold, italic, underline, and other styles or attributes.
- ❖ By changing the text color.
- ❖ By changing the text alignment.
- ❖ By changing the font and font size of the entire spreadsheet.

To change the font, the font size, or the font styles or attributes of a selected cell or range of cells, select a cell or a range of cells by using the mouse or the keyboard. Make a selection from the Font, Size, or Style submenus, found under the Format menu. The contents of the selected cell(s) now display with the formatting you have chosen.

When it comes to numbers, color has meaning. Green suggests the possibility of money and red the lack of it. Black denotes a certain amount of stability. Use the Text Color command to apply various colors to selected cells.

To change the color of the text of a selected cell or a range of cells, follow these steps:

1. Select a cell or a range of cells by using the mouse or the keyboard.
2. Pull down the Format menu and move to the Text Color submenu. The Text Color submenu displays, as shown in figure 4.12.

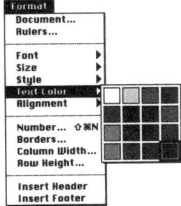

Figure 4.12. *The Text Color dialog box.*

> **Tip**
>
> To duplicate cell formatting, select the cell you want to duplicate and then choose the Copy Format command from the Edit menu, or press Command-Shift-C. Next, select the destination cell and choose the Paste Format command from the Edit menu, or press Command-Shift-V.

3. Click on a color. Text in the selected cells now displays in the color selected.

To change the default font a spreadsheet, enter your preferences in the Default Font dialog box, located on the Options menu.

1. Pull down the Options menu and choose the Change Default Font command. The Default Font dialog box displays, as shown in figure 4.13.

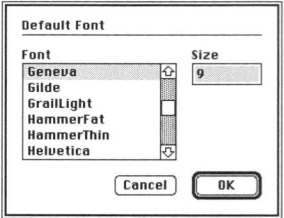

Figure 4.13. *The Default Font dialog box.*

2. Click on the cell in which you will enter information.
3. Scroll through the Font list and select a font.
4. Type a font size into the text box.
5. Click on the OK button or press the Return or the Enter key. The spreadsheet now displays in the default font.

Adding Borders and Solid Lines

You can apply borders selectively to all or part of a selected area in a spreadsheet document or frame.

To apply a border to part of a spreadsheet, follow these steps:

1. Select an area of the spreadsheet or the spreadsheet frame.
2. Pull down the Format menu and choose the Borders command. The Borders dialog box displays, as shown in figure 4.14.

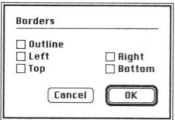

Figure 4.14. *The Borders dialog box.*

3. Click on the areas where you would like to apply a border.

4. Click on the OK button or press the Return or the Enter key. ClarisWorks displays the table with borders, as shown in figure 4.15.

	A	B	C	D	E
1		January	February	March	South
2	East	200	300	400	500
3	West	300	350	500	450
4	North	400	400	600	700
5	South	500	450	700	

Figure 4.15. *A spreadsheet with borders.*

To quickly apply an outline, right, or bottom border, press the button on the Shortcuts palette, as shown in figure 4.16.

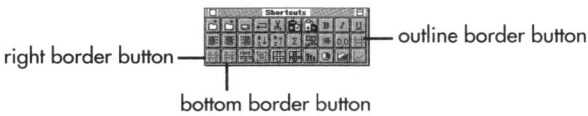

Figure 4.16. *The spreadsheet Shortcuts palette.*

Changing Cell Alignment

You can specify the alignment of cell contents. The alignment determines how the cell contents flow. You can align cell contents to the left or right side of a cell, or center the contents of a cell. Generally, the default setting, aligns text cell entries to the left and numeric cell entries to the right.

To change the alignment of cell entries, follow these steps:

1. Select a cell or a range of cells.
2. Pull down the Format menu and move to the Alignment submenu. The Alignment submenu displays.
3. Choose the General, Left, Center, or Right alignment command. The cell contents realign.

To prevent the contents of a cell from extending into another cell or appearing clipped, choose the Wrap command on the Alignment submenu. You may need to increase the row height to view the entire contents of the cell.

Shortcut
To quickly change the alignment of cell entries, press the button on the Shortcuts palette, as shown above in figure 4.16.

Formatting Numeric Entries in Spreadsheets

Formatting numeric entries does more than the formatting of text. Numeric entries can be formatted in many ways, including by currency, date,

and time. Sometimes values in a cell appear to display incorrect information because you've used the wrong number format. When this happens, you need to choose the appropriate numeric format.

Since a spreadsheet only deals with the value of the numbers you type in, visual formatting devices such as dollar signs and the number of decimal places really don't add meaning to the calculations.

Table 4.2. *Numeric Formats*

Type	Description	Example
General	ClarisWorks displays all decimal places filled by a number other than 0. When the numeric entry is too large for the cell, ClarisWorks will first try to render it in scientific format. If that fails, the cell fills with # (number signs). To correctly display the number, you may have to widen the column or specify fewer decimal places.	50.56678
Currency	ClarisWorks adds the dollar sign ($) and displays two decimal points.	$50.56
Percent	ClarisWorks calculates the percentage by multiplying the number by 100 and inserts the percentage sign (%).	5056%
Scientific	ClarisWorks displays the cell entries in the scientific notation which allows larger numbers to be expressed compactly.	5.06e+1
Fixed	ClarisWorks rounds up the number, based on the number of decimal places specified.	50.57

To change the formatting of numeric entries, follow these steps:

1. Select a cell or a range of cells.
2. Pull down the Format menu and select the Number command, or press the Command-Shift-N keystroke. The Numeric dialog box displays, as shown in figure 4.17.

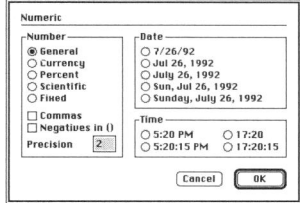

Figure 4.17. *The Numeric dialog box.*

3. Select the type of number formatting, date formatting, and time formatting, as well as the number of decimal places, whether to use commas to separate thousands, or if negative amounts should appear in brackets.
4. Click on the OK button or press the Return or the Enter key. Figure 4.18 shows how the same entries change after applying selections from the Numeric dialog box.

Figure 4.18. *Samples of numeric formatting.*

Using the Time and Date Formats

You can express both times and dates in several formats by making various selections from the Numeric dialog box. You can specify whether time is divided into A.M. and P.M. or uses the 24-hour notation favored in Europe and some industries.

Dates are calculated as the sum of days after January 1, 1904. If your entries become unformatted, they will display numbers, rather than dates. Reapply the date format to display the numbers as dates.

Using Formulas

One of the chief joys of working with an electronic spreadsheet is the ease, accuracy, and rapidity with which a computer calculates the results of formulas.

Rather than add specific sums, a spreadsheet adds the contents of specific cells and references them by their address. This way, when you change the contents of a cell, ClarisWorks automatically recalculates the totals.

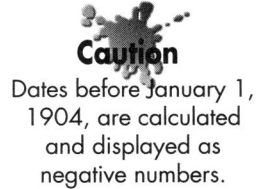

Caution
Dates before January 1, 1904, are calculated and displayed as negative numbers.

Relative and Absolute Cell References

Each cell is referred to by its address. Formulas often refer to a cell or a range of cells' address. Relative cell referencing, the normal mode, enables you to copy a formula from one column to another. Relative cell references are related by their position to the active cell.

For the most part, relative referencing is all you need. For those times when you need to anchor a cell reference to the contents of a specific cell, use absolute references. By typing a dollar sign ($) in front of the column and row address, you ensure that a formula will refer to a particular cell.

Copying Formulas With the Fill Down and Fill Right Commands

Creating formulas in ClarisWorks is pretty easy. Since you often repeat the same formulas in a spreadsheet, you can duplicate formulas with a Fill Down or a Fill Right command.

To duplicate the formula or text in a cell, follow these steps:

1. Click on the cell whose contents or formulas you want to duplicate.
2. Drag a range of cells below or to the right of the selected cell.
3. Pull down the Edit menu and select the Fill Down or Fill Right command, or press the Command-D or Command-R keystrokes, respectively. The formula or cell contents are duplicated in the range you selected.

Simple Formulas: Adding a Range of Cells

To create a simple formula in ClarisWorks, you must first decide where the total will be. Specify the range, including the cell, where total amount is to be entered. Choose the AutoSum command. ClarisWorks calculates the results.

To add a range of cells, follow these steps:

1. Pull down the Edit menu and choose the Show Shortcuts command from the Shortcuts submenu. The Shortcuts palette displays, as shown in figure 4.19.
2. Select a vertical or a horizontal range of cells, including an empty cell where the total can display. If you select from the

bottom up or from right to left, you will see the formula display in the Entry bar.
3. Click on the AutoSum button.
4. Press the Enter key or an arrow key. ClarisWorks calculates and inserts the total in the last cell of the range.

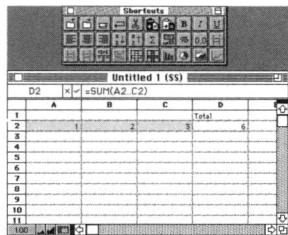

Figure 4.19. *A simple calculation and the spreadsheet Shortcuts palette.*

Note that a range of cells is indicated by two periods between the beginning and the end of the range. For example, the range A1..A10 includes all cells between A1 and A10.

Simple Formulas: Multiplying, Dividing, or Subtracting a Range of Cells

Calculating simple multiplication, division, or subtraction formulas is easy. The process is identical to creating a simple sum, except that you edit the formula and enter a numeric operator, such as "-" for subtracting, "*" for multiplying, "/" for dividing, and "^" to create an exponent.

To multiply, divide, or subtract the contents of selected cells, follow these steps:

1. Pull down the Edit menu and choose the Show Shortcuts command from the Shortcuts submenu. The Shortcuts palette displays.
2. Select a vertical or a horizontal range of cells, including an empty cell where the total can display. If you select the range from the bottom up or from right to left, you will see the formula display in the Entry bar.
3. Click on the AutoSum button.
4. Edit the formula to include a numeric operator (-, /, *, ^), as shown in figure 4.20.

5. Press the Enter key or an arrow key. ClarisWorks calculates and inserts the total into the last cell of the range.

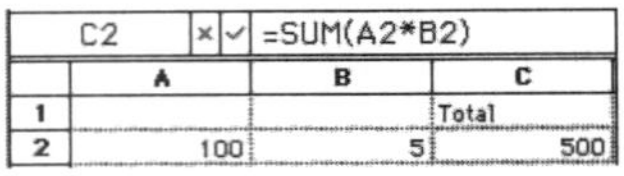

C2	×✓	=SUM(A2*B2)	
	A	B	C
1			Total
2	100	5	500

Figure 4.20. *An edited formula.*

How ClarisWorks Solves Formulas

When a formula has only one type of calculation in it, you can understand how ClarisWorks calculates the results. In formulas making use of more than one type of operation (addition, subtraction, multiplication, or addition), ClarisWorks solves the formula by calculating the various parts of the formula in the following order.

- ❖ Percentage.
- ❖ Exponentiation.
- ❖ Multiplication, division.
- ❖ Addition, subtraction.
- ❖ Total or final relationship.

More Complex Formulas: Using Functions

Spreadsheet programs come with a set of predefined formulas so that you don't have to enter formulas for calculating averages or standard deviations. Functions are useful because they help prevent errors in formulas. A function is not an entire formula. To use a function, you must paste a function and indicate its argument or the cell references it should use to calculate.

To insert a function into a formula, follow these steps:

1. Click in the cell that will hold the total.
2. Pull down the Edit menu and select the Paste Function command. The Paste Function dialog box displays, as shown in figure 4.21.
3. Scroll through the list of functions and make a selection.
4. Click on the OK button or press the Return or Enter key.
5. The Function displays in the Entry bar, as shown in figure 4.22

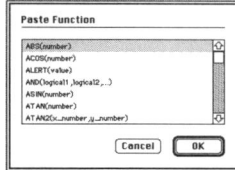

Figure 4.21. *The Paste Function dialog box.*

Figure 4.22. *Pasted function in the Entry bar.*

6. Select the argument "number 1, number 2" from the Entry bar.
7. Move to the spreadsheet and highlight the range of cells to be calculated. The formula in the Entry bar is updated, as shown in figure 4.22.
8. Click on the Accept button or press the Enter key or an arrow key. ClarisWorks calculates and inserts the total in the last cell of the range.

ClarisWorks Functions

ClarisWorks supplies 100 functions in eight categories that you can use in your spreadsheets and databases. The categories are: business and financial, date and time, information, logical, numeric, statistical, text, and trigonometric. All of these functions are available to you in your spreadsheet designs.

Functions that point to cell references such as: ALERT, HLOOKUP, INDEX, ISNA (is not available), LOOKUP, MATCH, NA (not available), ROW, VLOOKUP, and some others are not available in databases where there is no cell structure. You can tell which functions are not in the database environment by scrolling the functions list in the Enter Formula function scroll box of the Define Fields dialog box. Refer to chapter 5 for more information about calculation fields.

Table 4.3 lists an abbreviated description of ClarisWorks's functions.

Table 4.3. *ClarisWorks functions*

Category	Function Name	Explanation
Business and Financial	FV	Future Value
	IRR	Internal Rate of Return

Continues

Table 4.3. *Continued*

Category	Function Name	Explanation
	MIRR	Modified Internal Rate of Return
	NPER	Number of Periods
	NP	Net Present Value
	PMT	Payment
	PV	Present Value
	RATE	
Date and Time	DATE	
	DATETOTEXT	
	DAY	
	DAYNAME	
	DAYOFYEAR	
	HOUR	
	MINUTE	
	MONTH	
	MONTHNAME	
	NOW	
	SECOND	
	TEXTTODATE	
	TEXTTOTIME	
	TIME	
	TIMETOTEXT	
	WEEKDAY	
	WEEKOFYEAR	
	YEAR	
Information	ALERT	
	BEEP	
	CHOOSE	
	COLUMN	
	ERROR	
	HLOOKUP	Horizontal lookup
	INDEX	
	LOOKUP	
	MACRO	
	MATCH	
	NA	Not available
	ROW	
	TYPE	
	VLOOKUP	Vertical lookup
Logical	AND	
	IF	
	ISBLANK	
	ISERROR	
	ISLOGICAL	
	ISNA	

Category	Function Name	Explanation
Numeric	ISNUMBER	
	ISTEXT	
	NOT	
	OR	
	ABS	Absolute value
	EXP	Exponential
	FACT	Factorial
	FRAC	Fraction
	INT	Integer
	LN	Natural logarithm
	LOG	
	LOG10	Log base 10
	MOD	Modulo
	PI	
	RAND	Random
	ROUND	
	SIGN	
	SQRT	
	TRUNC	Truncate
Statistical	AVERAGE	
	COUNT	
	COUNT2	
	MAX	Maximum
	MIN	Minimum
	PRODUCT	
	STDEV	Standard deviation
	SUM	
	VAR	Variance
Text	CHAR	Character
	CODE	ASCII code
	CONCAT	Concatenate
	EXACT	
	FIND	
	LEFT	
	LEN	Length
	LOWER	
	MID	Middle
	NUMTOTEXT	
	PROPER	
	REPLACE	
	REPT	Repeat
	RIGHT	
	TEXTTONUM	
	TRIM	
	UPPER	

Continues

Table 4.3. Continued

Category	Function Name	Explanation
Trigonmetric	ACOS	Arc Cosine
	ASIN	Arc Sine
	ATAN	Arc Tangent
	ATAN2	Arc Tangent 2
	COS	Cosine
	DEGREES	
	RADIANS	
	SIN	Sine
	TAN	Tangent

No doubt many of these functions are already familiar to you from school, projects, or other endeavors. Space precludes a full explanation of how to use these functions. The Claris Help System (covered in chapter 2, "Some Basics") contains single-page explanations of each function by name that should be sufficient to help you determine their uses.

Formula Errors

Sometimes you may set up a formula incorrectly. If you have created a circular reference, the contents of a cell will be framed by bullets. In a circular reference two cells which are part of formulas depend on each other. When you create a circular reference, you will see an alert, as shown in figure 4.23.

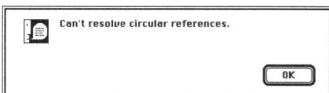

Figure 4.23. *The Circular Reference message box (alert).*

When you get the alert, look at the cells indicated by the bullets and re-enter the formulas.

ELEMENTS OF GOOD SPREADSHEET DESIGN

An effective spreadsheet is designed so that upon looking at it, you can understand what that spreadsheet is trying to convey, whether you look at spreadsheets everyday or open a file infrequently. Elements of good spreadsheet design include:

❖ A descriptive title that reveals the purpose of the spreadsheet at a glance.
❖ Clear labeling of columns and rows.
❖ Information presented in an orderly fashion.
❖ Row height and column widths adjusted so that the information is clearly readable.
❖ Effective use of text formatting and color.
❖ The use of formulas in blocks that can be referenced in cells.

Good spreadsheets are planned. Before you create a spreadsheet, write down the information the spreadsheet needs to contain. Jot down column and row labels. Indicate what information is to be used for calculations. Title the spreadsheet clearly across the top and include the date the spreadsheet was last modified.

By adding borders and suppressing the display of grid lines, you can create documents that don't look like a traditional spreadsheet.

Figure 4.24 displays a sample spreadsheet.

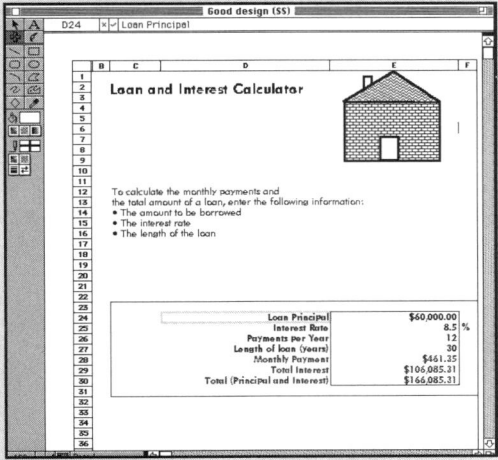

Figure 4.24. *A sample spreadsheet with various design elements.*

Using Variables Correctly

If you define a variable in a formula, whenever the value or variable changes it will throw off your entire spreadsheet. A better design involves the use of what is called a P-block, or parameter block. Put all of your variables into that block, and reference the cells that contain those values throughout your spreadsheet. Then, whenever your variables or values change, a single change in the P-block will suffice to implement the change wherever it occurs throughout the spreadsheet. The P-block is an important spreadsheet concept that will save you considerable headaches and is likely to enable you to rework a spreadsheet without having to start over from scratch.

Changing How a Spreadsheet Displays Onscreen

Depending on what you are using a spreadsheet document or frame for, you may want to change the way it displays onscreen by hiding or displaying row and column numbers, cell grids, and formulas. When you hide row and column grid lines, your spreadsheet looks like a table; hiding grid lines gives the document the appearance of a blank sheet of paper. Displaying formulas is useful when you want to review the accuracy of the formulas used throughout a spreadsheet.

To suppress the row and column headings, cell grids, solid lines, or display formulas, follow these steps:

1. Click anywhere in the spreadsheet.
2. Pull down the Options menu and choose the Display command. The Display dialog box displays, as shown in figure 4.25.

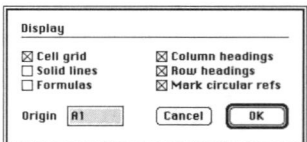

Figure 4.25. *The Display dialog box.*

3. Click on the appropriate checkbox.
4. Click on the OK button or press the Return or the Enter key. ClarisWorks updates the display of your entire spreadsheet.

Caution

When you hide the row and the column headings, you will not be capable of resizing column width or row height with the mouse. To change a column width, you will need to use the Column Width command from the Format menu.

Protecting Your Spreadsheet

A spreadsheet can reflect a lot of cumulative effort. Designing a spreadsheet, entering formulas, and inputting information all take time. It is wise, then, to do whatever you can to protect the integrity of the data in a spreadsheet. Saving your work frequently and maintaining additional backup copies of your work should be ingrained habits by now.

With a spreadsheet, you have the additional option of protecting selected cells. When you protect cells, anyone using the spreadsheet will be unable to make changes to those cells unless he first unlocks them.

To protect selected cells, follow these steps:

1. Select a cell or a range of cells.
2. Pull down the Options menu and choose the Protect Cells command, or type the Command-H keystroke. If you try to make changes to the protected cells, you will see the alert shown in figure 4.26.

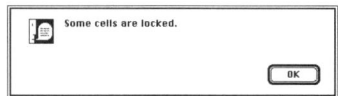

Figure 4.26. *The Protect Cells dialog box.*

3. To unlock the cells, pull down the Options menu and choose the Protect Cells command, or type the Command-Shift-H keystroke.

Rearranging the Worksheet

As you work on a spreadsheet, you may find it necessary to add or delete cells, rows, and columns. In ClarisWorks, you also can move the contents of a cell or a range of cells to a new location on the spreadsheet. In addition, you can cut, copy, and paste information from one spreadsheet document or frame to another.

> **Tip**
> Other ways of protecting your document include saving it as a Stationery document type in the Save As dialog box. When you open the document, it will open as a new, untitled worksheet. In the Finder, you can select the name of the file, pull down the File menu, select the Get Info command, and click on the Lock checkbox. When you open the document, you will not be permitted to input any changes.

Using the Cut, Copy, and Paste Commands in a Spreadsheet

Cutting, copying, and pasting are easy ways to duplicate or move information between files. If you are not sure how to do this, refer to chapter 2, "Some Basics."

A cell can hold formatting, formulas, text, and the results of a calculation, and there are several ways to cut, copy, and paste these various data types into the individual cells of a spreadsheet.

Use the ordinary Cut, Copy, and Paste commands to copy the following from one cell to another:

- ❖ Text.
- ❖ Numeric entries.
- ❖ Formulas.

To copy cell formatting, follow these steps:

1. Select the cell or a range of cells you want to duplicate.
2. Pull down the Edit menu and choose the Copy Format command, or press Command-Shift-C.
3. Select the destination cell or a range of cells.
4. Pull down the Edit menu and choose the Paste Format command, or press Command-Shift-V. The format is copied to the selected cells.

To copy the result of a formula, follow these steps:

1. Select the cell containing the material you want to duplicate.
2. Pull down the Edit menu and choose the Copy command, or press Command-C.
3. Select the destination cell or a range of cells.
4. Pull down the Edit menu and choose the Paste Special command. The Paste Special dialog box displays, as shown in figure 4.27.

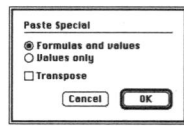

Figure 4.27. *The Paste Special dialog box.*

5. Click on the Values Only radio button.
6. Click on the OK button or press the Return or the Enter key. The value is pasted into the selected cells.

Inserting and Deleting Rows and Columns

Inserting and deleting cells enables you to create space to add information or to delete gaps or delete information.

To insert a row or column of cells, follow these steps:

1. Click on a row or column heading to select an entire row or column.
2. Pull down the Calculate menu and choose the Insert Cells command, or press Command-Shift-I. ClarisWorks inserts a row above the row you selected or a column in front of the column you selected.

Inserting and Deleting Cells

If you don't want to add an entire new row or column, you can choose to insert or delete a single cell or a range of cells.

To insert a cell or a range of cells, follow these steps:

1. Select a cell or a range of cells.
2. Pull down the Calculate menu and choose the Insert Cells command, or press Command-Shift-I. ClarisWorks displays the Insert Cells dialog box, as shown in figure 4.28.

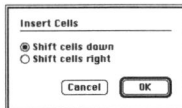

Figure 4.28. *The Insert Cells dialog box.*

3. Indicate whether to shift the selected cells down or to the right.
4. Click on the OK button or press the Return or the Enter key. ClarisWorks inserts the same number of empty cells above or to the left of the cell or the range of cells you selected.

Shortcut
Use Command-X to cut, Command-C to copy, and Command-V to paste.

Tip
To insert or delete cells quickly, press the button on the Shortcuts palette, as shown in figure 4.16.

To delete a cell or a range of cells, follow these steps:

1. Select a cell or a range of cells.
2. Pull down the Calculate menu and choose the Delete Cells command, or press Command-Shift-K. ClarisWorks displays the Delete Cells dialog box, as shown in figure 4.29.

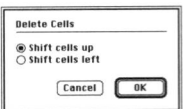

Figure 4.29. *The Delete Cells dialog box.*

3. Indicate whether to shift the selected cells up or to the left by clicking on the appropriate radio button.
4. Click on the OK button, or press the Return or the Enter key. ClarisWorks deletes the same number of empty cells above or to the left of the cell or the range of cells you selected.

Sorting

Because spreadsheet information is organized both vertically and horizontally, you can sort the contents of rows or columns easily. Sorting enables you to rank information which can help you analyze the contents of your spreadsheet.

ClarisWorks sorts text in alphabetical order (A to Z) and numeric entries in numeric order (ascending order).

When sorting horizontally or vertically, ClarisWorks keeps the data of selected cells together.

To sort the contents of a selected range of cells, follow these steps:

1. Select the range of cells you want to reorder by sorting.
2. Pull down the Calculate menu and choose the Sort command. The Sort dialog box displays, as shown in figure 4.30.

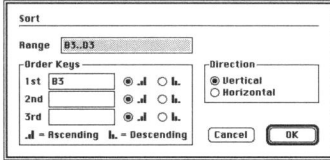

Figure 4.30. *The Sort dialog box.*

3. In the Order Keys area of the dialog box, indicate the order in which you want to sort the selected range.
4. Indicate whether you are sorting in ascending order (1,2,3; a, b, c) or descending order (3,2,1; c, b, a) for each order key.
5. Click on the OK button or press the Return or the Enter key.

Transposing Columns and Rows

Sometimes, it may be more useful to reorder your worksheet by transposing entire columns and rows.

To transpose columns and rows, follow these steps:

1. Select the cells and the labels you want to reorient.
2. Pull down the Edit menu and choose either the Copy command or the Cut command, or press the Command-C keystroke or the Command-X keystroke, respectively.
3. Highlight the range where you want to paste the re-oriented cells.
4. Pull down the Edit menu and select the Paste Special command. The Paste Special dialog box displays.
5. Click on the Transpose checkbox, as shown in figure 4.31.

Shortcut
To quickly sort in ascending or descending order, press the button on the Shortcuts palette, as shown above in figure 4.16.

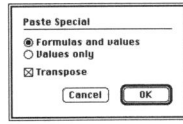

Figure 4.31. *The Paste Special dialog box with the Transpose option.*

6. Click on the OK button or press the Return or the Enter key. ClarisWorks re-orients your data as shown in figure 4.32.

	A	B	C	D	E
1		January	February	March	South
2	East	200	300	400	500
3	West	300	350	500	450
4	North	400	400	600	700
5	South	500	450	700	
6					
7					
8		East	West	North	South
9	January	200	300	400	500
10	February	300	350	400	450
11	March	400	500	600	700
12	South	500	450	700	

Figure 4.32. *Transposed columns and rows.*

Transposing columns and rows is especially helpful if you want to create a chart.

Charting Your Data

Spreadsheets can organize and manipulate information effectively, but their gridlike structure is not always the best format in which to present information—especially to groups. ClarisWorks easily converts selected information from a spreadsheet into a chart or a graph. Charts and graphs present information in a way that is immediately understandable to the viewer. The spreadsheet environment offers you the capability to change chart types easily. You also can use the graph tools to add arrows and text.

Creating a Chart

Creating a chart is as easy as selecting a range of information in a spreadsheet and then choosing the Make Chart command from the Options menu. A chart is linked dynamically to the spreadsheet, so any changes made to the range in the spreadsheet that are illustrated by the chart are reflected in the chart.

To create a chart, follow these steps:

1. Select a range of cells in a spreadsheet document or frame.
2. Pull down the Options menu and choose the Make Chart command. The Chart Options dialog box displays, as shown in figure 4.33.
3. Click on a chart type from the Gallery area of the dialog box.
4. Click on the OK button or press the Return or the Enter key. ClarisWorks places the chart in your worksheet, as shown in figure 4.34. You can drag the chart to a new onscreen location if you prefer.

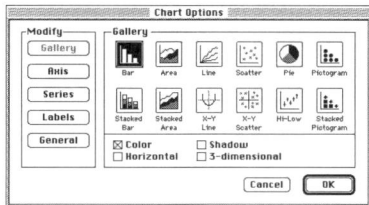

Figure 4.33. *The Chart Options dialog box.*

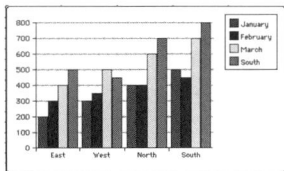

Figure 4.34. *A sample chart representing a range of cells.*

The Elements of a Chart

A chart presents information that is organized along two axes. The X-axis measures one set of data on the horizontal line in a chart or graph. Information on the Y-axis is located on the vertical line in a chart or graph. Tick marks indicate increments along either the X-axis or the Y-axis. Labels for the X-axis and Y-axis communicate important information to the viewer, such as the incremental measurements the tick marks represent, and should be descriptive.

The Chart Types

The Gallery portion of the Chart Options dialog box, provides you with a choice of 12 distinct chart types.

Bar charts show the differences between data in bars or columns. Bar charts can be horizontal or vertical, as shown in figures 4.35 and 4.36.

A stacked bar chart consolidates information, as shown below in figure 4.36.

Area charts are similar to line charts, but they use the areas between the lines to emphasize the relationships of data to each other, as shown in figure 4.37.

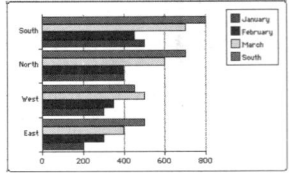

Figure 4.35. *A horizontal bar chart.*

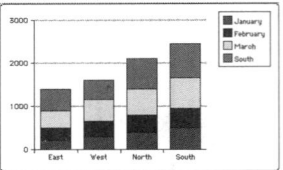

Figure 4.36. *A stacked bar chart.*

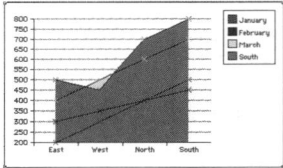

Figure 4.37. *An area chart.*

Stacked area charts add the various areas together. This is a good format to display cumulative values over time, as shown below in figure 4.38.

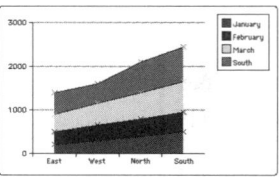

Figure 4.38. *A stacked area chart.*

Line charts show changes in data or in categories of data over time. They can be used to document trends. Newspapers, for instance, use them to chart stock market trends, as shown in figure 4.39.

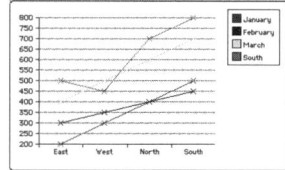

Figure 4.39. *A line chart.*

Scatter charts display information from a range of cells as points on a chart, as shown below in figure 4.40.

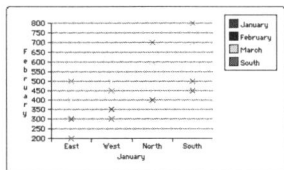

Figure 4.40. *A Scatter chart.*

Pie charts demonstrate percentages in relation to a whole, as shown below in figure 4.41.

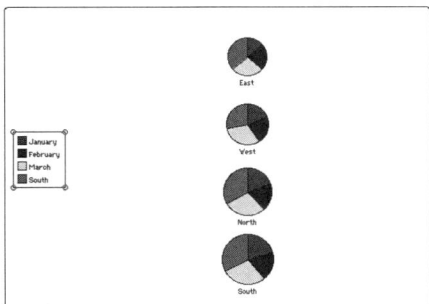

Figure 4.41. *Four pie charts.*

High-low charts plot the high point and the low point for each selected range of cells, as shown in figure 4.42. This kind of chart is useful for documenting commodity prices and for recording temperatures.

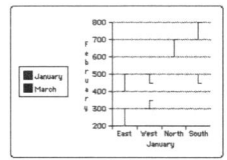

Figure 4.42. *A high-low chart.*

Pictogram charts give you a visual method for providing an image of what is being measured, as shown below in figure 4.43. For example, the pictograms in figure 4.43 represent trees. You can edit the pictograms.

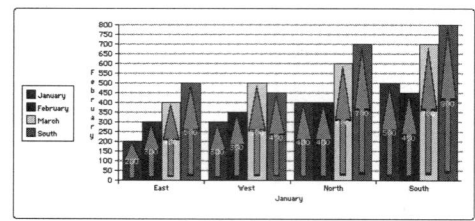

Figure 4.43. *A pictogram chart.*

Changing Chart Types

Change chart types when you think a different chart format will better communicate your data.

To change the type of an existing chart, follow these steps:

1. Click on the chart with the pointer tool to select it.
2. Pull down the Options menu and choose the Modify Chart command, or press Command-Shift-I. The Chart Options dialog box displays as shown in figure 4.33.
3. Click on the type of chart you want and select any other modifications.
4. Click on the OK button or press the Return or Enter key.

> **Tip**
> To quickly change an existing chart type to a bar, a pie, an area, or a line chart, press the button on the Shortcuts palette, as shown in figure 4.16.

Adding a Chart Title

To help orient the viewer, you should always include a title for each chart.

To add a title to a chart, follow these steps:

1. Click on the chart with the pointer tool to select it.
2. Pull down the Options menu and choose the Modify Chart command, or press Command-Shift-I. The Chart Options dialog box displays, as shown in figure 4.33.
3. Click on the Labels button. The Chart Options's Labels dialog box displays, as shown in figure 4.44.

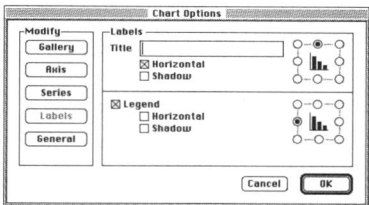

Figure 4.44. *The Chart Options's Labels dialog box.*

4. Type the name of the title into the Title text box.
5. Click on one of the placement circles in the graphic.
6. Click on the OK button or press the Return or Enter key.

Customizing the Chart Axes

You can customize the appearance of the axes by adding labels, displaying grid lines, setting the interval values, and placing the tick marks.

To modify the axes, follow these steps:

1. Click on the chart with the pointer tool to select it.
2. Pull down the Options menu and choose the Modify Chart command, or press Command-Shift-I. The Chart Options dialog box displays as shown in figure 4.33.
3. Click on the Labels button. The Chart Options Axis dialog box displays, as shown in figure 4.45.

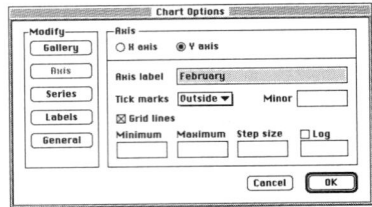

Figure 4.45. *The Chart Options Axis dialog box.*

4. Type the name of the title in the Title text box.
5. Click on one of the placement circles in the graphic.
6. Click on the OK button or press the Return or Enter key.

Customizing the Series Options

The Series options enable you to label the data points with values from the spreadsheet.

To customize a chart's series options, follow these steps:

1. Click on the chart with the pointer tool to select it.
2. Pull down the Options menu and choose the Modify Chart command, or press Command-Shift-I. The Chart Options dialog box displays, as shown in figure 4.33.
3. Click on the Series button. The Chart Options Series dialog box displays, as shown in figure 4.46.

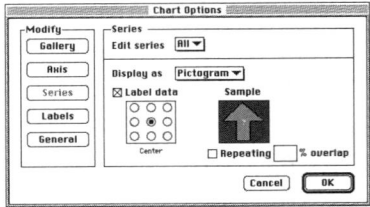

Figure 4.46. *The Chart Options Series dialog box.*

4. Select the series you want to edit from the pop-up list.
5. Select how you want the information to appear from the Display As pop-up menu.
6. Click on one of the placement circles in the graphic to indicate where the label will be entered.

7. Choose a symbol from the palette and specify its size.
8. Click on the OK button or press the Return or Enter key.

Changing the Data Range in a Chart

You can change the range of spreadsheet cells a chart is based on without creating a new chart.

To edit a data range for a chart, follow these steps:

1. Click on the chart with the pointer tool to select it.
2. Pull down the Options menu and choose the Modify Chart command, or press Command-Shift-I. The Chart Options dialog box displays as shown previously in figure 4.33.
3. Click on the General button. The Chart Options General dialog box displays, as shown in figure 4.47.

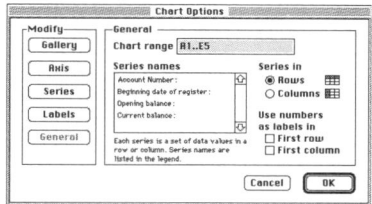

Figure 4.47. *The Chart Options General dialog box.*

4. Type the new range of cells you want the chart to illustrate.
5. Indicate whether the series should be in rows or columns.
6. If you want to use numbers as labels (for example, "1st Quarter"), click on the appropriate checkbox.
7. Click on the OK button or press the Return or Enter key.

CREATING A CHECK REGISTER

With persistence, you can create a check register that automatically subtracts all checks from the opening balance and adds all deposits to the opening balance, to give you a current balance amount. Figure 4.48 displays a sample register created in ClarisWorks.

The following register added borders to some areas of the spreadsheet and turned off the display of grid lines.

To create a check register follow these steps:

1. Create a new spreadsheet document.
2. Type in your personal information.
3. Enter the labels: Check No., Date, Payee, Description, Checks (-), Deposit (+), and Current Balance.
4. Apply currency formatting to the appropriate columns. Now you are ready to build the formulas that will calculate your new balances.
5. Enter the opening balance amount.
6. In cell G14, type this formula: =F14+G14.
7. In the second line of the Current Balance column (G15), enter the following formula: =G14-E14+F14.
8. Using the Copy and Paste Special commands, duplicate this formula in each of the cells in this column.
9. To create the current balance at the top of the page, enter this formula: =G14-SUM(E15..E37)+SUM(F15..F27). You now are ready to enter your checking account information.

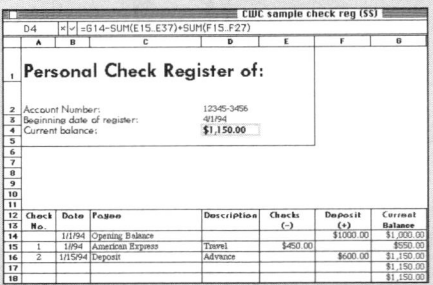

Figure 4.48. *A check register created in ClarisWorks.*

Printing a Spreadsheet

You can print your spreadsheet document by using the Print command from the File menu. If you want to use charts as a part of a presentation, print them onto transparencies for use on an overhead projector. When you print, ClarisWorks prints out all the data contained in each cell, including hidden text. You may need to use the Page Setup command on the File menu to change your page to landscape mode so that you can fit more columns onto each page.

Printing a Range of Cells

Since a spreadsheet can hold much information, it is sometimes more effective to print only a specific cell range of a worksheet.

To print a cell range, follow these steps:

1. Pull down the Options menu and choose the Print Range command. The Print Range dialog box displays, as shown in figure 4.49.

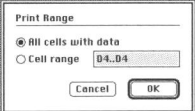

Figure 4.49. *The Print Range dialog box.*

2. Type in the range of cells you want to print.
3. Click on the OK button or press the Return or Enter key.
4. Pull down the File menu and choose the Print command. The Print dialog box displays, as shown in figure 4.50.

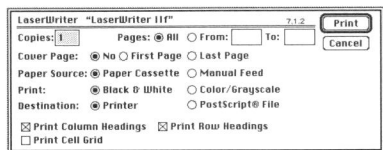

Figure 4.50. *The Print dialog box.*

> **Tip**
> If you select a cell range and choose the Print command, the printing job will be limited to the selected range of cells.

5. Type in the number of copies you want to print in the Copies text box.
6. Indicate if you want to print all pages by clicking on the All radio button or a range of pages by entering specific page numbers into the From and To text boxes.
7. Indicate whether you want to print column headings, row headings, or cell grids.
8. Click on the OK button or press the Return or Enter key.

Inserting Page Breaks

You may want to organize information by inserting page breaks.

To insert a page break, follow these steps:

1. Select the cell that is to be the last cell on the page.
2. Pull down the Options menu and choose the Add Page Break command.

Remove page breaks by choosing the Remove Page Breaks command from the Options menu. Choosing Remove All Breaks from the Options menu removes all manually inserted page breaks.

Summary

ClarisWorks' spreadsheet environment offers you powerful tools to create spreadsheet documents (worksheets) and spreadsheet frames that organize, sort, chart, and calculate your data. In this chapter, you learned how to create a worksheet, move around in a spreadsheet, how to enter information into worksheets, and how to select cells. You also learned how to add formatting, solid lines, and number formatting options.

Step-by-step procedures for creating formulas and pasting functions illustrated how convenient it is to let the computer do number crunching. By combining good spreadsheet design tips and basic formulas, you discovered how you can use ClarisWorks to create a personal check register (see sidebar).

A spreadsheet's structure lends itself to sorting and makes it easy to rearrange the contents of a worksheet.

Like spreadsheets, databases can organize, calculate, and sort information. In the next chapter, you'll learn how to use ClarisWorks' powerful database environment to manage information, such as client addresses, that you use every day.

You also will learn how to organize data within a database so that you can search, organize, analyze, and build reports that give you detailed information. These are different capabilities than you've used here for spreadsheets.

Chapter 5
Organizing Information With a Database

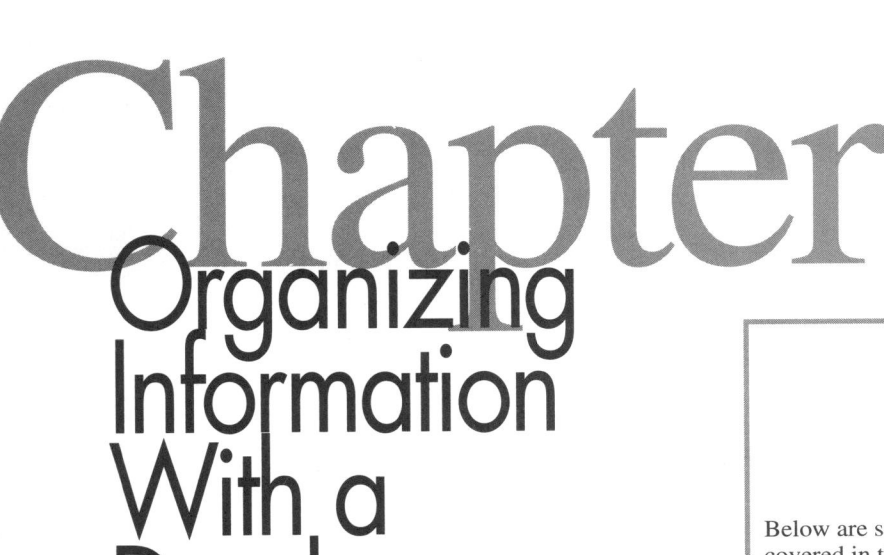

This chapter introduces the database environment. A database is an application used to organize, find, sort, search, and analyze related pieces of information. You will learn how to set up database fields and records,

Below are some of the how-to topics covered in this chapter:

How to create a database	126
How to define fields	132
How to enter data into fields and records	136
How to automate data entry	137
How to add, modify, and delete fields	139
How to view data in a database	141
How to find or select sets of records	145
How to sort records	148
How to create a layout	150
How to use parts on a layout	155
How to create and work with summary data and parts	156
How to add headers and footers to a layout	156
How to set up columns of data	160
How to remove unwanted space in layouts	161
How to import and export data from other files and applications	162

enter data, and display data in layouts that you design. Analyzing data by using reports is also described here.

In a database you can accomplish tasks that cannot be done manually. At home, you can organize your compact disc library, find a phone number in your address book in a blink of an eye, or finally balance your checkbook. For your business, you can manage sales records, print invoices and statements, and find just those three of your customers in Newton, Massachusetts, who purchased a gold-plated widget from you in the past three months.

What Is a Database?

A database is a collection of related information in electronic form. When you create a database you define a regular structure or filing system into which you can store compactly large amounts of information (see figure 5.1). Databases are used for a variety of tasks in your everyday life; some databases are instantly apparent, others are hidden from your view.

Your address book and Rolodex file are personal databases. When you go to your travel agent to make an airline reservation, they log onto a reservation service like American Airlines's SAABRE system, which is a remote database stored on several mainframe computers. Online information services also store information in a database. Even the automated teller machine (ATM) at your bank is a terminal for remote databases. Suffice it to say that databases are one of the most important and empowering uses to which you can put your Macintosh.

Databases provide a structure for storing related information that you define. The most important underlying concept of a database is a record. A record is the group of facts that you choose to store in your database file. For example, in an electronic address book, each person's information is a record. In a database, you define various fields into which you place your data. Every record in a database has the same set of defined fields. The data you enter into each of those fields can be unique, can be duplicated, or can be left vacant, as you choose.

The first step in designing a database is to determine what kinds of information you need to collect. You can do this exercise on paper. Write down the names of the fields you want to create; the kind of data each field should contain; and whether you want data automatically entered, or to have a list of choices for values, and so on. Break up your data into small chunks so that it is more convenient to work with. For example, you could have a single field for each person's name, but if you do, you will not be able to sort your database easily. Similarly, you can have a number field for telephone numbers, but you will be unable to search for just a part of that phone number. Number, date, and time fields have data entry restrictions that text fields do not. Don't worry, these are facts you will learn as you read further in this chapter. Changes, however, are made most simply in the beginning, when you are first setting up your database and before you have entered a lot of data into it.

Write down the tasks for which you need to use your information. Databases are useful for printing labels, sending invoices and statements, doing data entry, and performing other tasks. Each task most likely requires a separate layout that you will need to design. You might begin by sketching each layout with the required fields. A preview sketch helps you ascertain how to automate the layouts by including calculations, summaries, entry options, and other techniques.

Figure 5.1. *Databases have a structure that enables them to store information compactly.*

About Records and Fields

A ClarisWorks database document consists of *records*—groups of related facts or pieces of information. You can define a record as whatever makes the most sense for the project you are undertaking. For example, a phone book normally has a record for each person. However, a realtor's records might be by house, with the person who lives in the house stored as information in one of the record's fields. A realtor could just as well create records based on individual home owners, paying no design penalties for this alternate construction. Records are added to your database in subsequent order (one after another) by a manual procedure.

Tip

You can use a spreadsheet document to create a list of fields and their definitions. Use columns labeled: field name, data type, formula (if any), auto entry options, data format, text format, tab order, and notes. Using a spreadsheet frame enables you to sort by various columns.

You also can use a drawing document (see chapter 6) to design your layouts. Use shaded boxes for fields. You can select all of the objects in the drawing document and then copy them to the Clipboard. Next, switch to your database, create a new layout, and paste the drawing objects into your database layout.

Fields are the fundamental storage containers for data in database documents. Fields are defined by field name, data type, value, and other properties. You define fields within the Define Fields dialog box, as described later in this chapter in the "Defining Fields" section. Each record contains one or more fields.

A field name and its attributes are called the field's *definition*. Fields can accept text, numbers, dates, and time data. You can also define fields that calculate and summarize data for you.

You can format the data you enter into database fields to maximize its usefulness to you. Two types of formatting are possible: formatting that is based on the data type, and text that is formatted through the use of fonts, font sizes, and font styles or attributes. You can enter a number into a field that has a predetermined set of decimal places or percentage value. You also can apply word processing-like formatting to any or all of the characters in a field. For more information on formatting, see "Working With Data," later in this chapter.

Views of a Database

Databases are *modal*—that is, you select various views of your database file to accomplish specific tasks. Modality is perhaps for novices the most confusing aspect of databases. Therefore, it's crucial that new users read this section carefully. By changing the view of your database, your capability to perform certain actions changes. This chapter first offers an overview of the principles of database modality and later gives more detailed explanations.

Databases display fields on your screen in a layout form. In the Layout mode, you can design how your screen display and printed output will look. You can decide what fields should appear where, and how records are displayed. For example, one per screen, one record next to another in a list, or as a set, like mailing labels on a sheet. You build the layout a component at a time.

You cannot enter data in the Layout mode. To enter data, you switch to the Browse mode, with or without the page-view feature turned on. The Browse mode is what you see when you enter data onscreen. The Browse mode view may or may not differ from what you print. To see data you are going to print, select the Page View mode from the View menu. (Page View automatically is turned on in the word processing environment.)

Layout Mode

Layout mode is the screen display and print-output design mode (see figure 5.2). To switch to the Layout mode, select the Layout command from the Layout menu, or press Command-Shift-L. You switch between various layouts in a database by choosing the name of the layout from the bottom of the Layout menu.

> **Shortcut**
> The Layout mode can be selected by using the Layout command on the Layout menu, or by pressing Command-Shift-L.

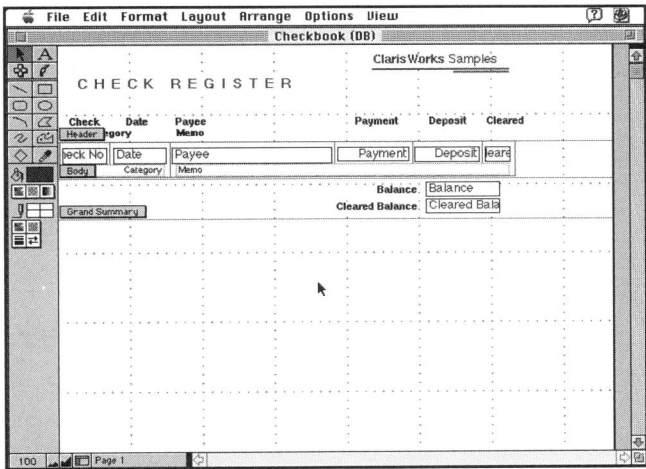

Figure 5.2. *A sample layout.*

The particular layout you see in Layout mode corresponds to the layout you choose from the bottom of the Layout menu. Layouts have various parts that determine what gets displayed or printed. Constructing layouts is described more fully in "Using Layouts," later in this chapter. You know you are in the Layout mode when you see field names and drawing tools, and there is no Bookmark icon in the status panel. You also can enter data in the Browse mode. You can create any number of layouts for various purposes. Layouts are named, and added to the bottom of the Layout menu. To switch between layouts and to change how you view your data, select a layout by name.

Browse Mode

Browse mode is the screen-display data entry mode, shown in figure 5.3. Most of the time you spend in a database is spent in the Browse mode.

Shortcut
The Browse mode can be selected by using the Browse command from the Layout menu, or by pressing Command-Shift-B.

By default, your database always opens in the Browse mode of the last layout that was onscreen, enabling you to enter data into the file without delay.

Figure 5.3. *The sample layout viewed in Browse mode.*

Every layout can be viewed in Browse mode. You can tell you are in the Browse mode when you see the Bookmark icon in the status panel, along with the number of records and their condition displayed. Browsing data is described later in this chapter, in "Browsing Data in a Database."

Find Mode

Find mode is where you enter criteria used in a search. A find screen looks identical to a browse screen, except that you enter your search parameters into one or more fields, as in figure 5.4. To enter the Find mode, select the Find command from the Layout menu, or press the Command-Shift-F keystroke. When you perform the find procedure, you view the Browse mode all records in the database that meet your search parameters.

Shortcut
Switch to the Find mode by selecting the Find command from the Layout menu, or by pressing Command-Shift-F.

ClarisWorks uses a construct called "query by example." You search your database by entering search parameters into the fields of interest. Each set of search parameters is called a "request." You can narrow the focus of a search by creating a find operation with more than one request. Finds and searches enable you to examine a subset of the records in your database. A subset of your database might be one, several, or all of the database's records, depending upon the parameters you set for the search.

ClarisWorks enables you to work with the selection of records you found. When you close your database and reopen it, you view your database in the condition it was in before it was closed. If you think you have lost some records, check below the Bookmark to see whether you are working with a partial or complete selection of records. To view missing records, perform another find, or select the Show All Records command on the Organize menu to view all of your records. For more information about searching your database, refer to "Finding and Selecting Records" later in this chapter.

Shortcut
Select the Show All Records from the Organize menu, or press Command-Shift-A to view all of your records in Browse mode, in the order that the records were created.

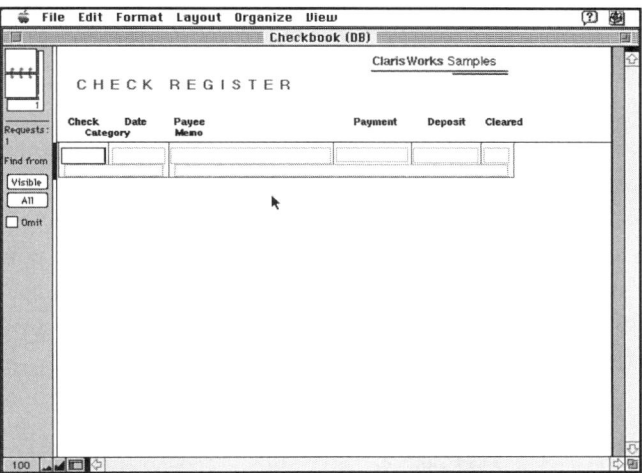

Figure 5.4. *The layout's Find screen.*

Page View Mode

Page View enables you to preview how your database records will print. Unlike many databases, ClarisWorks lets you enter data in the Page View mode (see figure 5.5). You switch to Page View mode by selecting the Page View command from the View menu, or by pressing Command-Shift-P. Page View equals the Page Preview option found under the File menu in other Macintosh programs.

Figure 5.5. *Page View mode.*

You need to work with Page View because what prints out doesn't always match what you see onscreen. In the Layout mode, you can add various fields that may or may not print, depending upon the condition of your database. That is, while you see headers and footers in both the Browse and Page View modes, sorts and finds affect various constructs, such as summary fields, which can have page or section breaks associated with them. The only way to know for sure what you will be printing is to use Page View.

Defining Fields

You define fields in your database file in the Define Fields dialog box. (see figure 5.6). When you first create a database, ClarisWorks automatically opens the Define Fields dialog box. You then can create all of your initial fields. After you close the Define Fields dialog box, you can always reopen the dialog box to make additional modifications or add new fields by using the Define Fields command on the Layout menu, as described in the section "Adding, Modifying, and Deleting Fields."

To add fields to your database document:

1. Select the New command from the File menu, click on the Database radio button in the New Document dialog box, and

press the OK button. This creates a database document and automatically opens the Define dialog box.

Alternately, from inside a database document, select the Define Fields command from the Layout menu. The Define Fields dialog box appears, as shown in figure 5.6.

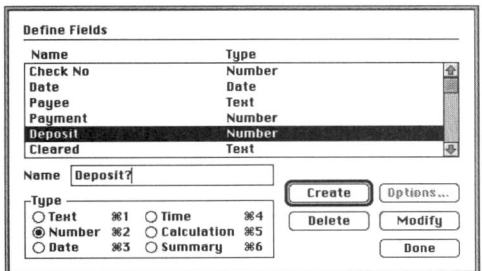

> **Shortcut**
> The Command-Shift-D keystroke opens the Define Fields dialog box in a database document.

Figure 5.6. *The Define Fields dialog box.*

2. Type a field name up to 63 characters long in the Name text box.

3. Select the field type by either clicking on the appropriate radio button, or pressing the Command key equivalent to the right of each field type.

   Use the following keystrokes for rapid field type selection: text, Command-1; number, Command-2; date, Command-3; time, Command-4; calculation, Command-5; and summary, Command-6.

4. Click on the Create button to define a field. If you dismiss the Define Fields dialog box in a new database document without creating any fields, ClarisWorks creates a default field, called "Field 1," for you.

5. Continue to create fields, repeating steps 2, 3, and 4, until you are through. Then click on the Done button to view your database document.

If you defined a calculation or summary field, additional steps are required in the above procedure. These fields compute value based on a formula you define. Calculation and summary fields can calculate totals, perform multiplication, do date and time arithmetic, and even perform text manipulation. A calculation or summary field can have as a result a text, number, date, or time value.

To define a calculation or summary field:

1. Perform steps 1 through 4 on the previous page, if needed. When you click on the Create button for a calculation or summary field, the Enter Formula dialog box, shown in figure 5.7, appears.

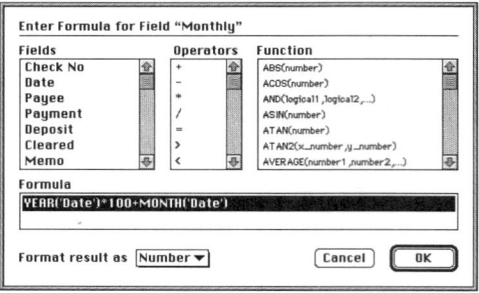

Figure 5.7. *The Enter Formula dialog box.*

2. Select the Format Result As option from the pop-up menu at the lower-left of the Enter Formula dialog box by clicking on that menu and then dragging your selection.

   You can choose either Text, Number, Date, or Time. Your selection shows a check mark when selected, and appears in the box when you release your mouse button.

3. Enter your desired formula in the Formula text box. Formulas are built up from field names, operators, and functions. If you enter a formula from your keyboard, make sure that field names are precise and enclosed in a single quotation mark, and that the syntax of functions are followed exactly.

   You can enter a formula by double-clicking on field names from the Fields scroll box, operators from the Operators scroll box, and functions from the Function scroll box. ClarisWorks helps you by enclosing field names in single quotation marks automatically, and providing you with appropriate function syntax.

4. Click on the OK button to enter your formula and return to the Define Fields dialog box. ClarisWorks checks the formula for valid expressions when you close the Enter Formula dialog box, and alerts you to potential problems. If the formula is valid, ClarisWorks places a calculated value in every record for a calculated field. Summary fields are only calculated when a database is sorted into groups of records.

Note
ClarisWorks uses the same formulas for databases and spreadsheets. Refer to the "Using Formulas" section of chapter 4 for a full description.

Tip
You can use the Copy (Command-C) and the Paste (Command-V) keystrokes to enter a formula into the Formula text box.

5. Your formula is shown to the right of the field name in the Define Fields dialog box.
6. Click on the Done button or press the Escape key to close the Define Fields dialog box.

You can define data entry options for text, number, date, and time fields. These options perform automated data entry, providing default values, serial numbers, and data validation for values you enter. Setting entry options increases the speed and accuracy of data entry.

Field Types

You can define fields to contain the following kinds of information:

- Text. Any alphanumeric character or symbol in a string up to 500 characters long may be entered in a text field. Numbers typed into a text field are treated as text.

    If you apply a style to characters in a text field, ClarisWorks reduces the number of characters that are possible. Examples of text fields are names, addresses, and notes.

- Numbers. A number field contains any numeric character with or without a decimal point up to 254 characters in length. Non-numeric characters typed into a number field are ignored in numeric calculations.

    Numbers must fit on a single line and cannot include a Return character. Number fields are used for cost, weight and height, age, and so on.

- Dates. A date field stores dates based on the Macintosh serial date system. Dates you enter are converted into a number so that date arithmetic may be performed on those values.

    Dates, like numbers, must be entered on a single line without a Return character. Examples of date fields are date of birth, starting date, termination date, and so on.

- Time. A time field stores times based on the Macintosh serial date system. This system converts times you enter into a numeric value so that time arithmetic can be performed on those values.

    Time, like numbers and dates, must be entered on one line without a Return character.

Tip
Double click on the name of a calculation or summary field to open the Enter Formula dialog box.

Note
Did you forget where a character is found? Try using the Key Caps desk accessory on the Apple menu. Key Caps shows you auxiliary characters that are available in your current font. Hold down the Command, Option, Shift, and Control modifier keys to see additional characters. Characters you type in Key Caps may be copied and pasted into ClarisWorks.

Text, number, date, and time fields are the only kinds of data that you can enter directly into a ClarisWorks database. At the present time ClarisWorks does not support picture fields, a capability that is found in Claris's dedicated database, FileMaker Pro. ClarisWorks has two other field types, but they are derived from data you enter into the text, number, date, or time fields. They are:

- ❖ Calculation fields. These are calculated values, drawn from field data in the same record and based on a formula or expression that results in any of the four primary data types mentioned above.
- ❖ Summary fields. These are calculated values drawn from fields across a group of records.

The distinction between calculation and summary fields is a critical one. You can define a calculation field and a summary field to have exactly the same formula, and each will yield very different results. Calculation fields act on values found in the same record and their placement in a layout rarely changes their displayed value. Summary fields act on values contained in a group of records. You get different values in summary fields, depending upon which group of records you are looking at, which part of a layout the summary field was placed in, and how the database was sorted. These differences are more fully explored later in this chapter.

Data Entry Options

Whenever possible, use data entry options to speed data entry, reduce typing errors, and keep your data consistent. You can set data entry options that:

- ❖ Auto-enter data into a field.
- ❖ Verify data for accuracy.
- ❖ Provide a list of values for selection.

All of these choices are set within the Entry Options dialog box, which is accessed from the Define Fields dialog box, as shown in figure 5.8. Open the Entry Options dialog box by selecting a field and clicking on the Options button, or by double-clicking on the given field name. Note that entry options are not available for calculation or summary fields, only for fields where you enter data into text, number, date, or time fields.

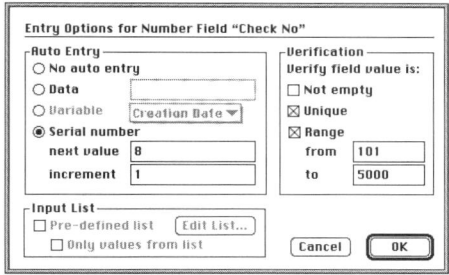

Figure 5.8. *The Entry Options dialog box.*

When you set an auto-entry option, data automatically is entered into that field whenever you create a new record. You can select the data and modify it later, as needed. Among your data type choices for auto-entry are:

- Data. Any set of characters, text, number, date or time you enter into the Data text box.
- Variable. The date or time a record is created or modified can be auto-entered. ClarisWorks uses your Macintosh System's date and time for its values. You also can enter the name of the person who creates or modifies a record into a field.
- Serial Number. A serial number is an incremented set of numbers used to label a record. Serial numbers are used for tagging forms, transactions, part numbers, and so on.

You can have a field display a list of values from which you choose. The values are entered into the Input List section of the Entry Options dialog box (see the lower-left corner of figure 5.8). Having a list provides speedy and accurate data entry because a value can be selected from that list when you tab into the field. If you click on the Only Values From List checkbox, no other values besides those you define will be accepted. Otherwise, you can enter any value, whether it is on the predefined list or not.

To add a value list:

1. Click on the Predefine list checkbox to select it. An "X" appears in that checkbox, and the Edit List button and Only Values From List checkbox are enabled.
2. Click on the Edit List button. The Values dialog box for the field's predefined list appears, as shown in figure 5.9.

Note
To change your system's time, select the Alarm Clock desk accessory from the Apple Menu, or use the General Control Panel. To change an owner's name, use the Sharing Setup Control Panel (System 7) or the Chooser Desk Accessory (System 6).

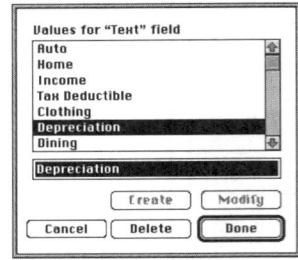

Figure 5.9. *The Values dialog box.*

3. Enter a value in the text box below the scrolling list.
4. Click on the Create button or press the Return key.

   To modify a value: Click on that value in the scrolling list, edit it in the text box, and then click on the Modify button.

   To delete a value: Click on that value in the scrolling list, then click on the Delete button.

5. Click on the Done button or press the Escape key when the value list is complete. You are returned to the Entry Option dialog box.

One last set of entry options enables you to verify data that you enter into a field. When you enter data into a verified field, ClarisWorks checks the required values against your data for a possible mismatch. An alert box is posted for a mismatch, which you can either ignore (override) or change the value accordingly.

You have the following verification options (see the verification section of figure 5.8):

❖ Not empty. The field must contain a value and cannot be left blank. Setting the key field to this option is worthwhile. For example, if your database tracks people by their Social Security numbers, you need to make sure that field is filled in during data entry.

❖ Unique. The field must not contain a value. ClarisWorks compares the value in a record to the value in the same field in all other records to see if there is a match.

   For a database of individuals where there can be only one record for each person, it is a good idea to set a unique value.

Tip

You can use the Paste command (Command-V) to enter data into the Data text box or to paste data into the Values dialog box.

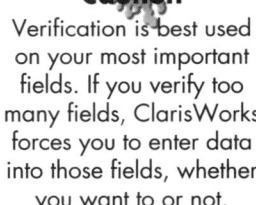

Caution

Verification is best used on your most important fields. If you verify too many fields, ClarisWorks forces you to enter data into those fields, whether you want to or not.

❖ Range. Enter a starting value in the From text box and a final or ending value in the To text box. You can set a range for number, date, and time fields.

Adding, Modifying, and Deleting Fields

Fields are added, modified, or deleted easily. You only need to reopen the Define Fields dialog box to make these changes. Some of these changes have important and irreversible consequences to which you need to pay special attention.

To add a field:

1. Open the Define Fields dialog box by selecting the Define Fields command from the Layout menu.
2. Enter the name of the new field into the Name text box and click on the data type radio button.
3. Click on the Create button. Remember to set any entry options, and to create a formula if it's a calculation or summary field. You can continue creating new fields as desired.
4. Dismiss the Define Fields dialog box by clicking on the Done button or by pressing the Escape key.

There are no serious implications in creating new fields. You sacrifice performance for database files that have hundreds of fields, but no pre-existing data will be compromised by creating new fields.

To modify a field's definition, do so from within the Define Fields dialog box. Select the Define Fields command from the Layout menu, then click on the name of the field that you wish to modify in the scrolling Field Name text box to select it.

To change the name of the field, edit the name in the Name text box, and then click on the Modify button. There are a few implications to changing a field name. If the field name is used as part of a formula in a calculation or summary field, then ClarisWorks automatically adjusts that formula when you modify the field.

To change the field type, click on the new Type, then click on the Modify button.

If you change a previously defined field type, there can be serious implications of which you need to be aware. When a text field is converted to either a number, date, or time field, the data in that field will be trun-

Note
You can set more than one verification option for a field. Often (such as in the situation mentioned above) this is desirable.

cated in all records after the first 254 characters. Any characters after a Return character are also truncated. Only valid dates and times will be recognized.

When you change a number field into a date or time field, the conversion results in the translation of that number as to a serial date or time. The reverse translation of a date or time value field into a numeric field displays the serial date or the number itself.

When you change a text, number, date, or time field to either a calculation or summary field, ClarisWorks deletes all values in those fields and substitutes the results of the formula you enter.

To modify a calculation or a summary formula:

> Double-click on the field name in the Field scroll box, or click once on the field name and then click on the Modify button.
>
> In the Enter Formula dialog box, edit the formula for the field. Effect your changes by clicking the OK button to close the dialog box. ClarisWorks recalculates the field in all existing records, based on the new formula. There are no implications to changing a field's formula, other than getting another calculated value displayed. You can always experiment with different formulas.

To delete a field:

1. Click on the field name in the Name scroll box, then click on the Delete button. ClarisWorks posts an alert box that tells you that the field and all of the data it contains in all records will be permanently deleted from your database.

2. Click on the OK button to delete the field and its data. Alternately, click on the Cancel button to return to the Define Fields dialog box without deleting the field.

Deleting a field definition removes that field from any layouts the field was in and removes all the data from every record in the database.

Deleting a field definition is not the same thing as deleting a field from a layout. When you delete a field from a layout only the display of that field on that layout is removed. If the field appears in other layouts, it remains displayed. The field and its data still is contained in the database and can be added back into the layout whenever you desire.

Caution

Pay special attention to changing a field type. You can permanently delete and loose data from your file. This is an operation that cannot be undone. Therefore, make a backup copy of you database before trying field conversion in case you make an error.

Caution

The deletion of a field definition cannot be undone. Be sure that before you delete a field definition you will not need that field or its data again. Consider saving a copy of the database file before you delete a field. If you then later need the deleted information, you can work from your backup file.

Working With Data

You view data in the Browse and in Page View modes. In either mode, you can create new records, enter data into fields, and edit data in pre-existing records. The following sections tell you how.

Browsing Data in a Database

When you are browsing data in a database, you may see more than one record on a screen. This is true for some layouts, such as lists, and not for others. A list layout is the default arrangement. In list view, one record appears above another. When you click on a record in the list view, the record is highlighted. You may only want to see one record on your screen at a time. Single screen viewing is less confusing for the display of forms, such as invoices.

To view records as a list, select the List View command from the Layout menu. ClarisWorks places a check mark on the command when List View is active.

To view records one at a time, select the List View command again to remove the check mark next to the command name.

Only one record is active in your database at a time. You can tell which record is active by looking at the Bookmark to determine the record number; however, knowing the record number may not make the active record obvious. The active record has a field with the insertion point in it, and in the List View you see a black bar at the left of the record in the Browse or Page View modes.

You can select multiple records at a time by dragging through the set of records in a List View, Shift-clicking on records to get a contiguous range of records, or Command-clicking on individual records as part of a non-contiguous range of records. You deselect a range of records by pressing the Enter key. You can cut, copy, and paste records as a group from one database to another (common field data types must match), to a spreadsheet, or to a word processor. You also can delete a set of records in this manner.

To move from record to record, use the Bookmark. Click on the top page to move back a record (previous), click on the bottom page to move forward a record (later), and drag the Bookmark itself to move through the

Shortcut

Press Command-Return to move to the next record and Command-Shift-Return to move to the previous record.

records. With the Bookmark at the top of the book, you are on the first record in the database, your original record. When you move the Bookmark to the bottom of the book, you arrive at the last or most recently created record. You can use the Command-Return keystroke to advance a record or the Command-Shift-Return keystroke to move backward a record.

If you see a record you want to activate, use your cursor to click anywhere on that record. To activate a field, click on it. ClarisWorks places the insertion point in the field you click on. Selected fields have solid borders; unselected fields have dotted-line borders, as shown in figure 5.10.

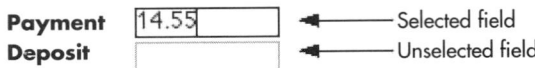

Figure 5.10. *A selected field box versus an unselected field box.*

To go to a specific record:

1. Select the Go To Record command from the Organize menu. The Go To dialog box appears, as shown in figure 5.11.

Shortcut

Select the Go To Record command or press Command-G to select a specific record by its record number.

Figure 5.11. *The Go To Record dialog box.*

2. Enter the number of the record you seek in the Go To Record text box.
3. Click on the OK button. You then are taken to the desired record. The record returned is the number of the record in all records.

If you know the number of the record you wish to activate, you can use the Bookmark in the status panel to go to that record. Drag the Bookmark until the number of the record shows just below the book. Alternately, click on the number of the current record to highlight it, type the number of the record, then press the Return or the Enter key.

You can choose to hide selected records in the Browse mode so that they are not viewed as part of a browsed set by using the Hide Selected command on the Organize menu or use its Command-(keystroke equivalent. Use the Hide Unselected command on the Organize menu or Command-) when the selected records are the ones with which you want to work. The effect of Hide Unselected is the same as if you omitted these records during a find procedure. To view all the records in your database, select the Show All Records on the Organize menu or press the Command-Shift-A keystroke.

Entering Data by Creating or Modifying Records

You enter data in the active record by moving from field to field. You also can enter data in other records or create new records for data entry.

To move from field to field:

1. Type the characters you want into that field and press the Tab key.

You enter data into fields in a ClarisWorks database in the order in which you created the fields in the Define Fields dialog box. When you switch to a new layout, a new record, or the next record, the insertion point appears in the first defined field, wherever that appears on the layout. Pressing the Tab key moves you to the next field in the sequence, called the tab order. The default tab order is likely to be inconvenient. You may have moved fields about on the layout, or even omitted fields. ClarisWorks enables you to set a tab order of your choosing.

To set the Tab Order:

1. Select the Tab Order command from the Layout menu.

    The Tab Order dialog box shown in figure 5.12 appears, with your field creation order in the Tab Order scroll box.

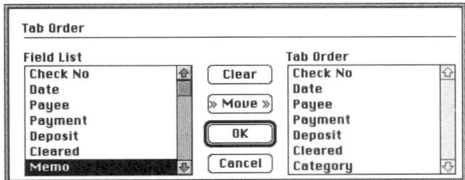

Figure 5.12. *The Tab Order dialog box.*

Shortcut
Use the Hide Selected command on the Organize menu, or Command-(to remove selected records from view. Use the Hide Unselected Records command or Command-) to remove unselected records from your browsed set.

Tip
To place a tab character inside a field, use Command-Tab. When ClarisWorks exports that character, the application places a quotation mark around the tab to indicate that it is a text character and not a field-separation symbol.

2. Click on the Clear button to remove all fields from the tab order. Or click on a field in the Tab Order scroll box to highlight its name, then click on the Move button to remove just that field from the tab order. You can also double-click on a field name to remove it from the tab order.

3. Click on a field name in the Field List scroll box, then click on the Move button to transfer that field to the end of the Tab Order scroll box. You also can double-click on a field name to move it into the tab order.

The tab order goes from top to bottom, with the bottom field being the last field in the tab order. When you press the Tab key with the last field selected you cycle back to the first field in the tab order.

4. Click on the OK button to set the tab order and return to your layout.

To add a new record to your database, in the Browse mode, select the New Record command from the Edit menu or press the Command-R keystroke.

Whenever you create a new record, that record is added to the end of all of the other records in your database. The number of records in the status area increments by one, any serial number field increments by one, and the new record becomes the active record. The first field in that record gets the insertion point and becomes the active field.

To duplicate your current record, in the Browse mode, select the Duplicate Record command from the Edit menu or press its keystroke equivalent, Command-D.

As before, you create a new record that is added to the end of your file. That record becomes the active record. All data in the new record is copied from your previous record, with the exception of serial number fields, which jump incrementally by a value of one. Duplicating a record can save you time and increase accuracy.

Finding and Selecting Records

You can search your database for specific information and any record or records that match the search criteria you enter. You create a find request in the Find mode, and the find operation returns records that match the search criteria in the Browse mode, hiding records that don't match the search criteria. In another find operation, called "record matching," only records in your current browsed set are searched and returned for matches.

> **Tip**
> To move a contiguous group of fields at once, hold the Shift key, then click on the first field in the range followed by the last field in the range, then click on the Move button. To move several non-contiguous fields into the tab order at once, hold the Command key, click each field one at a time, then click on the Move button.

> **Shortcut**
> The New Record command on the Edit menu can be selected by using Command-R. That command is only enabled in the Browse mode.

Search criteria entered into a field in a find can be a value or an expression that uses a ClarisWorks operator. When you enter a value, ClarisWorks searches for that value. For example, using the text string "John" finds "John", "john", "Johnson", and so on. A value search is not case-sensitive and finds any occurrence. Other commonly used operators are the equal sign (=), which finds an exact match; the less-than symbol (<); the greater-than symbol (>); the less-than or equal symbol (≤) [use the Option-< keystroke to type this symbol]; and the greater-than or equal symbol (≥) [type Option->]. Thus, "=John" finds only "John" or "john", not "Johnson." With the greater-than or less-than (and equal) symbols you can search for numbers, dates, and times that are smaller or occur earlier, respectively. For example, ≤ 8/27/52 returns all values on or before that date. If you wish to find records that do not match the search criteria, click on the Omit checkbox in the status panel of the Find screen.

To find records you enter the Find mode, a screen similar to ClarisWorks's Browse mode. You enter a value or expression in any field(s) that serve(s) as the search criteria. A set of search criteria represent a find request. You can string find requests together to narrow a search.

Multiple search criteria in a find request represent a Boolean AND statement; both criteria must be true for a record to satisfy the search. Multiple find requests represent a Boolean OR statement; either find request may be true to satisfy the search. The records that are returned by a search are called the found set.

To perform a search:

1. Switch to a layout that has all the fields you want to search by choosing the name of that layout from the bottom of the Layout menu. You cannot search fields that are not contained in a layout.
2. Select the Find command from the Layout menu or press Command-Shift-L. A blank Find screen of your active layout appears. (See figure 5.13 for an example of a Find screen with some sample criteria entered into two find requests.)
3. Enter the find criteria into the field(s) you want to search.
4. To create an additional find request, select the New Request command from the Edit menu or press Command-R. Another blank Find screen appears.

Shortcut
Use Command-D to activate the Duplicate Record command on the Edit menu. The Duplicate Record command is only enabled in the Browse mode.

Tip
If no layout contains the fields you want to search, you can temporarily add a field to a layout in the Layout mode; perform a search; and then later remove that field. Your selected records will remain in view.

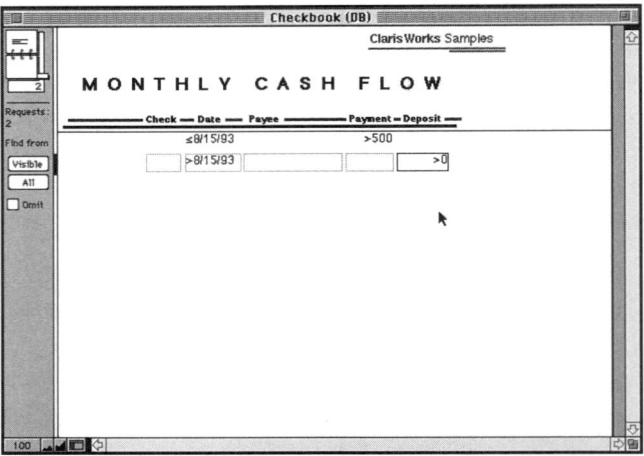

Figure 5.13. *A Find screen with search criteria entered.*

5. Enter the find criteria into the field(s) you want to search. Click on the Omit checkbox if you wish to search for records that do not match the request criteria (Boolean NOTs and NORs).

6. Continue creating new requests and entering search criteria, as needed.

7. Click on the All button to search all records in the database for matches. Or click on the Visible button to search only those records that are in your current browsed set. This omits records from the browsed set that don't match the search criteria.

In the Find mode, you see the number of find requests in the Bookmark. To switch to another request:

❖ Click on the pages of the Bookmark;
❖ Move the Bookmark up or down;
❖ Enter the request number under the Bookmark;
  or
❖ Use the Command-Return keystroke to move to the next request and the Command-Shift-Return keystroke to move to the previous request.

These are the same techniques you used to navigate browsed records in your database.

Shortcut
Use the New Request command from the Edit menu or its Command-R keystroke equivalent to create a new find request.

If no records matched your search criteria, you are prompted via an alert box to modify your search criteria and perform the find again or to cancel your search.

When records are returned, you see the number of records found below the Bookmark in the status panel. The number of records in the database appears in parentheses next to the number found, as shown in figure 5.14.

Figure 5.14. *The Bookmark after a set of records has been found.*

With a Match Records search you can perform searches based on a formula you create. The Match Records feature enables you to create searches that do not depend upon any layout and works with all of the fields across your database. With appropriate formulas you can omit records, perform searches based on multiple criteria, and use various search logics. All of the fields, operators, and functions are available to you in the Match Records dialog box. You can consider the Matching Records feature as the equivalent of a universal find command.

1. In the Browse mode, select the Match Records command from the Organize menu. The Match Records dialog box appears, as shown in figure 5.15. This dialog box is identical to the dialog box in which you to define calculation fields.

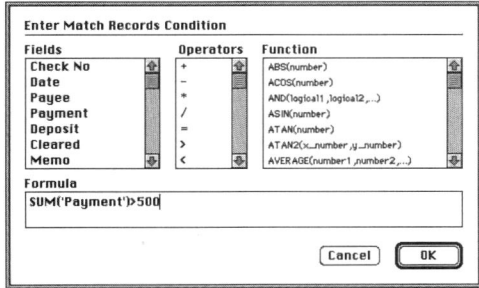

Figure 5.15. *The Enter Match Records Condition dialog box.*

2. Enter the formula you wish to search for by typing it into the Formula text box or by double-clicking on fields, operators, and functions in the three scroll boxes.

   Remember that fields are surrounded by single quotation marks in the formula and that text is surrounded by double quotation marks.

3. Click on the OK button.

Records are selected based on their evaluation of your formula. If the formula is true, the record is selected. Searches are best performed on formulas that can be evaluated as true or false. Use time and date values converted to text with the TimeToDate and DateToText functions. See "Using Functions" in chapter 4.

Organizing Records by Sorting

You can use the values in fields to change the order in which your records appear in your database, a process called sorting. Sorting records serves several purposes. By sorting values into a given order, you can analyze more easily the data in your file and make sense of trends. Sorting also puts like values together so that they can be grouped. As you will learn subsequently, subsummary parts are used in layouts to group records that have the same value in a sorted field. A subsummary part sorted by last name would appear after or before any group of records that have the same last name.

> **Note**
> When you sort a database, you sort records for all of the layouts in that database.

You sort by the sorting order: ascending, 0 to 9 and A to Z, and earlier dates or times to later dates or times; or descending, 9 to 0, Z to A, and later dates and times to earlier dates and times. Sorts look at the first character, the second, then the third, and so on. In the United States, sorts are performed by using a character sequence called the ASCII code. Other languages and countries use various character-sorting sequences.

> **Note**
> Remember that dates and times are stored internally in your Macintosh as a number: serial dates and times. The sorting of dates and times is performed internally as a number sort, and then displayed as a date or a time.

To sort a set of browsed records in a database:

1. View all of the records that you want to sort.
2. Select the Sort Records command from the Organize menu or press Command-J. The Sort Records dialog box appears, as shown in figure 5.16.

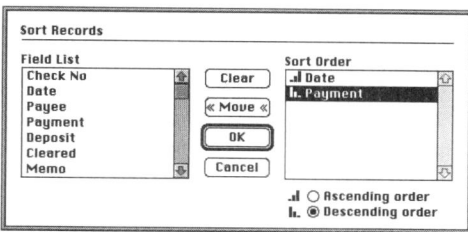

Figure 5.16. *The Sort dialog box.*

3. Add a field to the Sort Order by clicking on its name in the Field List scroll box to highlight it, then click on the Move button. Or double-click on a field name to move it directly. You can select multiple field names by Shift-clicking or Command-clicking on field names.

4. With the name of the field in the Sort Order highlighted, click on the Ascending or Descending radio button below the Sort Order scroll box.

5. Add additional fields to the sort order as desired.

Adding additional fields creates what is called a multilevel sort. Your database is sorted first by the last (bottom) field in the Sort Order, then by the next field, and finally the top field in the Sort Order. The last sort is the primary sort, the next to last is the secondary sort, and so on.

6. Click on the OK button to sort your records. ClarisWorks sorts your browsed set and places the word "Sorted" in the status panel. Records are renumbered according to their sorted order.

> **Shortcut**
> Select the Sort Records command from the Organize menu or press Command-J in the Browse mode to sort a set of browsed records.

Using Layouts

Layouts are the way you view your data when in the Browse or Find modes. You can have one or more layouts in your database; they are independent of the data and fields in your database. What you see in a layout is dependent upon how you design the layout in the Layout mode. You can add any field, text labels, graphics, or other objects to a layout and format those objects for your purposes. Working in the Layout mode is similar to working with a drawing document—many of the tools and procedures are the same in both instances.

> **Shortcut**
> Press Command-Shift-L to switch to the Layout mode.

To view a layout in any of the database modes, you choose the layout by name from the bottom of the Layout menu. To change features in a layout, you must be viewing that layout, and then switch to the Layout mode by using the Layout command (Command-Shift-L) from the Layout menu.

Parts and fields are added to layouts through the use of the Insert Parts and Insert Fields command on the Layout menu. Selections are then made in dialog boxes to determine which parts and fields you want. These procedures are detailed in following sections.

All other graphic objects—lines, squares, circles, text, patterns, fills, line widths, and so on—are added by selecting a tool from the Tool panel, clicking and dragging the object, and then making the appropriate attribute settings from either the Tool panel or the Format menu. You may want to turn on the ruler from the View menu, the grid from the Options menu, and other drawing aids to help you in your work. Since all of these procedures are covered in the next chapter, refer to chapter 6, "Adding Graphics to Your Work."

Creating and Deleting Layouts

A database must always have at least one layout. You will not be able to delete the last layout of your database.

To create a new standard layout, duplicate the active layout, or create a blank layout:

1. Select the New Layout command from the Layout menu. The New Layout dialog box, shown in figure 5.17, appears.

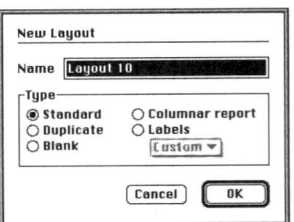

Figure 5.17. *The New Layout dialog box.*

2. Enter a name in the Name text box for your layout. ClarisWorks uses the default name Layout #, where # refers to the number of layouts that exist in your database after this layout appears.

3. Click on the radio button for the type of layout you want. Five different layouts are possible: Standard, Duplicate, Blank, Columnar report, and Labels. A standard layout is the default choice. Layout types are described subsequently and in more detail.

4. Click on the OK button to create the layout and return to the layout window. The layout name is added to the bottom of the Layout menu. Or click on the Cancel button to go back to your previous layout without creating a new layout.

If you selected the Standard, Duplicate, or Blank layouts, when you click on the OK button in step 4, the new layout appears onscreen.

A standard layout is shown in figure 5.18. In a standard layout all fields appear in the creation order from top to bottom with a text label to their left. A standard layout is good for data entry with a file that has just a few fields in it. A blank layout is shown in figure 5.19. Blank layouts are a good starting point for creating forms. Both of these layouts are created with just a body part. Normally both of these layouts are used one record at a time, instead of showing a list of records.

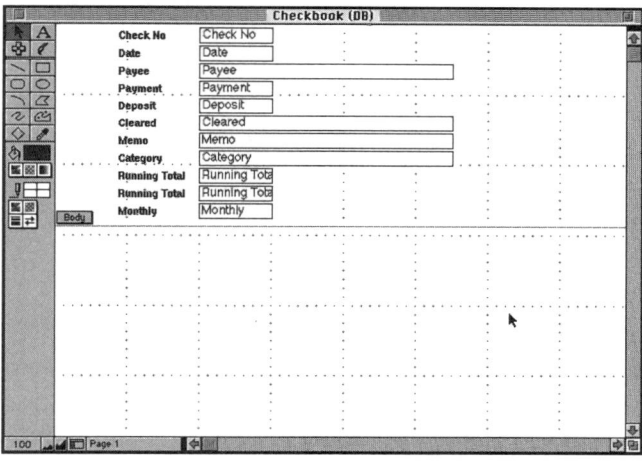

Figure 5.18. *A standard layout in the Layout mode.*

If you selected the Columnar report and the Label layouts some additional steps are required to determine which field(s) will appear in the layout. In the case of the Label layout, the label size must be set for a custom label.

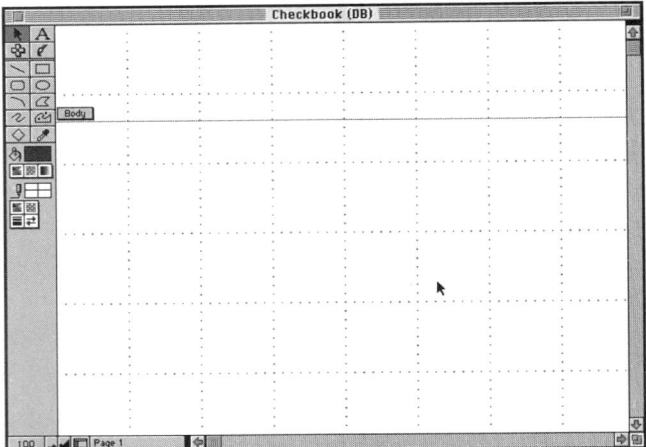

Figure 5.19. *A blank layout.*

To create a Columnar Report layout (or an Avery label):

1. Follow steps 1 through 4 above, selecting the Columnar Report layout by clicking on its radio button (see step 3). The Set Field Order dialog box shown in figure 5.20 appears. Continue to step 5 below.

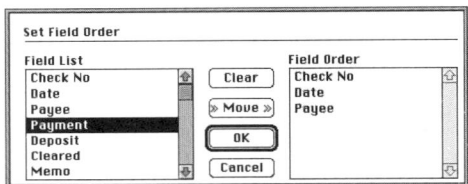

Figure 5.20. *The Set Field Order dialog box.*

5. Move fields from the Field List scroll box to the Field Order scroll box by double-clicking on the field name. You also can use Shift-clicking or Command-clicking techniques to move several fields at once into the Field Order list box.

6. Click on the OK button to create the columnar report. A sample columnar report in the Layout mode is shown in figure 5.21. The layout name is added to the bottom of the Layout menu. Alternately, click on the Cancel button to return to the previous layout.

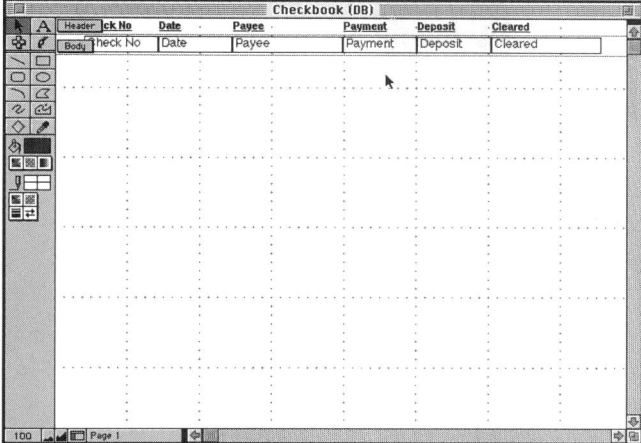

Figure 5.21. *A sample columnar report layout in the Layout mode.*

In a columnar report the field names appear in the header, and the field data appears as a list in the body, below. (See the next section for a description of parts of a layout.) A columnar report is a good way to display many records of a few fields. When you add too many fields to a layout, the fields wrap around to the next line.

If you wish to create an Avery label layout, you need to select the label name from the pop-up list in the New Layout dialog box. Then follow the same steps to create an Avery label layout as you did for creating a new columnar report layout (see above).

You also can create custom label layouts, and the procedure varies slightly from that just given for a columnar report or an Avery label layout. If you need custom margins, use the Choose Document command from the Format menu to create them. You also can vary the space between labels by resizing the parts on the custom layout you create.

To create a custom label layout:

1. Follow steps 1 through 4 (above) for creating a standard layout. In step 3, click on the custom Label radio button in the New Layout dialog box.

   When you click on the OK button in the New Layout dialog box (step 4) the Label Layout dialog box shown in figure 5.22 appears. Proceed to step 5.

Tip
Since Avery makes a large range of labels, you may find that your custom label size and arrangement already exists within the Avery series.

154   Chapter 5 • Organizing Information With a Database

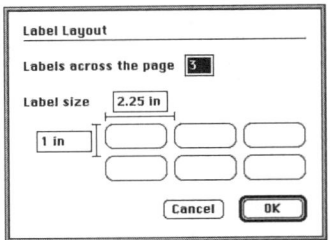

Figure 5.22. *The custom Label layout dialog box.*

5. Enter the number of labels across the page in the Labels Across the Page text box, and the height and width (in inches) in the Label Size text boxes.

   The label width is measured from the left edge of a label to the left edge of the next label; label height is measured from the top edge of the first label to the top edge of the next label.

6. Click on the OK button. The Set Field Order dialog box appears. You complete the custom label layout as you would an Avery label layout from this point on.

7. Move fields from the Field List scroll box to the Field Order scroll box by double-clicking on the field name.

8. Click on the OK button to create the custom label layout. Or click on the Cancel button to return to your previous layout.

You may occasionally need to rename a layout or to delete a layout from your file. To rename a layout:

1. Select the layout you want to rename from the Layout menu.

2. Select the Layout Info command from the Layout menu. The Layout Info dialog box appears, as shown in figure 5.23.

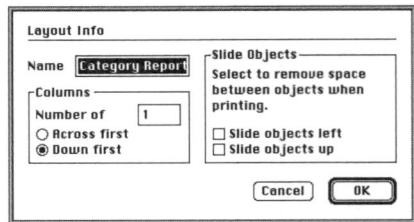

Figure 5.23. *The Layout Info dialog box.*

3. Enter a new name in the Name text box.
4. Click on the OK button.

To delete a layout:

1. Select the layout you want to delete from the Layout menu.
2. Select the Delete Layout from the Layout menu. ClarisWorks posts the dialog box shown in figure 5.24 asking if you want to delete the layout.
3. Click on the OK button to permanently delete the layout.

> **Caution**
> Deleting a layout is irreversible and cannot be undone. About this time, don't you wish you had a backup of your database?

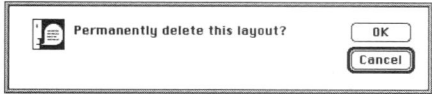

Figure 5.24. *The delete layout dialog box.*

Parts of a Layout

By adding parts to a layout you control how your page appears in the Browse mode and in printed output form. You use parts in all ClarisWorks documents: headers, footers, and the main section of the document, which in database documents are called the body part. Databases offer additional subsummary and grand summary parts to help you present and summarize data.

The parts of a layout are:

- ❖ Header. A header appears at the top of your screen display when you view data in the Browse mode or print at the top of every page when you print the document.
- ❖ Body. Body parts appear for every record displayed or printed. Normally body parts contain data for each record.

If you choose to create a summary report, then the body part is omitted from your layout. To return the body part, use the Insert Field command to place a field on the layout, as described in the next section.

- ❖ Subsummary. Subsummary parts are defined for groups of records and allow summary fields placed on that part of the document to summarize that group of records. To have a subsummary part appear and function, you need to sort the database by the field for which the subsummary part was defined. You see as many subsummary parts as there are unique values in the field for which the subsummary report was defined.

- ❖ Grand Summary. Grand summary parts apply to all records you are browsing or printing. Placing a summary field in this part reports the total of a field that the summary field summarizes.

Subsummary and grand summary parts can be either leading or trailing the set of records that they summarize.

- ❖ Footer. This part appears once at the bottom of your screen display, or once at the bottom of each printed page. No fields may be placed on a footer.

Figure 5.25 shows a sample layout with all of these defined parts.

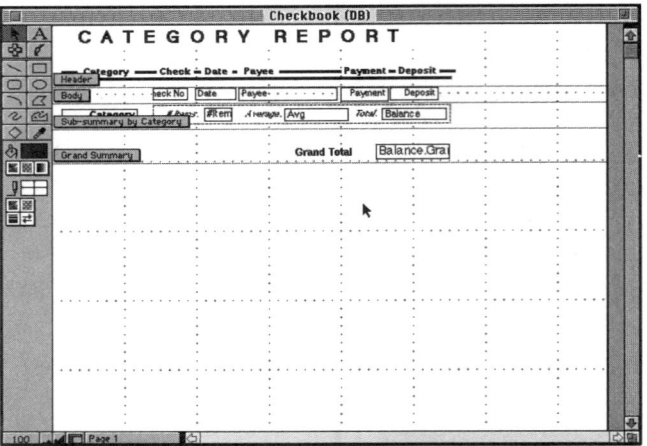

Figure 5.25. *A sample layout with parts.*

To create a new part:

1. In the Layout mode with the layout you want to modify showing, select the Insert Part command from the Layout menu.

    The Insert Part dialog box appears, as shown in figure 5.26.

2. Click on the radio button for the part type you want. If you wish to create a subsummary part, then continue with step 3. For any other part type, click on the OK button to add the part to your layout.

3. For a subsummary part, click on the field you wish to summarize in the scroll box.

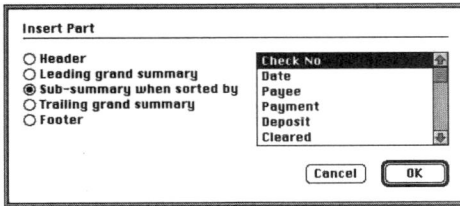

Figure 5.26. *The Insert Part dialog box.*

4. Click on the OK button. A Part Position dialog box appears.
5. Click on either the Above or Below button to have the subsummary part appear before or after the records it summarizes.

Don't forget to add summary fields to your summary parts, as needed. You also can use subsummary parts to divide groups of records. You may find it useful to place a horizontal line in the subsummary part as a divider.

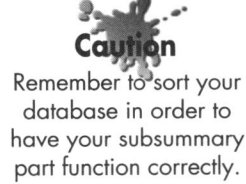

Caution
Remember to sort your database in order to have your subsummary part function correctly.

To resize a part on a layout:

1. Move the pointer over the part border; the cursor changes to a line.
2. Then click on the part and drag it up or down.

To delete a part:

1. Select all objects on the part by clicking on them or by click-dragging them, and then press the Delete key.
2. Move the pointer over the part border; the cursor changes to a line.
3. Then, click on the part and drag it up until the part disappears.

Adding and Removing Fields

Any field in your database can be added to any layout. To add a field to a layout that doesn't exist, create the field first in the Define Fields dialog box, as described in "Defining Fields."

To add a field to a layout:

1. Select the layout by name from the Layout menu, if that layout isn't already onscreen.
2. Switch to the Layout mode by selecting the Layout command from the Layout menu, if necessary.
3. Select the Insert Field command from the Layout menu. The Insert Field dialog box appears as shown in figure 5.27.

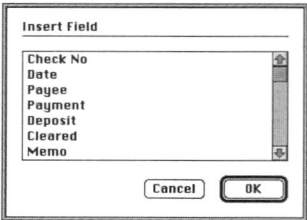

Figure 5.27. *The Insert Field dialog box.*

4. Click on the name of the field you want to add to your layout to select that field and highlight its name. Only fields not already on your layout appear in the scrolling list.
5. Click on the OK button. The field appears in the center of the body part of your layout.

To delete a field:

1. Select that field by clicking on it in the Layout mode, then press the Delete key.

Fields in the Layout mode are like objects in the drawing environment. You can click on their handles when they are selected to resize them, apply various line borders (strokes), line colors, and patterns, transparent fills, and fill colors and patterns. For information about applying graphic characteristics to objects, see chapter 6, "Adding Graphics To Your Work."

You can set the default text characteristics of a field by selecting the font type, font size, font style, alignment, and line spacing by using menu commands from the Format menu. Whatever the default font characteristics of a field, you can apply individual character formatting in the Browse mode, just as you would in a word processing document. All field data types allow this kind of layout formatting.

Number, date, and time fields, as well as calculation and summary fields that result in these data types can be additionally formatted so that they display data in a more meaningful way. You can enter data in the Browse mode and have that data appear in a form of your choosing when you tab out of the field.

To set the data formatting of a number field:

1. Double-click on the number field in the Layout mode or select the field, and then choose the Field Format command from the Options dialog box.

   The Number Format dialog box shown in figure 5.28 appears.

2. Click on the appropriate radio button and enter the Precision value to set the number formatting.

3. Click on the OK button.

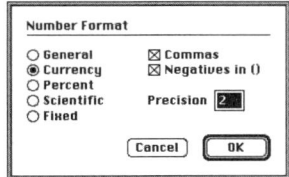

Figure 5.28. *The Number Format dialog box.*

Numbers can appear as entered, in currency, in percentages, as scientific notation, as fixed numbers, with or without commas, and with parentheses to indicate negative numbers. You also can select how many numbers that you have entered are displayed by typing a number into the Precision text box of the Number Format dialog box.

Similarly, follow the same procedure to select a date format for a date field. When you choose the Field Format command a Date Format dialog box appears, as shown in figure 5.29. Short, medium, and long date formats are available. Time fields offer a set of time formats shown in figure 5.30. Both 12- and 24-hour time formats are available.

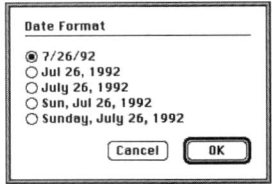

Figure 5.29. *The Date Format dialog box.*

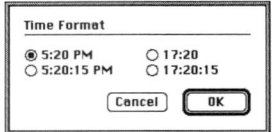

Figure 5.30. *The Time Format dialog box.*

Using Columns

To browse and print your records in columns, use the Layout Info dialog box (see figure 5.23) and select the command from the Layout menu. The number of columns entered into the Columns box appears in Page View mode as a set of equal-sized columns that divide your page. A gray vertical line separates each column. As much of a record appears in each column as the size of the layout will allow.

You can select whether records appear down a column and then over to the next (right) column or appear across a row (left to right) and then continue down to the next column. Figure 5.31 shows the two text-flow (filling) patterns.

Tip
To conserve printed labels, use the Fill Across option.

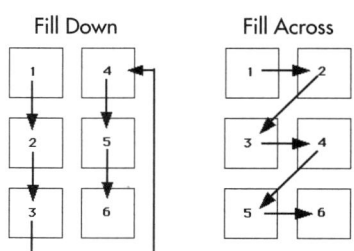

Figure 5.31. *Fill Down columns versus Fill Across columns.*

Removing Unwanted Space

In many instances, you want to have parts of your documents close up when there is blank space. On a label, it looks much more attractive when the lines of an address close up a blank address-field line. Similarly, when printing a list of records you can have a more attractive report when parts are closed up to eliminate blank spaces. The feature, called "slide object," enables you to eliminate blank spaces by shifting objects either left or up when a blank field occurs. The enclosing part is also reduced in size. Figure 5.32 shows an example of sliding objects.

Figure 5.32. *Examples of labels with and without sliding objects.*

Sliding objects only appear in printed output, although they can be viewed in Page View mode. You will not see the effects of sliding objects in the Browse mode.

To remove spaces due to blank fields when you print:

1. In the Layout mode, select the Layout Info from the Layout menu. The Layout Info dialog box appears, as shown in figure 5.23.
2. Click on the Slide Object checkbox(es).
3. Click on the OK button.

For sliding objects left to work properly, the fields need to be the same size in the sliding direction. That is, to slide left the field heights must be identical; to slide up, the field widths must be identical.

> **Tip**
> When using the Slide Objects option, always preview your page(s) by using the Page View mode before printing.

Importing and Exporting Data

You can insert data from other data files into a ClarisWorks database document. Inserting data brings all of the data of that file into ClarisWorks. The following file formats are supported in version 2.0 of

ClarisWorks: AppleWorks DB; ASCII text; DBF (dBASE format); DIF (spreadsheet format used by Lotus 1-2-3 and others); Microsoft Works 2.0 DB; and SYLK (formatted spreadsheet format used by Resolve, Wingz, and Excel).

To import data:

1. Open your ClarisWorks database document, if necessary.
2. In the Browse mode select the Insert command from the File menu. The Insert dialog box appears, as shown in figure 5.33.

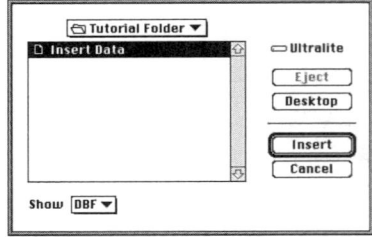

Figure 5.33. *The Insert Data dialog box.*

3. Select the document type from the Show pop-up menu.
4. Select the document name that is the source of the imported data by double-clicking on the file name.

    The Import Field Order dialog box appears, as shown in figure 5.34.

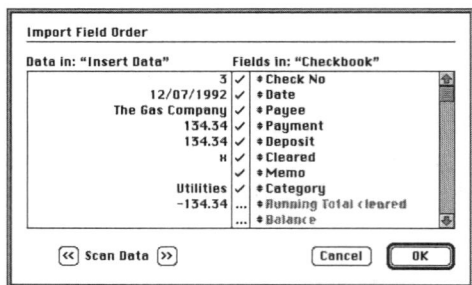

Figure 5.34. *The Import Field Order dialog box.*

DBF and DIF show field names as the first record. You use the Import Field Order dialog box to match data to the ClarisWorks database fields into which they are to be imported. Use the Scan buttons to move a record forward or backward in the data source file.

5. Click on and drag the double-headed arrows next to ClarisWorks' fields up or down to match the fields to the data.
6. Click on the check mark to stop a field from receiving data. Click again to place the check mark to have that field import data in the insert operation.
7. When the order is correct, click on the OK button. ClarisWorks adds the records to the end of your database file and adjusts increments of the number of records in your file.

You import data from other files when you want to convert those files into a ClarisWorks document. This is different than inserting data into an existing ClarisWorks document, which appends the data to a file you already have open. ClarisWorks uses a set of translators to import data into a new ClarisWorks document. The word "converted" is added to the file's title. Use the Open command on the File menu, choose the document type you wish to create, and the file type you wish to open in the Open dialog box. ClarisWorks does the importing automatically if it has the appropriate translator. Save the file and name it, if you want to keep it.

To export a ClarisWorks document, simply save that document by using a new file format. The Save As dialog box offers you the following file formats: ASCII text, DBF, DIF, Excel, and SYLK. If you want to export only a subset of your data, save a copy of your file, and delete the records you want to export. Then, use Save As to create the file format you need.

You can copy the data in summary fields to the Clipboard, and paste them into other documents. Remember to sort your database first to have the subsummary parts function correctly. To copy summary fields, you first need to be in Page View mode. Then select the Copy Summaries command from the Edit menu to copy those values.

Summary

In this chapter you learned about databases. Databases have a fields and records structure that compacts a large amount of information for storage. You create field definitions for recording and storing various data, and for automatic data entry, calculations, data summary, and data validation.

Databases can be viewed in various ways. By using the Layout mode, you design your display of data and printed output. Layouts are created for a variety of purposes: data entry, browsing, reporting, printing, and so on. You view data in the Browse mode, as well as create records and enter data in that mode. You can also check your work in the Page View mode.

Information is retrieved by using the Find mode. You can search your database for matching records by using criteria, or parameters, that you specify. A found or browsed set of records that satisfies your search criteria is returned. This feature makes databases valuable indeed. You also can organize data by using a Sort command. Sorting your database records lets you examine trends and group like information together.

The next chapter explores working with graphics in ClarisWorks. It also teaches you to apply what you learn about drawing tools to design attractive database layouts.

Chapter 6
Adding Graphics to Your Work

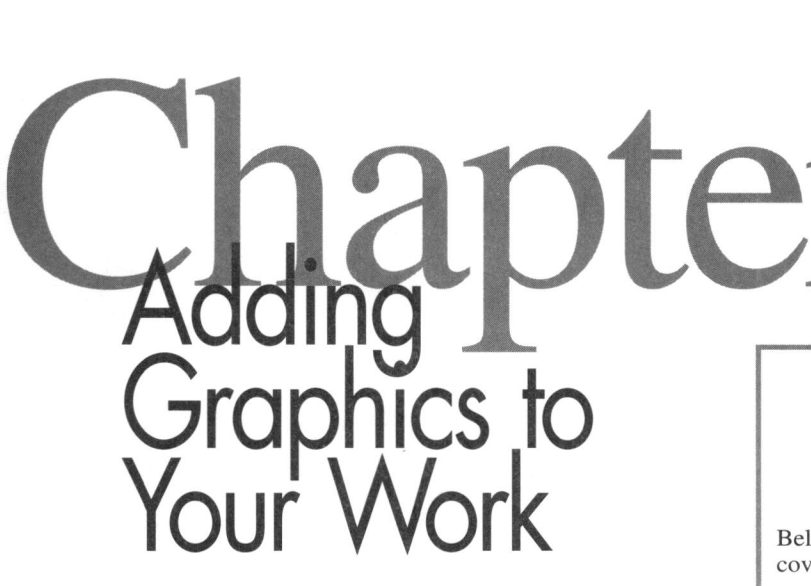

It's said that, "A picture is worth a thousand words." Save yourself about three pages of writing and use the ClarisWorks drawing and painting environments to add impact, clarity, and understanding to every document that you create. In this chapter, you will learn which graphics to use for the purpose you intend, and how to create, modify, and use drawings and paintings in your ClarisWorks documents.

This chapter also explains the use of drawing and painting tools within word processing documents and spreadsheets, and for designing database layouts. It's

Below are some of the how-to topics covered in this chapter:

How to choose between a drawing or a painting	166
How to change the attributes of an object	169
How to change the stacking order of objects	170
How to change environments with the Tool panel	171
How to create objects	172
How to select objects	175
How to move and resize objects	176
How to position objects	180
How to group and lock objects	181
How to transform objects	182
How to assign line and fill attributes	183
How to create a multiple spread	187
How to set a painting's resolution and color depth	188
To make an object opaque, transparent or blend	189
How to work with painting tools	189
How to edit images	191
How to transform areas of your painting	193
How to make screen captures	195

this capability to share tools between environments that makes ClarisWorks such an easy program with which to work.

Understanding the Difference Between Painted Images and Drawn Objects

There are two basic types of graphics in the computer world, and ClarisWorks creates both kinds. A drawing document consists of mathematically-defined objects, like circles, boxes, and curves. Thus, drawing documents are usually called *object-oriented graphics.* When you *draw* a circle using the Circle tool, ClarisWorks uses the formula for a circle to create that circle, either onscreen or on a printer. Because the software uses a formula, it can display the object to the best capability of the printer or monitor being used. This is a feature called *device-independence.* Drawings have a precision and scalability that makes them ideal for high-resolution purposes such as graphic design, technical illustrations, and high-resolution output.

A paint document consists of a set of square dots called *pixels.* A paint document consists of rows and columns of pixels, each of which has a specific color assigned. These grids of colored pixels are also called *bitmaps.* A bitmap has a specific number of pixels per inch—usually 72 pixels per inch, which is the number of pixels that a Macintosh monitor can display. (This is called the bitmap's *resolution.*) The computer doesn't know anything about what image those pixels create; it just knows what color to make each pixel. Figure 6.1 should help clarify the difference between objects and bitmaps.

Figure 6.1. *A drawn circle (object) versus a painted circle (bitmap), magnified 400 percent.*

When you *paint* with the Circle tool, ClarisWorks creates a pattern of pixels that approximates the circle. You can think of pixels as the dots in a pointillist painting. Paint documents enlarge poorly; the application has to insert more pixels to create a larger image, but it doesn't know the best way to do that, so it just makes the existing pixels larger. This creates a very blocky image. To improve a paint document's texture, you increase the resolution of the bitmap, store more pixels, and increase the file size. Paintings convey a graininess that makes them effective for natural images, textures, backgrounds, logos, and other continuous-tone purposes.

Object-oriented graphics are defined as entities; a circle is a circle. With a bitmap, the result is a set of pixels that resemble a circle. In a bitmap, the circle's underlying description has no special meaning. Therefore, objects and bitmaps are edited very differently. In a drawing document, you could have several different documents that overlap; you could move them around, change their order, or whatever. Each square or circle is a separate entity.

In a bitmapped document, the computer only keeps track of individual pixels. To select a painted circle, you need to select the entire set of pixels that comprise the circle. Figure 6.2 shows what happens when you try to move part of a drawn object and part of a painted bitmap.

Figure 6.2. *Moving a drawn object versus moving a painted bitmap.*

The capability to define a drawn circle as an entity (object) means that when you assign attributes to a drawn entity, such as color, line width, and whether that object is in front of or behind another object, those attributes apply to the entire circle. You can't work with only part of a drawn circle unless you first break that circle into two separate objects.

A painted circle (bitmap) also can have color, line width, and other attributes assigned to it. However, these attributes are defined at the time you create the circle. Once it has been created, it's just a pattern of pixels. If you want to change the color of the circle, you have to change the color of the pixels. If you draw a square over part of a circle, that part of the circle is gone. If later you decide to remove the square, you'll only have part of a circle left.

Generally, drawn images have smaller file sizes than paintings. However, if you are trying to create a natural-looking image like a photograph using object-oriented graphics, the mathematics needed to draw that image would be incredibly complex, making the file size huge and requiring a lot of processing power. A drawing is not superior to a painting, or visa versa; each is just better for some purposes than the other.

Working in the Drawing Environment

If most of the work you want to do in your document is drawing, then you should work in a drawing document. Use the New command under the File menu, and click on the Drawing radio button to create your drawing document. Remember, a drawing document has (DR) in its Title bar. You also can tell you are in a drawing document when the text, spreadsheet, and painting environment tools draw a frame when you click and drag them.

You don't need to be in a drawing document to add drawn objects. You can create objects in a word processing, a spreadsheet, or a painting document by using the drawing tools, as discussed in "Creating Objects Using the Drawing Tools," later in this chapter. In the database environment, the drawing tools are available when you are in Layout mode (see chapter 5). The following discussion about drawn objects, using drawing tools, and working in the drawing environment, applies as well to using the drawing tools in the other environments in which the tools are available.

About Objects

Objects are what the drawing environment creates. An object is an entity that your computer stores and is unrelated to anything else in a document. An object has attributes, such as size, shape, position, borders, and fill patterns. All of these attributes are stored as mathematical equations, so that the onscreen drawn object or the printed object represents the solution to the mathematical equation. Therefore, drawings generally are compact and precise, but require a lot of computer processing power to be rendered.

Most of the attributes you can assign an object are controlled by features in the toolbox or by menu commands. You first create an object by using tools: text frames, spreadsheet frames, painting frames, lines, squares, ovals, arcs, polygons, bezigons (shapes made up of Bezier curves), and so on. Frames are objects, too. Line and fill attributes also can be applied using sections of the Tools panel. A line (also called a stroke) can be assigned width, arrow heads, color, and patterns. An object fill can have color, patterns, and gradients. A sample object with labeled attributes appears in figure 6.3.

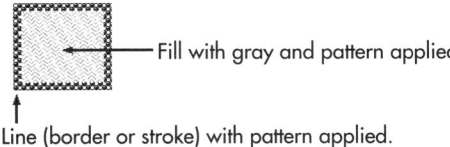

Figure 6.3. *Drawn object attributes.*

To manipulate or transform an object, you need to select it by clicking on it. Then you move, reshape (drag a handle), or transform the object by using either your mouse pointer or a menu command. Objects also appear in layers so that one object is always in front of another. You can reorder objects, group objects into a single compound object, lock objects into your drawing, and transform them in a variety of ways. The sections that follow tell you how.

Object Elements

One of the properties of objects is that they are drawn in layers; one object is in front of another. Objects are placed in *layers* in the order of their creation: the first drawn objects are in the back, the more recently drawn object is in the front. The object in front blocks objects that are behind it from view if the front-most object has a fill. Objects can have transparent fills or lines, which permit the object in back to show through. The layering of objects is called the stacking order. An example is shown in figure 6.4.

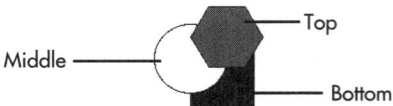

Figure 6.4. *Drawn object stacking order.*

> **Note**
> The Move To Back command will move an object behind a master page, as described in the "Creating Master Pages" section of chapter 8.

To change the drawn object stacking order, use the four Move commands on the Arrange menu, as shown in figure 6.5. They are: Move Forward, Move To Front, Move Backward, and Move To Back. Move Forward and Move Backward alter an object's position by one layer. Move To Front makes the selected object appear as if it were the last one created. Similarly, the Move To Back command makes the selected object appear as if it were the first one created. If you move several objects at once, they retain their relative position to one another.

Figure 6.5. *The Arrange menu.*

Creating Objects Using the Drawing Tools

You create objects by selecting a tool from the Tool panel. For the discussion that follows, refer to figure 6.6, where all of the Tool panel elements are labeled.

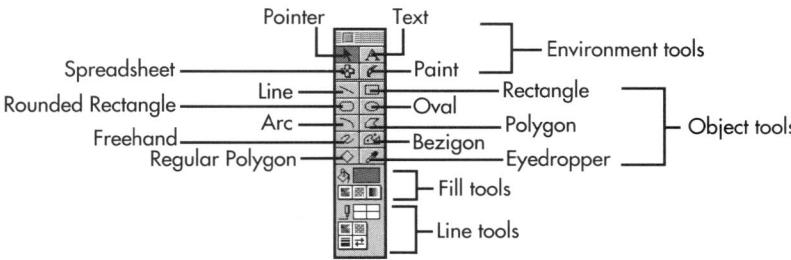

Figure 6.6. *The Drawing Tool panel.*

The Tool panel has a set of selection tools that are used to switch between environments. They are:

- The Pointer (black arrow). This tool is sometimes called a Selection tool in other drawing programs. The Pointer can select, move, and resize objects. For information about using the Pointer, see the next section, "Manipulating Objects."
- The Text tool (A). Use the Text tool to create a text frame and to switch to the word processing environment. Click on the insertion cursor inside of a pre-existing text frame to edit text as you would in a word processing document.
- The Spreadsheet tool (outlined cross). Use this tool to click and drag a spreadsheet frame and to switch to the spreadsheet environment. With the Spreadsheet cursor onscreen, you can click in a cell to enter or modify the cell's contents.
- The Painting tool (brush). Use the Painting tool to click and drag a painting frame and to switch to the painting environment.

All of the aforementioned tools are environment tools. ClarisWorks draws a double line in the Tool panel to indicate that they aren't drawing tools. When you select environment tools, your menus and capabilities change to reflect the switch to another environment. The Pointer is universal. Only the communications environment lacks a Tool panel. For more information about the capabilities of the text, spreadsheet, and painting environment tools, see chapters 3, 4, and the section "Working in the Painting Environment" later in this chapter.

The object tools appear on the Tool panel beneath the environment tools. Select an object tool (line, rectangle, rounded rectangle, oval, arc, polygon, freehand, bezigon, or regular polygon) to create an object. Your cursor changes to a crosshair.

To create a line, rectangle, rounded rectangle, oval, arc, freehand shape, or regular polygon object:

1. Select the appropriate tool box by clicking on it.
2. Click and drag the shape.
3. Release the mouse button to create the object. The object you created is selected, as is the Pointer, so that you can move or modify the newly created object.

Hold the Shift key to modify shapes by constraining them to the horizontal, vertical, or diagonal dimensions. You can change constraint values through the Graphic Preference dialog box to give you finer control and more variation over angles, as shown in figure 6.7.

The object tools are:

❖ The Line tool. Use the Line tool to click and drag straight lines. You can constrain your lines to either horizontal, vertical, or 45-degree diagonals by holding the Shift key while creating a shape.

❖ The Rectangle tool. Use the Rectangle tool to click-and-drag rectangles. If you hold the Shift key down while dragging a rectangle, you constrain its shape to a perfect square.

❖ The Rounded Rectangle tool. This tool creates rectangles and squares with rounded edges. The default curve is one-fourth inch.

❖ The Oval tool. Use the Oval tool to click-and-drag ovals. If you hold the Shift key down, you constrain the shapes it draws to perfect circles.

> **Tip**
> If you plan to create several shapes at the same time, double-click the appropriate tool to lock it. When a tool is locked, ClarisWorks won't switch to the Pointer tool after you draw a shape. A locked tool is highlighted in black; a selected tool is highlighted in gray. Click on another tool to deselect a locked tool.

> **Tip**
> To adjust the corners of a rectangle or a rounded rectangle, select the Round Corners command from the Options menu, or double-click on the object.

- ❖ The Arc tool. Use this tool to create an arc that connects your starting and ending points. If you use the Shift key to modify your drawn arc, you create arcs that are quarter segments of a circle.
- ❖ The Polygon tool. Use the Polygon tool to create shapes with straight-line edges. You can create regular and irregular shapes, and open and closed objects.

> **Tip**
> To modify an arc to any angle, select the Modify Arc command from the Options menu. Enter your starting and ending angles.

To create a polygon:

1. Select the Polygon tool.
2. Click to create a starting point for the polygon; you do not have to hold down the mouse button.
3. Click to create each subsequent point in the polygon.
4. To end the polygon, double-click to create the last point, or press the Enter key. To create a closed polygon, click on the first point you created.

You can have ClarisWorks automatically close polygons when you double-click. To set a graphic preference select the Preferences command from the Edit menu. Then click on the Automatic Polygon Closing radio button in the Graphics Preference dialog box (see figure 6.7). The last point of a polygon is then connected to the first point you clicked by a straight line.

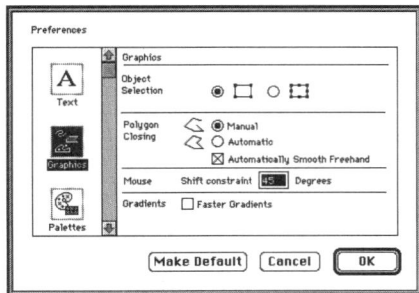

Figure 6.7. *The Graphics Preferences dialog box.*

174 Chapter 6 • Adding Graphics to Your Work

> **Note**
> Freehand shapes are set to the Automatically Smooth Freehand option in the Graphics Preference dialog box. With this option selected, ClarisWorks will alter your freehand drawing to make the curves smooth and even. If you want finer control over freehand shapes, deselect this option.

> **Shortcut**
> Select the Polygon Sides command from the Option menu or press Command-Shift-I to set the number of sides of a regular polygon.

> **Note**
> The Polygon Sides command is only available on the Options menu when the Regular Polygon tool is selected.

❖ The Freehand tool. Use the Freehand tool to create irregularly shaped lines and objects. In many programs, this tool has a pencil icon to indicate its purpose. Holding down the Shift key has no effect on what you draw.

❖ The Bezigon tool. This tool is used to create shapes that have Bezier curves or angles. Bezigons are created in the same manner as polygons; however, bezigon lines connect the points.

❖ The Regular Polygon tool. Select the Regular Polygon tool to click-and drag polygon objects that have equal, straight sides (rhombi, parallelograms). Hold down the Shift key to constrain the shapes to ones where some or all of the sides are either horizontal, vertical, or slanted.

To set the number of sides of the regular polygon (3 to 40), select the Polygon Sides command from the Option menu, or press Command-Shift-I . The Number of Sides dialog box, shown in figure 6.8, appears. Enter the number of sides: 3 for a triangle, 4 for a square, 5 for a pentagon, 6 for a hexagon, 8 for an octagon, and so on. Then dismiss the dialog box by clicking on the OK button.

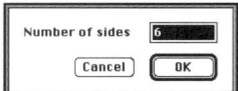

Figure 6.8. *The Number of Sides dialog box.*

❖ The Eyedropper tool. The Eyedropper tool does not create a shape. You use the Eyedropper tool to click and select a color, pattern, or gradient. The attributes of the object you clicked on can then be used to create new objects that have the attributes of the first object you clicked on. The Eyedropper is particularly useful in the painting environment for image editing. There it selects the color of the pixel you clicked on.

The remaining tools are the Fill Indicator, Fill Palettes, Pen Indicator, and Pen Palettes. They are attribute tools, and are discussed in the "Adding Colors, Patterns, and Gradients to Objects" section of this chapter.

You can create a duplicate of any object by selecting that object and choosing the Duplicate command (or pressing Command-D). An offset copy appears below and to the right of your original object. Duplicating an object does not change the contents of the Clipboard.

ClarisWorks has a duplication feature that is called "step and repeat" or "power duplication." If you move the duplicated object to a new position and then use the Duplicate command again, without doing anything else, ClarisWorks draws another copy the same distance away from the last copy, as illustrated in figure 6.9.

> **Tip**
> Press the Tab key to switch between the Eyedropper tool and another tool.

> **Tip**
> You can duplicate an object quickly by holding down the Option key, and then click-dragging an object.

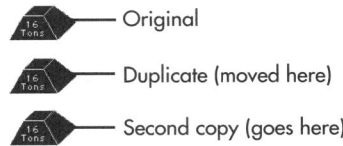

Figure 6.9. *ClarisWorks's step-and-repeat duplication feature.*

Manipulating Objects

When you click on an object or frame and select it, you see a set of small black squares on the object's outline, called *reshape handles*. Every object has four reshape handles that define the minimum rectangle that surrounds the object. That rectangle is called the object's *bounding box*. ClarisWorks enables you to set a preference to place a reshape handle at the midpoint of the bounding box. Click on the small rectangle with six reshape handles in the Graphics Preferences dialog box, shown in figure 6.7.

You manipulate objects by first selecting them. Once you have selected an object, you can move, resize, or apply various attributes to it.

- ❖ To select an object, click on its edge. If the object has a fill, even if it's a white fill, then you can click anywhere on the object to select that object.
- ❖ To select several objects, click-and-drag a selection marquee around them.
- ❖ Hold the Command key to select all objects that the selection marquee touches (rather than the objects completely contained within the selection marquee).
- ❖ Hold the Shift key and click on objects one at a time to add them to the range of objects selected.
- ❖ To select all like objects—all ovals, all rectangles, or whatever—click on the tool and then choose the Select All command from the Edit menu.

  When you click on the Polygon, Freehand, Bezigon, or Regular Polygon tool and Select All, ClarisWorks selects all objects of those types. So, if you click on the Regular Polygon tool and choose Select All, ClarisWorks will also select all Bezigons, polygons, and freehand objects as well.
- ❖ You can select all objects by using the Select All command when the Pointer tool is selected.

Shortcut
Use Command-A instead of choosing Select All from the Edit menu.

To deselect an object or frame, click outside the object. When more than one object is selected, hold down the Shift key and click again on an object to deselect it and remove it from the range of selected objects.

To delete an object or frame, select the object and either press the Delete key or select the Clear command from the Edit menu.

When you delete an object by using the Clear command, you preserve the contents of the Clipboard. You can use the Cut command to delete the object and place it in the Clipboard.

To move an object or frame, select the object, click on one of the object's edges (not a reshape handle), and drag the object to a new position. If an object has a fill, click anywhere on that object to move it. As you move an object, a dotted frame appears to indicate its new position.

To move an object one pixel in any direction, or "nudge," the object, press the appropriate arrow key. With the Autogrid option turned on, the arrow keys nudge the object one grid division.

You can use the Size palette shown in figure 6.10 to position an object exactly. Use the Object Size command from the Options menu to display the Size palette. The top four text boxes give the position of the object from (top to bottom): the left, top, right, and bottom of the page, respectively. Enter new values to move an object. The values in the boxes represent the distance from the edges of the bounding box to the edges of the paper.

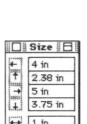

Note

If you are having difficulty with precise positioning, you may need to turn off the Autogrid by selecting the Turn Autogrid Off command from the Options menu, or by pressing Command-Y.

Figure 6.10. *The Size palette.*

To resize an object or a frame, click on a reshape handle and drag the handle outwards from the center of the bounding box to create a larger object. Drag the handle in towards the center of the bounding box to create a smaller object. Hold down the Shift key while click-dragging an object to change its shape proportionately. As you resize an object, a dotted frame appears to indicate the new shape.

You can use the Size palette (figure 6.10) to resize an object. The two bottom text boxes (top to bottom) indicate the width and height of the bounding box, respectively. Enter new values to resize an object.

To scale an object by a percentage:

1. Select the object.
2. Select the Scale Selection command from the Object menu. The Scale Selection dialog box appears, as shown in figure 6.11.

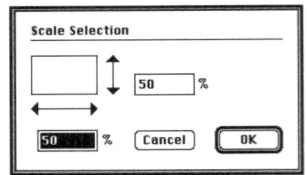

Figure 6.11. *The Scale Selection dialog box.*

3. Type the appropriate percentages into the Vertical and the Horizontal text boxes. Enter a percentage from 25 percent to 400 percent.
4. Click on the OK button.

Arcs, polygons, bezigons, and freehand objects require special handling before they can be reshaped. To reshape these objects, select them and choose the Reshape command (Command-R) from the Edit menu. Your cursor turns into a crosshair. You can then click on an ending or an anchor point to reshape the arc, polygon, bezigon, or freehand shape. Some examples are shown in figure 6.12.

> **Tip**
> To turn a straight line in a polygon into a curve, hold the Option key as you drag. To create another vertex in a polygon, click and drag a point on the line.

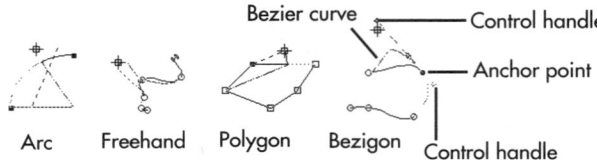

Figure 6.12. *Reshaping arcs, polygons, freehand curves, and bezigons.*

You will notice in figure 6.12 that bezigons, which are composed of Bezier curves, offer additional reshaping controls. Each clicked point on a Bezier curve, called an *anchor point,* has two additional control handles. To modify a bezigon:

> **Shortcut**
> Press Command-R to reshape an arc, polygon, freehand curve, or bezigon.

❖ Drag an anchor point to move it or use the arrow keys to nudge it.
❖ Drag either control handle to bend a curve segment.
❖ To add additional points on a bezigon, click on an edge.
❖ To delete an anchor point, click on it and then press the Delete key.

- ❖ To delete a control handle, Option-click on it. The result is a smooth curve.
- ❖ To add a control handle, Option-drag from the anchor point.

Bezier curves are tricky, and nothing beats practice for mastering them.

You can connect freehand curves, polygons, regular polygons, and Bezier curves together. Figure 6.13 gives an example.

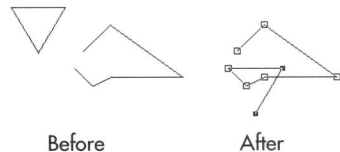

Before   After

Figure 6.13. *Connecting a regular polygon to a polygon.*

To connect a regular polygon object to a polygon object, do the following:

1. Select the first object, then choose the Reshape command from the Edit menu.
2. Cut or Copy that object to the Clipboard.
3. Select the object to which you want to join the first.
4. Click on the starting point to join the first object to the starting point of the second, or else the object is joined to the ending point.
5. Select the Paste command from the Edit menu to join the objects. The first point of the first object is joined to the second object. Hold the Option key before you paste to join the last point of the first object to the starting point of the second object.

ClarisWorks provides several methods for positioning objects. You can turn on a ruler, a visual grid, and the snap-to autogrid to aid you in placing objects as you are creating them. All of these features use the same units of measurement.

To show the ruler and set the units of measurement:

1. Select the Rulers command from the Format menu. The Rulers dialog box appears as shown in figure 6.14.

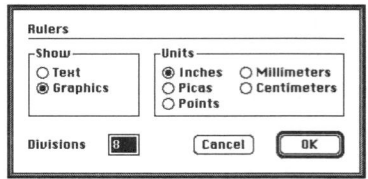

Figure 6.14. *The Rulers dialog box.*

2. Click on the Graphics button to show both the horizontal and the vertical rulers.
3. Click on the radio button for the unit of measurement you desire.
4. Click on the OK button.

The graphics rulers track the movement of the pointer by using a dotted line to indicate its current position. The text ruler has been discussed in chapter 3 and is most useful for working with text frames.

Two types of grids are available:

- ❖ The Graphics Grid. This is a visual grid that you see as dotted lines onscreen. Select the Show Graphics Grid command from the Options menu to display it, and the Hide Graphics Grid command to remove it. These two commands act like a toggle switch—one replaces the other. The default setting shows the Graphics Grid.

- ❖ The Autogrid. This invisible grid positions objects onto the grid when you click or drag them close to the imaginary horizontal and vertical lines that comprise the grid. This is called a *snap-to grid*. To turn the grid off, select the Turn Autogrid Off command from the Options menu. Select the toggle Turn Autogrid On again to restore the grid.

Shortcut
Select the Turn Autogrid Off command on the Options menu, or press Command-Y to remove the Autogrid. Press Command-Y or choose the Turn Autogrid On command to restore the autogrid.

Both the Graphics Grid and the Autogrid are on by default. To change the size of the grids, enter a new number in the Divisions text box of the Rulers dialog box shown in figure 6.15. The Options menu shown in figure 6.16 is where you find commands for positioning, object sizing, tool options, and frame linking. The Align to Grid command, also found on the Arrange menu (Command-K), moves selected objects to the closest point on the grid.

Figure 6.15. *The Options menu.*

To align objects to each other, use the Align Objects command found on the Arrange menu, or press Command-Shift-K. The Align Objects dialog box shown in figure 6.16 indicates the type of alignment chosen.

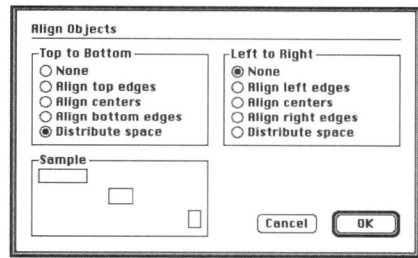

Figure 6.16. *The Align Objects dialog box.*

In many instances you may want to freeze the arrangement of a set of objects so that you can manipulate them as a group, rather than manipulating each component separately. To group selected objects, choose the Group command from the Arrange menu. Grouped objects are treated as a single object and show with one set of reshape handles, as shown in figure 6.17. To ungroup a group, use the Ungroup command. The grouping commands also work with imported PICT files.

Shortcut
Press Command-K to move selected objects to the nearest point on the grid.

Shortcut
Press Command-Shift-K to align objects with respect to one another.

182   Chapter 6 • Adding Graphics to Your Work

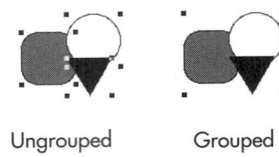

Figure 6.17. *Grouped and ungrouped objects.*

> **Shortcut**
> Press Command-G to group a set of objects. Press Command-Shift-G to ungroup a group.

If you want to free an object so that it can't be modified at all, use the Lock command on the Arrange menu. Frames cannot be locked. Use the Unlock command to modify these objects again. Locked objects show gray reshape handles when selected, as shown in figure 6.18.

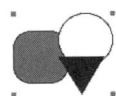

Figure 6.18. *A locked object.*

> **Shortcut**
> Press Command-H to issue the Lock command and prevent an object from being modified. Command-Shift-H issues the Unlock command.

In addition to being capable of placing and reshaping objects, you can both flip and rotate them. To turn an object left to right or upside-down, select the Flip Horizontal or Flip Vertical commands from the Arrange menu, respectively. To rotate an object 90 degrees clockwise, select the Rotate command from the Arrange menu, or press its Command key equivalent, Command-Shift-R. Figure 6.19 shows these transformations.

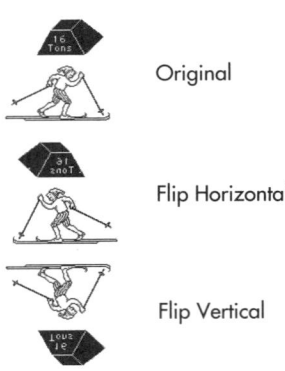

Figure 6.19. *Flip Horizontal and Flip Vertical.*

Other cool transformations in ClarisWorks are the Smooth and Unsmooth options. You can change a polygon's straight lines into curves by using the Smooth command from the Edit menu, or you can unsmooth a bezigon or freehand curve to change all of its curves to straight lines. Figure 6.20 shows you two examples.

> **Note**
> Press Command-Shift-R instead of using the Rotate command to rotate a selected object or a frame 90 degrees clockwise.

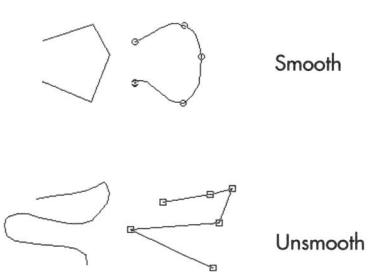

Figure 6.20. *The smooth and unsmooth transformations.*

Adding Colors, Patterns, and Gradients to Objects

As noted previously, objects and frames have line (also called stroke) attributes that you assign to their borders. They also have a fill attribute. Line (or stroke) attributes include width, color, transparency or opaqueness, and pattern. Object fills include attributes such as color, transparency or opaqueness, and a pattern or gradient. These assignments are made by using the attribute tools in the Tool panel.

The fill tools are located just under the object tools in the toolbox, as shown in figure 6.21. Use the fill tools as follows:

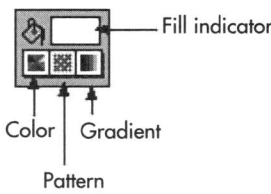

Figure 6.21. *The Fill tools.*

- ❖ The Fill Indicator. This indicates your currently selected color. It changes whenever you make selections from the other fill tools, or pick up a new fill by using the Eyedropper tool.

> **Tip**
> You can replace the 81-color palette with an editable 256-color palette by selecting that feature in the Palette section of the Preferences dialog box (from the Edit menu). If you don't see the color you need, double-click on a color to bring up the Macintosh color wheel. Then create the color you need.

> **Tip**
> You can edit a pattern by double-clicking on that pattern in the palette to open the Pattern Editor, or by highlighting that pattern and selecting the Patterns command from the Options menu.

❖ The Fill Color. Click on the Color icon to reveal a pop-up menu of 81 colors as shown in figure 6.22.

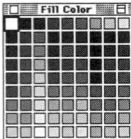

Figure 6.22. *The Fill Color floating palette.*

❖ The Fill icon. Use the Fill selections to make an object transparent, solid opaque, or opaque with a pattern applied. The Fill palette window is shown in figure 6.23. There are 62 possible patterns, plus icons to choose whether an object is opaque or transparent.

Figure 6.23. *The Fill palette floating window.*

❖ The Gradient icon. Select one of the 32 patterns and gradients to change your object fill, as shown in figure 6.24.

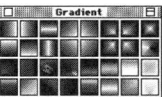

Figure 6.24. *The Gradient palette floating window.*

You can tear off any of the fill tools: color, pattern, or gradient, and create a floating palette. Click on and drag the icon for that pop-up menu onto your screen (see figure 6.24). To minimize the palette to just its title bar, click on the Zoom box. You can dismiss the palette by clicking on its Close box when you no longer need it. When you minimize several palettes, ClarisWorks stacks them in the upper-right corner of your document, as in figure 6.25.

> **Tip**
>
> To edit a gradient, you highlight it in the palette, select Gradients from the Options menu, and make selections in the Gradient Editor. You can change sweeps, colors, and angles, and the sample box shows you the results.

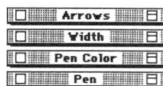

Figure 6.25. *Minimized palettes.*

The line tools are found below the fill tools in the Tool panel, as shown in figure 6.26. As with the Fill tools, all of the line tools (except the Line Indicator icon) can be dragged onto your screen to create floating palettes. The Color and Pattern icons are used in the same manner as fills. Use the other line tools as follows:

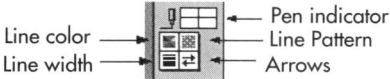

Figure 6.26. *The Line tools.*

- ❖ The Pen Indicator icon. This tool shows a crosshair (see figure 6.26, indicating the attributes of horizontal and vertical lines.
- ❖ The Pen Width icon. Click on and drag a selection. Your choices are: None, Hairline (1 point onscreen, 1/2 point printed on a laser printer), 1, 2, 3, 6, 8 points, and Other (which allows you to select a custom width).

- ❖ The Arrows icon. This tool adds arrows to the lines you select. You can have arrows at the starting point, the ending point, or at both ends of a line, as shown in figure 6.27.

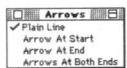

Figure 6.27. *The Arrows floating window.*

ClarisWorks sets some default attributes for objects. They are:

- ❖ Lines are black and 1 point in width.
- ❖ Objects have a white fill, with the exception of freehand objects, which are drawn with a transparent fill.

To reset these defaults, deselect all objects by clicking on a blank part of your drawing. Then make your selections in the Tool panel.

DRAWING A LOGO

Graphics can add a lot of impact to your personal and business communications. When you create a logo or a border for your stationery, most of the time you get better results from drawn objects than from painted objects. Painted logos can work well when you are looking for a texture or a splash effect. However, drawings print sharply and look more professional.

Logos are good projects to undertake. When you create a logo for business stationery, copy and paste the graphic onto a word processing document, then save the document as a template. For logos that you intend to use often and in a number of documents, copy the graphic and paste it into your Scrapbook. With your Scrapbook open, the Paste command places another page with your graphic in it. To use the logo again later on, go to that page in the Scrapbook, copy the graphic, and paste it into the document or file you want. Chapter 2 goes into more detail on creating stationery templates.

Adding Pages to a Drawing Document

You can work with large drawings that span more than one page in a drawing document. This is useful for posters, brochures, and other large-format projects. With a multipage spread, you can draw objects that span several pages. ClarisWorks shows you the page split and margins and the object is drawn split, but complete. You also can drag objects so that they span pages.

To create a multipage spread:

1. Select the Document command from the Format menu. The Document dialog box shown in figure 6.28 appears.

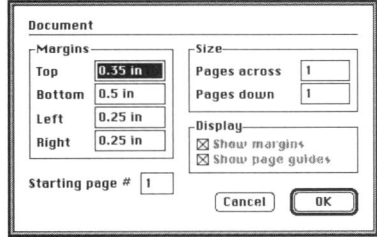

Figure 6.28. *The Document dialog box.*

2. Enter your document setup as follows:
    - ❖ Type the desired margins into the Margins text boxes.
    - ❖ Type the number of pages in the Pages Across and Pages Down text boxes.
    - ❖ Type a value in the Starting Page # text box.
3. Select the Page View command from the View menu.
4. Click on the OK button.

In Page View mode, you can see all of your pages. Zoom out (smaller magnification) to see multipage spreads. You may wish to hide margins and page guides. If so, deselect those checkboxes in the Display section of the Document dialog box (figure 6.28).

Working in the Painting Environment

Resolution is one of the key factors in determining the quality of your painting. Your Macintosh screen has a resolution of 72 dots per inch (dpi), so ClarisWorks uses that as the default resolution of a new painting document. That looks fine on your monitor, but will print poorly. You can increase the resolution of your image at the expense of larger file sizes. ImageWriters print (in Best mode) at 144 dpi, StyleWriters print at 360 dpi, LaserWriters at 300 to 600 dpi, and imagesetter quality ranges from 1200 to 2400 dpi.

To change the image resolution or color depth of a painting:

1. Select the Resolution & Depth command from the Format menu.
2. Click on the radio button for the resolution and color depth you want.
3. Enter the Origin of your painting in the two Origin text boxes for a Painting frame (in other document types).
4. Click on the OK button.

ClarisWorks scales your screen if there isn't sufficient memory to show the full-size image. Higher resolutions, large color depths, and larger document sizes can make tremendous demands upon your computer's memory.

The Painting Modes

The painting mode determines the manner in which many of the painting tools and transformations operate. Painting documents are only two-dimensional, but you can move selected areas over previously painted areas, and the two will interact. To change the painting mode, select the Painting Mode command from the Options menu, and make your selection in the Painting Mode dialog box, shown in figure 6.29.

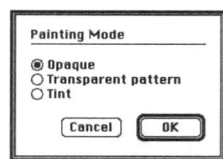

Figure 6.29. *The Painting Mode dialog box.*

> **Tip**
> Even if you increase the resolution, your monitor can only display 72 dpi. You'll have to zoom in on your painting to see (and edit) the increased resolution.

> **Tip**
> Allocate more memory to ClarisWorks in the Finder by first highlighting the ClarisWorks icon and then using the Get Info command from the File menu. (You'll have to quit ClarisWorks first!) Check your Macintosh documentation for more information. Try 2400K for depths of thousands of colors and 4200K for depths of millions of colors.

The three painting modes are:

- ❖ Opaque. Moving an opaque selection replaces the painted pixels beneath it. That is, you cannot see through the selection. Painting with an opaque tool replaces the area painted.
- ❖ Transparent. The white pixels of a selection are replaced by the underlying pixels when the selection is moved. Color pixels are not replaced.
- ❖ Tint. In tint mode, the color of the selected area you are moving, or the color of the tool you are applying, blends with the color of the area you are moving or painting to.

Using the Painting Tool Panel

The painting Tool panel adds some special tools for object selection; for creating points, lines, and patterns; and for erasing pixels that aren't in the Drawing Tool panel. This is in addition to the environment, object, fill, and line tools that you learned about already. These tools are shown in figure 6.30.

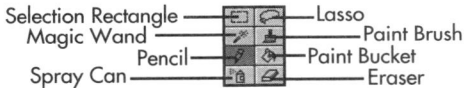

Figure 6.30. *The painting tools.*

When you select a painting tool by clicking on it, it remains selected until you select another tool (unlike the drawing tools). A summary of the painting tools follows:

- ❖ The Selection Rectangle tool. Use this tool to select a rectangular area. Just drag to create a marquee around the area you want to select. Hold down the Command key to modify this tool into the Lasso tool. You can also double-click on the Selection Rectangle tool to select the entire image. Hold down the Command key and double-click on the Selection Rectangle to select all painted (nonwhite) pixels in the image.
- ❖ The Lasso tool. The Lasso enables you to select an area of any shape. The selection border follows your cursor. When you release the mouse button, the selection area closes by connecting the endpoints with a straight line. Double-click on the Lasso tool to select all painted nonwhite pixels in your image.

> **Note**
> Every tool has a "hot spot" that is the focus of its action. For the Pencil tool, the hot spot is the pencil point; for the Paint Bucket tool, it is the pixel at the end of the dripping paint; and so on. When you use a tool, the hot spot determines exactly where you're clicking. For instance, when you fill an object using the Paint Bucket, the hot spot determines exactly where the paint will go.

Chapter 6 • Adding Graphics to Your Work

- ❖ The Magic Wand tool. With the Magic Wand tool selected, click on a pixel. All adjacent pixels of the same color are selected.
- ❖ The Brush tool. Create brush strokes using the Brush tool; the brush strokes are the color of the fill you've selected. Gradients are not used for this tool.

To modify the brush size and shape:

1. Double-click on the Brush tool, or select the Brush Shape from the Options menu with the Brush tool selected. The Brush Shape dialog box, shown in figure 6.31, appears.

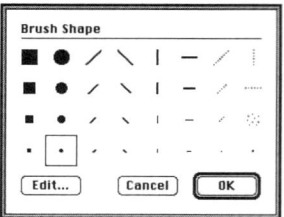

Figure 6.31. *The Brush Shape dialog box.*

2. Click on the shape you want. You also can create a custom shape by clicking on the Custom button and working with the Brush Editor.
3. Click on the OK button.

- ❖ Pencil tool. With the Pencil tool you click and drag lines. The Pencil is the default tool for a new painting document. The pencil uses the attributes from the Pen Indicator palette to draw lines. If you click first on a white pixel, a black or a colored line is drawn. If you click on a black pixel, a white line is drawn. Hold down the Shift key to constrain the line to the horizontal, vertical, or diagonal directions.
- ❖ Paint Bucket tool. The Paint Bucket tool fills all adjoining pixels of the same color with the currently selected fill color. Sometimes the Paint Bucket tool can have unexpected results. If one shape is connected to another shape or to the background that's the same color, by even one pixel, all connected areas will be filled with the fill

color. Don't forget that if you act immediately you can apply the Undo Paint command (Command-Z) to correct bad painting jobs.

To fill an area that already contains a pattern or gradient, don't use the painting tool. Instead select the area with either the Selection Rectangle, the Lasso, or the Magic Wand tool, and then choose the Fill command from the Transform menu.

- ❖ The Spray Can tool. Using the Spray Can tool you can create a mist of pixels. The slower you drag or the more often you drag, the darker the pattern in an area.
- ❖ The Eraser tool. Click and drag the Eraser tool to remove colored pixels from your picture. Hold the Shift key to constrain the motion of the Eraser tool to the horizontal or vertical axis—whichever direction you first moved the cursor. Double-click on the Eraser tool to completely erase your painting and start again fresh. Don't forget to use the Zoom tool to do fine erasing at the pixel level.

Editing Images

You can edit paintings by selecting areas or by editing one pixel at a time. You use the selection tools to select an area, and then move or transform that area. You can select and edit an area as small as a single pixel by using the window Zoom tool to get up close and personal. At maximum magnification (800 percent), individual pixels are easily modified using the pencil tool, and you are close to what many painting programs call the fat-bit mode.

To select an area, use the following:

- ❖ The Selection Rectangle tool to select a regular area.
- ❖ The Lasso tool to enclose an area surrounded by white pixels.
- ❖ The Magic Wand tool to select an area of colors similar to the pixel you clicked on.

Each of these tools have their own special purpose and utility. If you make a mistake, use the Undo Select command (Command-Z) on the Edit menu to return to your previous selection.

To deselect your painting, use the Pointer tool and click outside of your selection. If the entire image is selected, chose the Undo Select command from the Edit menu.

Tip
You can change the settings of the Spray Can by using the Edit Spray Can dialog box. Double-click on the Spray Can icon, or use the Spray Can command from the Options menu to open this dialog box.

Caution
Select all of your line and fill attributes before you paint. The only editing you can do to restore a painted-over area is to undo and remove your last work, or to erase the whole area and start over.

Note
When viewing a document close up, consider creating another view (from the View menu) in 100% view. Then when you make your changes close up, you can see the effect on your painting.

Chapter 6 • Adding Graphics to Your Work

> **Tip**
>
> You can quickly duplicate an area of your painting by holding down the Option key while you drag a selection. ClarisWorks leaves one copy behind as you drag the selection.

To move an area, select the area, then click on the Pointer cursor and drag the area to its new location. To nudge the area use the arrow keys. With the Autogrid turned off (the default for paintings), you nudge one pixel at a time. With the Autogrid turned on, you nudge one grid division.

For changing a painting one pixel at a time, use the Pencil tool. You use the Eraser tool to remove colored pixels in an area. For finely detailed color work in complex images, nothing beats working with the Magic Wand tool to select and modify small areas of similar colors. Remember that you can pick up a color and a fill by using the Eyedropper tool, and that you can use the Tab key to switch back and forth between an active tool and the Eyedropper. You can apply a fill by using the Fill command from the Transform menu to any selected area, but you must use the Eyedropper before applying this command.

The painting environment has a number of special effects that you can apply to selected areas, found on the Transform menu (see figure 6.32). In some instances, as with the Fill command, the effect is applied immediately, leaving the area selected as before. In other instances, such as the Shearing, Distorting, Perspective, Free Rotate, and Resize commands, selection handles appear with a bounding box. You apply the amount of the effect you want by clicking and dragging the handles. Some before and after images are shown with these transformations in figure 6.33. The Rotate and Scale Selection commands allow transformations where you enter specific values for the effects. You also can use the Flip Horizontal and Flip Vertical commands to mirror an image. The Scale Selection was described earlier for drawing documents (see figure 6.11), as was the Flip Horizontal and Flip Vertical transformations (see figure 6.19).

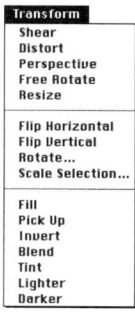

Figure 6.32. *The Transform menu.*

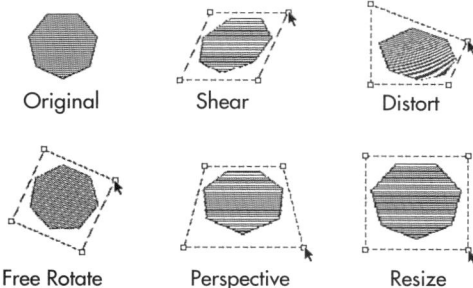

Figure 6.33. *Shearing, Distorting, Perspective, Free Rotate, and Resize transformations.*

Adding Colors, Patterns, and Gradients

The same Tool panel elements that you learned about in the drawing environment, in "Adding Colors, Patterns, and Gradients to Objects," are used in the painting environment as well. There also are a set of Transformation menu commands that you haven't seen before that you can apply to selections. They are:

- ❖ Fill. The Fill command applies your current fill, color, pattern, or gradient to a selection. Unlike using the Paint Bucket tool, the Fill command can fill part of an image and an image that is multicolored, such as a gradient.
- ❖ Pickup. The Pickup command enables you to select an area, move it to another area, and have the original image of your selection replaced by the area it is moved to. This command is useful for framing an area, making copies of an area, and so on.

  The Pickup effect is dependent upon your active painting mode. If you are using an opaque selection, replacement is what you get. With the transparent mode, the colors below are added to the selection. In tint mode you get a blend. See figure 6.34 for an example.

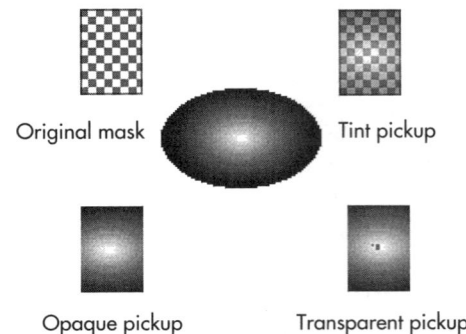

Figure 6.34. *The Pickup transformation.*

- ❖ Invert. The Invert transformation applies a negative image to your selection. Black goes to white, white to black. For colored pixels, the color equidistant across the from the center of the Macintosh Color Picker (color wheel) is used. Use Invert to create printing negatives from positives, and visa versa.
- ❖ Blend. This transformation takes the dark and light colors of a selection and adds intermediate colors to create a progression.
- ❖ Tint. Tint adds some of the current fill color to your selection.
- ❖ Lighter. Applies a tint using the color white.
- ❖ Darker. Applies a tint using the color black.

All of these commands are useful for working with continuous-tone images like photographs. Unfortunately, the current version of ClarisWorks lacks the Sharpen and Unsharpen commands, which are essential for image editing.

> ## CAPTURING AND EDITING A SCREEN
>
> To take a picture of your Macintosh screen, use the Command-Shift-3 keystroke. In standard Macintosh system software you hear the sound of a camera, and a PICT document called Picture 1 (or Screen 0, in System 6) appears in your top folder. In System 7 you can view this file by double-clicking on it; it opens in TeachText. To edit and view that screen capture using ClarisWorks, open the file from within ClarisWorks as a painting document. Remember that if you are working in color, you will probably have to adjust ClarisWorks's memory allocation.
>
> Other screen-capture utilities can also capture your screen as a PICT, or in some cases, as a TIFF file. Many utilities let you select an area of the screen by clicking and dragging to select a window, a dialog box, or other screen element to capture. Consider using commercial software such as Capture, Exposure Pro or shareware programs such as FlashIt! or SnapJot.

Summary

In this chapter you learned the differences between drawings and paintings. In a drawing, you create objects that are solutions to mathematical equations. Drawn objects have an individual identity, and are described by their attributes. Paintings create bitmaps, a two-dimensional mosaic of picture elements, or pixels. Drawings are precise; paintings show texture.

You create objects using the Tool panel. For lines and fills, attributes are assigned from selections made mostly in the Tool panel. For text, attributes are chosen from the Format menu. To modify, resize, move, and transform objects, you select them first and then either use the mouse or choose the appropriate menu command.

You can create painted graphics that look like shapes, but are collections of pixels or bits. Some additional tools enable you to create pencil lines, brush strokes, spray can graffiti, and to fill enclosed areas with your currently selected fill. You can erase areas of your painting, even one pixel at a time. Use selection tools to modify, move, or transform painted areas. Areas can be opaque, transparent, or blended with other areas.

In the next chapter you will learn how to use the communications environment to go online and transfer information by using a modem.

Chapter 7
The Communications Environment

Below are some of the how-to topics covered in this chapter:

How to select and set up a modem 198
How to create a communications document 200
How to connect to an online service or a BBS 201
How to disconnect from a session 203
How to capture text to your screen or to a file 207
How to receive a phone call 208
How to create, edit, and choose selections from the Phone Book 210
How to create a log on macro 211
How to send and receive files 214
How to connect directly to another computer 215
How to emulate a terminal to connect to other computers 216

ClarisWorks's communications environment enables you to reach out and touch someone, and have them touch you back. You can connect your Macintosh to online services, bulletin boards (BBSes), and other computers to do any one of a thousand tasks.

You can shop in an electronic mall, research an article in an electronic library, correspond with your office from a remote location, send and receive electronic mail, and accomplish many other tasks. People have met online, dated, and married. You can check the news, weather, sports, or the ski report; find a job, buy a home or a car; look at airline schedules and buy a ticket; whatever your fancy. It seems that every day brings new uses for communicating by computer.

ClarisWorks' communications environment is basic, but functional. You set up your communications document and automate your connection sequence by using a shortcut. Then your next connection to that service is only a menu command away.

A Communications Overview

Computers communicate by using binary digital information: essentially, sequences of ones and zeros. This causes problems for transmitting computer data over phone lines, because the phone lines are analog systems—they operate by changing sound into infinitely variable voltages, rather than just two as in digital communication. Therefore, a computer transmitting data must convert signals from digital to analog, and the computer receiving the data must convert the analog signal back to digital form. The devices that do this translation are called *modems*. Modem derives from the words modulator-demodulator, which is another description of translating the digital signal into analog form and back again.

Modems can be internal or external hardware devices. If the modem is external, you attach the modem to your Macintosh by using a standard serial cable. The modem then attaches to your phone line through a standard phone line. Internal modems attach directly from your Macintosh to your phone line.

Modem Terms

To ensure that each computer understands the analog translation of the digital signal, several protocols are used. These protocols are rules that describe exactly how the data is represented by the analog signal; they cover many details. For instance, different modem protocols create standards for transmission rates, error checking, error correction, and data compression.

To establish a communications session each computer must use the same frequency of bits per second, and the same protocols or an agreed-upon data transfer mode. The frequency of transmission is measured in bits per second, usually abbreviated to *bps*.

Today a 2,400 bps modem is slow, and a 14.4K (14,400 bps) modem is considered reasonably powerful. Through the use of data compression, you can get a two or three factor speed enhancement over the quoted speed.

To give you an idea of the relative data transfer speeds in practical terms, you can transfer an 800K file in about an hour when using a 2,400 bps modem. A 9,600 bps modem has a throughput of about 3.2M. A 14.4K modem, with data compression, gives you a throughput of more than 9.6M, or about twelve times that of a 2,400 bps modem. With the price of 14.4K data-fax modems falling to between $99 and $250, there is little reason to buy a less capable modem.

When you dial another system, you hear a set of emitted tones, and then another set of received tones. This tonal duet is called *handshaking*. Handshaking is the method modems use to agree upon data rates and protocols. If a fast modem is trying to shake hands with another, slower modem, or if the telephone line is noisy, then the faster modem can drop down in speed to establish communication with the slower modem.

Communications Software

Modems enable computers to transfer data, but they can't do it alone. Software is needed to control the operation of the modem, and to send and receive the data being transferred. That's what the ClarisWorks Communications module does: work with the modem to transfer information with another computer.

There are other kinds of software that do the same basic thing. There are commercial communications packages that work much the same as the Communications module, but that offer more advanced features. Bulletin boards—systems set up so that users can connect and transfer files, messages, and so forth—sometimes require special software that provides a customized interface and enhanced capabilities. Online services, which are commercial enterprises similar to but much larger than bulletin boards, almost always have special software that you need to connect.

Note
Often, the term "baud" is used synonomously with bps, but baud actually means something different—the electrical switching speed of the modem. At speeds greater than 300 bps, the baud rate is some fraction of the frequency. Bps is the correct term.

Tip
Buy the best modem you can afford. The savings you get by buying a slower modem are more than offset by the additional cost of longer connection times over the lifetime of the modem.

Some software enables you to connect your Macintosh to networks of other computers over the phone lines, enabling you to use a remote network just like you'd use the network at your office. Some kinds of modems can also send (and sometimes receive) fax transmissions, from another computer or a normal fax machine. These modems need special software to send and receive the faxes. Other, more specialized types of software exist, but these are the most common software types.

Getting Connected using ClarisWorks

You connect to another computer with ClarisWorks by opening a communications document and applying the Connect command from the Session menu (see figure 7.1). A session is the sequence of connecting to the other computer, called *logging on;* communicating; and disconnecting, called *logging off.* Various aspects of this process can be automated: settings and phone numbers are stored in your document, and logging on and logging off procedures can be captured as shortcuts.

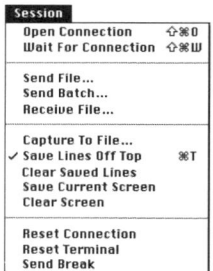

Figure 7.1. *The Session menu.*

Creating a Communications Document

Every communications session requires that a communications document be open onscreen. A communications document stores all of the settings that enable your Macintosh to speak the same language as the other computer to which you are connected. You use the same document every time you call up a given service, so it makes sense to name each document for the purpose it serves. If you call various services with the same set of settings, then create a phone-book entry for each service.

You create a new communications document by using the New command from the File menu and selecting the Communications radio button. An untitled communications window with (CM) in the title bar appears, as shown in figure 7.2. A communications window looks different than other ClarisWorks windows. You will notice a Status area underneath the Title bar, but no tool panel or zoom controls. The Status area shows a pop-up Phone Book, a Connect Time indicator, and, if you are using the communications environment for terminal emulation, you might see indicator icons and a Tab ruler, if you set those preferences.

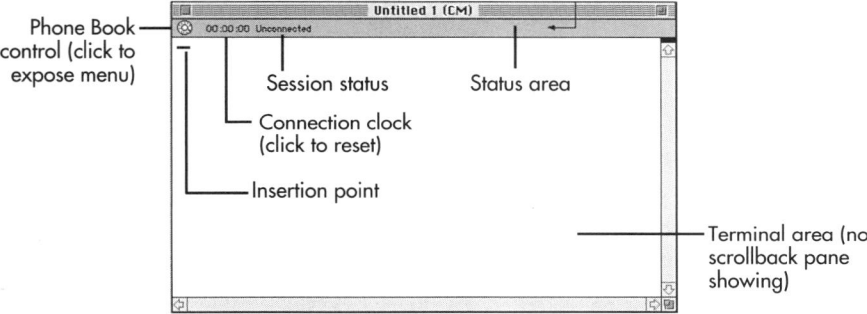

Figure 7.2. *A new communications document.*

The most important aspect of creating a new communications document is to enter the communications settings correctly, as discussed in the next section. You may need to check your service's documentation to get the needed information for the desired settings. Once your settings are entered, save your document. You only need to change settings infrequently, so most of the hard work is done only once.

To create a document for another service, you may want to make a copy of one of your pre-existing documents. Use the Save As command within ClarisWorks, or use the Duplicate command (both on the File menu) in the Finder.

To connect to an online service or bulletin board service for the first time:

1. Attach your modem to your Macintosh and the other end of your modem to a phone line. Then turn on your modem.
2. Create a communications document.
3. Assign all of the necessary parameters in the Connection Settings dialog box.

4. Select the Connection command from the Settings menu. The Connection Settings dialog box appears, as shown in figure 7.3.

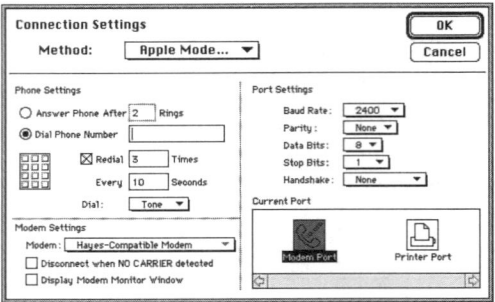

Figure 7.3. *The Connection Settings dialog box with the Apple Modem Tool selected.*

5. Enter the settings necessary to establish your connection, then click on the OK button. The most important settings are: the phone number, the modem type, the bps rate, parity, data bits, stop bits, and the handshake. These settings are discussed in detail in the next section.

6. Select the Open Connection command from the Session menu, or press Command-Shift-O. Your modem blinks, some make sounds, then the tonal duet of handshaking occurs.

The word "Connected" appears in the status area once your modem has established a connection. The word "Waiting" appears when your Macintosh is connected, but is still waiting for data.

What you see at this point depends on the type of service to which you are connecting. Normally you see a message in the communications window that indicates that you are connected, tells you the speed of the connection, and requests your name and sometimes a password.

7. Enter your name and password, if necessary, and follow any instructions that appear in the communications window. Your modem is now connected.

If you are connecting to an online service or BBS, and your communications document already exists, then open the appropriate communications document and follow steps 4-7 above.

Shortcut

Press Command-Shift-O to issue the Open Connection command and initiate a communications session. Use the same keystroke for the Close Connection command which appears in place of the Open Connection command if a session is active.

Once you are connected during a session, you can do the following things:

- ❖ Capture incoming data as text, and save it as a text file. See the section "Capturing Text" for more information on your options.
- ❖ Send or receive files. Refer to "Uploading and Downloading Files" for details.
- ❖ Print the data you receive by using the Print command on the File menu, as you would any Macintosh file.
- ❖ Copy tabular data to a spreadsheet or database, or copy text to your word processor via the Clipboard. Select the onscreen tabular data, then choose the Copy Table command from the Edit menu, and be sure to click on the Port radio button under the Capture From option in the communications section of the Preferences dialog box.

The procedure for disconnecting from an online service or a BBS is:

1. Type the command that signals the end of your communications session. Typical commands are: logout, logoff, exit, quit, off, or bye.
2. Select the Close Connection command from the Session menu, or press Command-Shift-O. Your modem shows the appropriate status lights as being on or off.

You also can establish a direct connection from one computer to another, called a "null-modem connection," or set up your computer to receive incoming calls. See the sections "Null-Modem Connections" and "Receiving Calls," respectively.

Setting Communications Settings and Preferences

Most of your setup work is done when you first create a new communications document. You might want to collect your documentation as you enter your settings. Enter your settings before you try to make a connection. Chances are that once you create your settings, you will never need to change them again. This section details the various communications settings.

Your most important settings appear in the Connection Settings dialog box (see figure 7.3). This dialog box uses tools supplied by the Apple Communications Toolbox, part of the System software. Additional tools can be added as extensions to your System folder. Three tools are supplied by Claris as part of ClarisWorks:

- ❖ The Apple Modem Tool for connection purposes.
- ❖ The VT102 Tool for terminal emulation (used as a VT100 emulator, as well).
- ❖ The XMODEM Tool for file transfers.

What you see in the Connection Settings dialog box depends on the selection you make in the Method pop-up menu for the tool. Your choices are the Apple Modem or the Serial Tools. The Apple Modem Tool is the default. It works with Hayes-compatible modems, an industry standard. (The Hayes command set is a very simple language used to control modems. Virtually all modems manufactured now use the Hayes command set.)

You also may want to change the settings for terminal emulation by using the Terminal command (see the "Terminal Emulation" section), and for protocols by using the File Transfer command (see "Uploading and Downloading Files"). Both are found on the Settings menu.

The most important of the settings in the Apple Modem Tool are:

- ❖ Answer Phone After... Rings. Enter the number of rings that the Macintosh should wait before answering the phone. See "Receiving Calls," later in this chapter.
- ❖ Dial Phone Number. Enter the phone number, with a comma for a 2-second pause, and any 8, 9, or 1's required to obtain access to outside lines or long-distance services. Use more commas for more pause time. Parentheses and hyphens are ignored.
- ❖ Redial... Times. Enter the number of times you want the computer to try redialing when a busy signal is detected.
- ❖ Dial: Tone, Pulse, or Mixed. This refers to the dialing method your phone lines use—pulse or Touch-Tone. The Mixed option uses both methods—for instance, if your phone lines require pulse dialing but you need to enter a calling card number with tone dialing.

- Modem Settings. Select the modem type from the pop-up menu. The generic Hayes-compatible modem is the default choice. Use that, unless you have a communication tool for your specific brand and model of modem. Communications tools, which specify the exact way the Macintosh communicates with the modem, are normally supplied on a disk by your modem manufacturer.
- Bps Rate. The speed of your modem, from 110 to 57,600 bps. For noisy phone lines, lower your setting.
- Parity. Allows data checking. None, Odd, or Even are your choices. This setting is determined by the service you are connecting to; most services use the None setting.
- Data Bits. Data bits indicate the width of a character in the bitstream. Your choices are 5, 6, 7, or 8 bits. Seven or 8 are most commonly selected. As with Parity, the setting you make here is determined by the service you're connecting to. Eight bits is the most common setting, with 7 coming in second.
- Stop Bits. The stop bit marks the end of a character. Your choices are 1, 1.5, or 2 stop bits, with 1 stop bit being the most common selection. Again, this setting is determined by the service you connect to.
- Handshake. The handshake is a method for data flow. Your choices are XON/XOFF, DTR & CTS, DTR only, CTS only, or None. None is the default; XON/XOFF is also common. This setting too is determined by the service you connect to.
- Current Port icon. Click on the Modem or Printer port icon—whichever port your modem is connected to. These ports are functionally identical. It doesn't matter which port you connect your modem to, only that you select the icon that corresponds to that port.

The communications Preferences dialog box enables you to set overall default preferences for the communications environment. The settings in this environment are more important than in other environments. Select the Preferences command from the Edit menu to display the Preferences dialog box shown in figure 7.4.

> **Note**
> If your modem's speed setting doesn't appear in the pop-up menu, use the next higher setting.

> **Note**
> Bps rate, parity, data bits, stop bits, and handshake are the most important settings you need to know to connect to another computer. The documentation for the service you want to connect to should tell you the correct settings for these options.

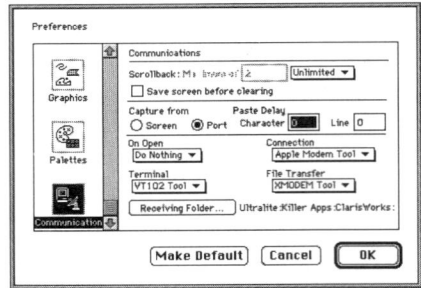

Figure 7.4. *The Preferences dialog box.*

A number of important settings appear in this dialog box:

- ❖ Scrollback. You can change the amount of data stored in the scrollback, which is normally an unlimited amount. See the discussion of scrollback preferences in the next section, "Capturing Text."
- ❖ Capture From: Screen or Port. Clicking on the Screen radio button captures only what you see onscreen; clicking on the Port radio button also captures control characters.
- ❖ On Open. Determines what ClarisWorks will do when you open the communications document. Your choices are Automatically Connect, Wait for Connection, or Do Nothing (the default setting).
- ❖ Terminal. Your choices are for VT102 or VT52 terminal emulation. This is determined by the service you connect to; VT102 is most common.
- ❖ Connection. Your choices are the Apple Modem Tool or the Serial Tool.
- ❖ File Transfer. The XMODEM Tool, Text Tool, or Claris Kermit Tool can be selected.
- ❖ Receiving Folder. Click to display a standard File dialog box. Select the default location where you want ClarisWorks to save received files.

Click on the OK button to apply these settings to your active document, and click on the Make Default button if you want to make these settings apply to any new documents you create. Your previously created documents are not affected by the new settings.

Capturing Text

Incoming text in a session appears in your communications window in the Terminal area. To prevent too much text from appearing in the Terminal area, ClarisWorks uses a text buffer of a certain size, and sends older data into an area called the *scrollback*. You see the scrollback if the option Save Lines Off Top command on the Session menu is selected (the default). Use the Command-L keystroke to select this command. With this command deselected, the scrollback window is hidden, but the text is stored anyway.

The scrollback is the older part of your session, and its size is unlimited. To limit the Scrollback pane size, enter that size as a Communications preference in the Preferences dialog box. When you save your text from a session, all of the text is saved as a text file.

You can open the Scrollback option and view its contents in the Scrollback pane, as shown in figure 7.5. The Scrollback pane creates a split window, and can be scrolled by using the scroll bar, or resized by using the Pane split control. (See chapter 2, "Some Basics," for information about working with window panes.) To see the scrollback, select the Show Scrollback command from the Settings menu. To hide the scrollback, select the Hide Scrollback command. Use the Command-L keystroke for both commands.

Shortcut
Select the Save Lines Off Top command from the Session menu, or press Command-T to show previously received text in the scrollback window. Use this keystroke again to not have received text in the Scrollback pane.

Note
Press Command-L to issue the Show Panes command and show previously received text in the Scrollback pane. Use Command-L once again to issue the Hide Scrollback command and remove the Scrollback pane.

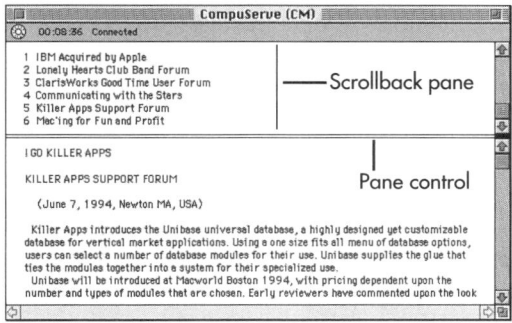

Figure 7.5. *The Scrollback pane.*

You can do the following with the Scrollback pane:

❖ Copy text from the Scrollback pane, just as you would from the Terminal area.

- ❖ Move data from the Terminal area to the Scrollback pane, and clear your screen by selecting the Save Current Screen command from the Session menu.

  To prevent an incoming Clear Screen command from the remote computer from removing your Terminal area data, click on the Save Screen Before Clearing checkbox in the Preferences dialog box.

- ❖ Clear the Scrollback pane by selecting the Clear Saved Lines command from the Session menu. The Clear Screen from the Session menu clears the terminal area, but leaves the Scrollback pane contents intact.

Normally you store previously received data in memory, and view it in the Scrollback pane. If you are low on memory, or know you want a permanent copy of the data, capture the data to a disk file. To capture data to a file, select the Capture File command from the Session menu, and name the data file in the Save dialog box that appears. Captured data can be saved in either port or screen format. The port format includes all control characters; the screen format is what you see onscreen. Use the Preferences command from the Edit menu to make either of these choices in the communications section of the Preferences dialog box, shown in figure 7.4.

Receiving Calls

To have your Macintosh receive incoming phone calls, you need to do some initial setup work. Make sure you tell the person who's going to call your computer the settings you are going to use so that the two computers can communicate.

To receive an incoming phone call:

1. Turn on your modem, and open or create the ClarisWorks communications document appropriate to your session.
2. Select the Connection command from the Settings menu (see figure 7.6).
3. In the Answer Phone After…Rings text box enter the number of rings desired.
4. Click on the OK button.

Figure 7.6. *The Settings menu.*

5. Select the Wait For Connection command from the Session menu, or press Command-Shift-W. Your modem initializes, its lights may flash, and a message appears indicating that your Macintosh is ready to receive a phone call. You will hear the phone ring, then the sound of handshaking when the connection is established.

6. End the session by selecting the Close Connection command from the Session menu, or press Command-Shift-O.

Automating Your Sessions

If you want to use the same communications document to dial various places or people, create a phone-book entry for each one.

To add the first entry to your phone book:

1. Select the Phone Book command from the Settings menu, or press Command-B. Or click on the Phone Book icon in the status area, and select the Edit Phone Book Entry command from the pop-up menu.

   The Edit Phone Book Entry dialog box appears, as shown in figure 7.7.

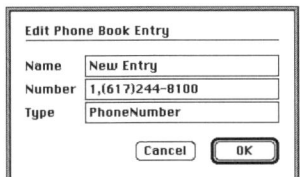

Figure 7.7. *The Edit Phone Book Entry dialog box.*

Shortcut
Press Command-Shift-W to issue the Wait For Connection command and prepare your computer to receive an incoming phone call.

Shortcut
Press Command-B to show the Edit Phone Book Entry dialog box.

2. Type a name and a phone number into the Name and Number text boxes, respectively. (The Type text box contains information relevant to the communication tool you're using, so don't worry about it.)

3. Click on the OK button. The Phone Book dialog box shown in figure 7.8 appears.

4. To add another name and number to the phone book, click on the New button.

5. To dismiss the Phone Book dialog box, click on the Done button.

To edit the Phone Book:

1. Select the Phone Book command from the Settings menu.

   Or, select the Edit Phone Book command from the Phone Book pop-down menu in the status area. The Phone Book dialog box shown in figure 7.8 appears.

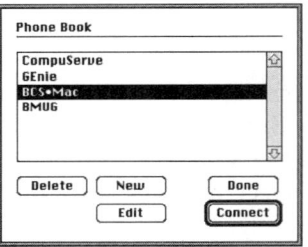

Figure 7.8. *The Phone Book dialog box.*

2. Select the entry by clicking on it, then click on the Edit button and make your changes in the Edit Phone Book dialog box that was shown in figure 7.7. You can click the Delete button to delete an entry or add an entry by using the New button.

3. Click on the Done button.

To connect using the Phone Book, click on the Phone Book icon and select the name of the service or person from the pop-up menu, as shown in figure 7.9. A connection is opened, and the phone call is made by using the settings that exist in your communications document.

Figure 7.9. *The Phone Book pop-up menu.*

The most valuable automation you can create for a communications document is a log-on macro. Macros are discussed in detail in chapter 9, "Advanced Topics." To record a macro:

1. Within your communications document, select the Record Macro command from the Shortcuts submenu or use its keystroke equivalent, Command-Shift-J. The Record Macro dialog box appears, as shown in figure 7.10.

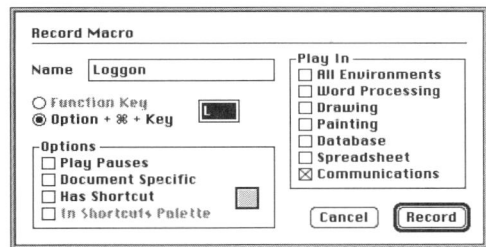

Figure 7.10. *The Record Macro dialog box.*

2. Enter a name into the Name text box, and a keystroke in the Function key text box (optional).
3. Click on the Record button.
4. Select the Connection command from the Session menu, enter the appropriate phone number and bps rate into the Connection Settings dialog box. Then click on the OK button.
5. Select the Open Connection command from the Session menu.
6. Select the Macro Wait command from the Shortcuts submenu under the File menu. The Macro Wait dialog box appears, as shown in figure 7.11.

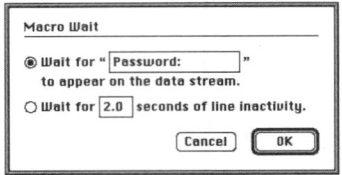

Figure 7.11. *The Macro Wait dialog box.*

Have your macro wait until the text string appears that requires your first keyboard entry. That string might be: "Name:", "UserID:", or something similar. The string is case-sensitive. You also can set a time delay, but this is less precise than a text string entry.

7. Click on the OK button to record the Macro Wait in your sequence.

8. When the text string appears prompting you for an entry, type in your information. For many services, two entries are required: a name and a password. The second string requires a second Macro Wait step in the sequence; add another one as described in steps 6 and 7.

9. Finish recording your macro.

10. Select the Stop Recording command from the Shortcuts submenu, or press Command-Shift-J.

To run the macro, select the Play Macro command from the Shortcuts submenu, and double-click on the macro name. Alternately, use the assigned keystroke for the macro instead.

Uploading and Downloading Files

You transfer files during a session by using a transfer protocol or a file-transfer method, and issuing the Send File or Receive File command from the Session menu. Each computer must use the same transfer protocol. You change protocols by using the File Transfer Tool, and make your selections from the File Transfer Settings dialog box shown in figure 7.12. The XMODEM Tool is the default choice, and is used by nearly all Macintosh services.

> **Caution**
> Your log-on macro will disclose your password to anyone that uses it. If you're using a machine that others can easily use, think twice before recording a password in a macro.

The most important choices for file transfers are:

- ❖ Method. The Method pop-up menu selects among variations of the XMODEM protocol. Your choices are the MacBinary, MacTerminal 1.1, Straight Modem, and XMODEM Text methods. MacBinary is the most popular standard in the Macintosh world.
- ❖ Timing Options. These options set retry transmission delays and attempts. Both are set to the number 10 as a default—ClarisWorks will try 10 times to connect, and will wait 10 seconds between attempts.
- ❖ Transfer Options. The XMODEM Tool allows for some error checking. Your choices are: Standard, CRC-16, 1K Blocks, and CleanLink. Standard is, as they say, standard. Use 1K Blocks for faster and more reliable performance, if the remote computer supports it.
- ❖ Received File Options. This section attaches attributes to incoming files. Your choices are: Creator ID, Use FileName Sent by Remote Computer, and Enable Auto Receive. The Creator ID automatically creates an association for the file with an application, and asks you to name the file when the transfer is complete. Use FileName accepts the name, and is only available for the MacBinary or MacTerminal methods.

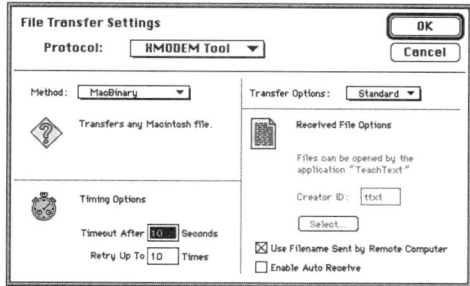

Figure 7.12. *The File Transfer Settings dialog box.*

To send a file:

1. Select the File Transfer command from the Settings menu. The File Transfer settings dialog box appears, as shown in figure 7.12.
2. Set the options you want, then dismiss the dialog box by clicking on the OK button.
3. With your session established, select the Send File command from the Session menu. An Open dialog box appears.
4. Navigate the standard file dialog box, then double-click on the file name you wish to send. Alternately, click once to highlight the name, then click on the Send button. Clicking on the Cancel button ends the procedure.

The File Transfer Status dialog box appears, as show in figure 7.13.

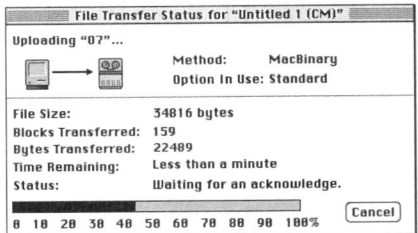

Figure 7.13. *The File Transfer Status dialog box.*

Null-Modem Connections

Connecting directly from one computer to another without the use of a phone line does not require the use of modems to create intermediary analog signals. You can directly connect the serial port of one computer to the serial port of the other, commonly called a "null-modem" connection.

Note
For data transfer on a regular basis, an established network is preferable to null-modem transfers. It's a lot easier, and faster as well.

Null-modem connections frequently are used for file transfers from a PowerBook to a desktop Macintosh, or from a Macintosh to an IBM PC or PC-compatible computer. Serial connections can operate at higher data transfer speeds than modem connections. First try the maximum setting for bps rate, 57,600 bps.

To connect to another computer directly:

1. Open your ClarisWorks communications document.
2. Select the Connection command from the Settings menu. The Connections Settings dialog box appears.
3. Select the Serial Tool setting from the Method pop-up menu. The Serial Tool options now appear, as shown in figure 7.14. Make appropriate settings changes to match the receiving computer.

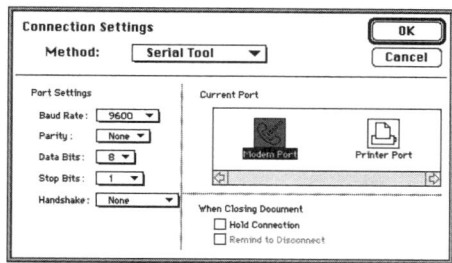

Figure 7.14. *The Connection Settings dialog box with the Serial Tool selected.*

4. Select the Open Connection command from the Settings menu. A connection is established.
5. You will see the other computer type characters, or you can type characters yourself and see them onscreen and have them transmitted.

    If you don't see your typed characters, then turn the Local Echo on by clicking the checkbox in the General section of the Terminal Settings dialog box, as shown in figure 7.15. If you see repeated characters, lliikkee tthhiiss, turn this option off.
6. Alternately, you can send (upload) or receive (download) files from the other computer.
7. End the session by selecting the Close Connection from the Session menu. "Unconnected" appears in the Status area.

Terminal Emulation

Terminal emulation enables your Macintosh to connect to another computer, such as a mainframe, and act as a terminal. You can enter characters from your keyboard, and have them translated into the characters the other computer expects. The VT102 Tool is the default terminal type, and is a common terminal standard. You change the terminal tool by selecting the Terminal command from the Settings menu, and making selections from the Terminal Settings dialog box shown in figure 7.15.

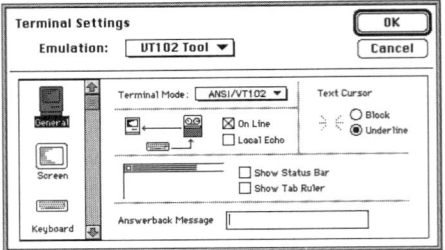

Figure 7.15. *The Terminal Settings dialog box.*

You most important choices are:

❖ Emulation. Your choices are the VT102 (or VT100), VT52, or TTY Tools. The VT emulation is for Digital Equipment Corporation computers, and compatible terminals; the TTY emulation is for dumb terminal emulation. Each emulation gives you several choices for each of the devices in the scroll box.

❖ General. Click on the General icon to see these settings. Settings in this section enable you to select character sets, stay On Line, use a Local Echo, change the Status bar, select a Text Cursor, and supply an Answerback Message. Figure 7.16 shows the Status area with the rulers and indicators turned on.

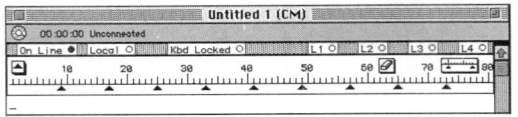

Figure 7.16. *Terminal emulation ruler and indicator bars.*

- ❖ Screen. Click on the Screen icon to see its settings. Settings in the Screen section enable you to change the character display width (80 or 132 characters), enter a character Size (9 or 12 point), Show Control Characters, Auto Wrap to Next Line, Insert Characters, change Scroll Text behavior, and display Inverse Video.
- ❖ Keyboard options. Click on the Keyboard icon to see these settings. These options set the action of the numeric keypad or cursor keys. For computers without keypads or cursor keys, use the Keypad or Cursor commands on the Keys menu and make selections from the pop-up menus. Figure 7.17 shows the pop-up keypad. Click sounds, repeat behavior, and line feed are other options available.

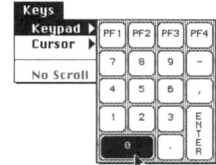

Figure 7.17. *The Keypad pop-up menu.*

- ❖ Character Set. Click the Character Set icon to display these settings, scrolling down if necessary. Character sets are used for various languages.

You may have to experiment with your terminal settings to get them right.

CONNECTING TO AN ONLINE SERVICE

The communications environment isn't as advantageous as it used to be. These days most online services require, or work best when used with, their own dedicated software.

You can connect to services such as CompuServe by using ClarisWorks to run a session, navigate through the service, send and receive mail, and accomplish just about any task there is to accomplish. However, doing so is a chore. CompuServe sells the CompuServe Information Manager (CIM) and CompuServe Navigator, both of which are graphical front ends to the service. When using CIM and the CompuServe Navigator, you just double-click on an icon or choose a menu command to perform a task—skills which are much easier to learn.

Other services have similar programs. America OnLine, GENie, AppleLink, and Apple's new eWorld all use their own dedicated software. You still can use a communications document to connect to BBSes, and many still use text-based systems. Even in the BBS world, though, the use of interface software such as FirstClass from SoftArc is increasing, and there are fewer text-based BBSes in operation.

Summary

In this chapter you learned the basic principles of communicating with and transferring data to and from other computers. A communications session requires a communications document, with an appropriate set of settings, protocols, and parameters. You also must connect your Macintosh to a modem and a phone line. For direct communications with another computer, only a serial cable is required to communicate: Modems are not required.

In the next chapter you will learn how to make the various ClarisWorks environments work together to create compound documents and to do specialized tasks.

Chapter 8
Making It All Work Together

Now that you have learned how to use each of the several environments available to you in ClarisWorks, you are probably ready to figure out how to make those environments work together for you. This chapter provides you with tips and techniques on creating compound documents by using different types of frames in various kinds of documents.

If you work with files supplied by others, you will find the discussion of importing and inserting files useful. The chapter ends with step-by-step procedures for creating merged documents, labels, and printed envelopes.

Below are some of the how-to topics covered in this chapter:

How to create compound documents with frames 220
How to tell which frames you can use 220
How to link text frames to create newsletters 222
How to import files 227
How to insert a document in another document 228
How to merge to documents to create form letters 230
How to print envelopes 231
How to create mailing labels 233

Composing Compound Documents With Frames

One of the most powerful ways to make use of ClarisWorks' integration is to create a document, such as a newsletter or report, that integrates several kinds of frames into a single document.

Not all environments support the use of frames, and some environments, such as the drawing environment, create objects instead of frames. Table 8.1 summarizes how documents handle other environments. This section helps you learn how best to understand and use these environment limitations and capabilities.

Table 8.1. *Frames Available for Each of the ClarisWorks Environments*

Document type	Can include these frames	With these restrictions
Communications	none	
Database	SS, WP, PT	You can only work with frames while in the Layout mode.
Drawing	SS, DB, PT, WP	
Painting	SS, DB, WP	As soon as you stop working on a frame, it becomes a painting object. This means that you cannot edit its contents.
Spreadsheet	SS, DB, PT, WP	Insert a word processing frame by holding down the Option key as you select the spreadsheet environment tool.

Note
Compound documents may not be created in the communications environment.

Document type	Can include these frames	With these restrictions
Word processing	SS, DB, PT, WP	Insert a word processing frame by holding down the Option key as you select the word processing environment tool.

If a frame contains objects, you can edit those objects directly from within your document. You do not need to enter the frame's environment. The object must be contained in the frame, and not be floating on top of it. You add an object to a frame by first holding down the Control key, and then drawing the object. You can in this manner add a square or a circle to a spreadsheet or a painting frame. To edit that square or circle, simply hold the Control key and click on that object. Then make your changes.

Text Frames

Text frames behave a little differently than the spreadsheet and painting frames. You don't have to draw the outline of a text frame.

To create a text frame:

1. Select the Text tool from the Tool panel.
2. Click in the existing document. Don't worry about sizing the frame correctly; you can always resize the frame later on.
3. Type or paste in your text. Figure 8.1 displays an empty text frame.

Figure 8.1. *An empty text frame.*

As you type, the frame gets bigger, growing down.

To resize the margins of the text frame:

1. Select the Pointer tool.
2. Click on the frame to display its resize handles.

Tip
To create layouts, you can insert spreadsheet frames into spreadsheet documents and word processing frames into word processing documents by holding down the Option key when creating the frame.

Tip
To select a frame, click on it. To enter a frame's environment, double-click on the frame.

3. Click on a handle and drag the frame to the size you want. ClarisWorks reflows your text. The text frame will be only as deep as needed to show the text.

A frame is a specialized type of object. All of the commands for moving and resizing objects apply to frames. You may want to review the discussion in the "Manipulating Objects" section of chapter 6, "Graphics," to refresh your memory on the subject.

One of the best ways to put text into a text frame is to use the Copy and Paste commands. To paste text into a text frame, follow these steps:

1. Locate the text you want to copy.
2. Select the text, then pull down the Edit menu, and choose the Copy command.
3. Open the destination document.
4. Click on the text frame, then pull down the Edit menu and choose the Paste command. ClarisWorks copies the text into the frame. If the text did not fit in the frame, you will see a little box with an "X" in it at the lower-right of the frame, as shown in figure 8.2.

When·you·type·in·

Figure 8.2. *A filled text frame and text frame indicator.*

When you see the text flow indicator, you can resize your frame to the text. You also can link several text frames together, to create an attractive multicolumn layout or a story that spans more than one page.

Linking Text Frames to Create Newsletters

When you read the first page of a newspaper, you'll find that many stories continue, or "jump," to subsequent pages. By splitting up stories, the newspaper is able to spark interest in a variety of subjects that receive coverage elsewhere in the paper. This practice also helps magazines draw your attention to advertisements, probably the primary purpose for jumping pages in a magazine.

To create multicolumn and multipage stories on your computer, you used to have to purchase expensive page-layout programs such as Aldus PageMaker or QuarkXPress. You can create the same layout in

Caution
If you plan on using linked frames in a document, you must create and link those frames. You cannot link existing frames.

ClarisWorks by creating linked text frames. ClarisWorks fills each of the linked frames automatically, in the sequence that you indicate.

To create linked text frames, follow these steps:

1. Open your document.
2. Pull down the Options menu and choose the Frame Links command. When this command is activated, each frame is linked as it's created.
3. Click on the Text tool in the Tool panel.
4. Click in the document and drag the dimensions of the text frame. A linked text frame displays, as shown in figure 8.3.

> **Shortcut**
> Select the Frame Links command from the Options menu or press Command-L to link the text frames that you create.

> One of the best ways of putting text into a text frame is to used the Copy and Paste commands. To paste text into a text frame, follow these steps:

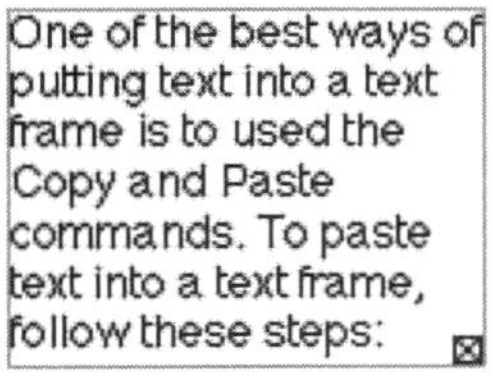

Figure 8.3. *First linked text frame.*

5. Now paste or type text into the frame. When the text frame is full, you will see a box with the "X" indicator in the lower-right of the frame, as shown in figure 8.3.
6. Create a subsequent linked text frame by clicking on the Continue indicator (the downward arrow icon) and by clicking elsewhere in the document.

   ClarisWorks continues the text in the new linked text box, as shown in figure 8.4, and marks linked frames with Link indicators (the chain icon). The top of the first linked frame has a Top-of-Frame indicator (a blank indicator box).
7. Continue clicking in the document to create additional frames.
8. When you have finished creating linked frames, pull down the Options menu and choose the Frame Links command, or press Command-L to complete the operation.

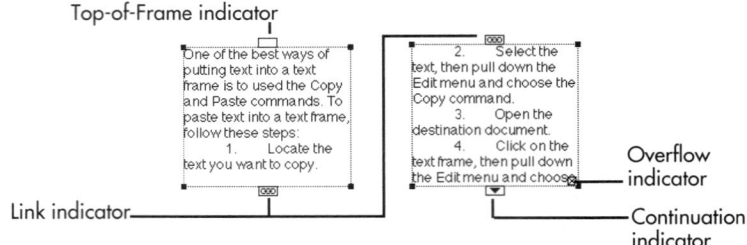

Figure 8.4. *Linked text frames showing the Top-of-Frame and the Continuation indicators.*

As you work with linked text frames, you may want to resize them. Unlike regular text frames, linked text frames do not flow to meet the dimensions of the text.

To resize linked text frames, follow these steps:

1. Click on the frame you want to resize.
2. Drag on the handles and then release. You must drag by clicking on the black reshape handles, not on the Continuation indicator.

To delete a linked text frame, follow these steps:

1. Click on the frame you want to delete.
2. Press the Delete or the Backspace key. Alternately, select the Cut command from the Edit menu. The frame is deleted, but the text is intact.

Graphics Frames

The graphics tools on the Tool panel are available to you most of the time. There is no way to create a drawing frame, but you can create a painting frame (see figure 8.5). Drawing tools create objects that float over your document. You may create and move drawn objects in the word processing, spreadsheet, database, and drawing documents.

Figure 8.5. *A painting frame.*

You can use the Modify Frame command to change the resolution, color depth, and origin of painting frames. Select the frame, and choose the Modify Frame command from the Options menu. The Resolution and Depth dialog box appears. This dialog box was discussed in detail in chapter 6, in the section "Editing Images."

Shortcut
Press Command-Shift-I to issue the Modify Frame command and display the Resolution and Depth dialog box for a selected painting frame.

Spreadsheet Frames (Using Tables and Charts in Reports)

One effective way to use spreadsheet frames is to add them to word processing, database, spreadsheet, or drawing documents. These frames can be used to display tables of information or charts.

To create a spreadsheet frame, follow these steps:

1. Pull down the View menu and choose Show Tools. The Tool panel displays.
2. Click on the cross-shaped Spreadsheet tool. The text pointer changes to a spreadsheet pointer.
3. In the window, hold down the mouse button and drag an area in the shape a rectangle. This creates the spreadsheet frame, as shown in figure 8.6.

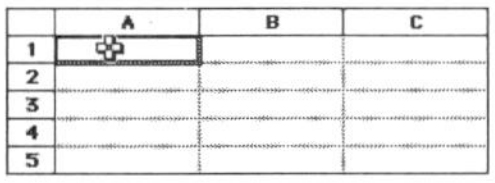

Figure 8.6. *A spreadsheet frame.*

Spreadsheet frames can only be the exact size of the closest number of columns and rows. A spreadsheet frame is a window into the spreadsheet environment. When you select a spreadsheet frame your menus change, spreadsheet environment functions become available, and you can graph or chart data in the spreadsheet.

Use the Modify Frame command from the Option menu (Command-Shift-I) to change the appearance of the Spreadsheet display. That dialog box is shown in figure 8.7.

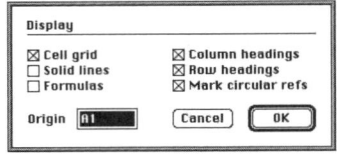

Figure 8.7. *The spreadsheet environment Display dialog box.*

Linking Frames

Frames may be linked to provide the following advantages:

- ❖ Text frames can be linked to create autoflowing columns for newsletter formats.
- ❖ Spreadsheet frames can be linked to provide access to a spreadsheet document.
- ❖ Painting frames can be linked to provide access to a painting document.

Creating Master Pages

A master page may contain headers, footers, logos, watermarks, or words such as "copy," "do not duplicate," or "confidential." With ClarisWorks, you can set up one master page per document. The master page actually is a drawing document.

To create a master page, follow these steps:

1. Create a drawing document.
2. Pull down the Options menu and select Edit Master Page. Master Page displays in the lower-left of the screen, as shown in figure 8.8.

Figure 8.8. *Page indicator for a master page.*

> **Tip**
> When creating the elements of the master page, use light shades in the main text area to keep the text readable. Consider placing master page items in the margin area for clarity.

3. Type, format, or draw the information that will appear on every page of the document.
4. Pull down the Options menu and select Edit Master Page to return to the working area of the main document.
5. Add text or spreadsheet frames and insert the information that will appear in the foreground.

To preview the document contents and the master page, as shown in figure 8.9, pull down the View menu and select Page View.

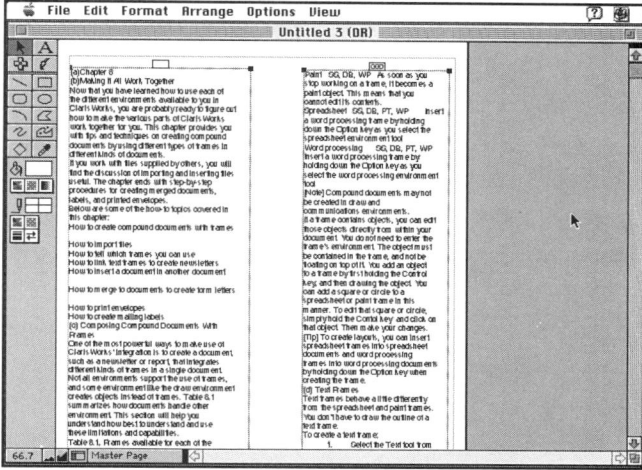

Figure 8.9. *Text with master page.*

Importing Files and Inserting a Document Within Another Document

If you are putting together a project such as a report or newsletter that depends on contributions from multiple individuals, you may need to either import information from other programs or insert a ClarisWorks file into another file.

To import a file into ClarisWorks, you must first ascertain if the file was created on a machine other than a Macintosh. If this is the case, you will need to use the Apple File Exchange utility, MacLink, DOS Mounter, or another program to convert the file so it is readable by your Macintosh.

When you installed ClarisWorks, you also installed file format translators so that you would have the capability to interpret files created by other programs.

To import a file, follow these steps:

1. Launch ClarisWorks, if it's not already open.

2. Pull down the File menu and choose the Open command. The Open dialog box displays.

3. Open the Document Type pop-up menu and select the type of document you want to import. If you don't select a Document Type, folders in the Open dialog box may appear empty.

4. Select the file you want to import into ClarisWorks.

5. Open the File Type pop-up menu and select the file type of document you want to import.

6. Click on the OK button (or press the Return or Enter key). The document opens in ClarisWorks and the word (converted) displays in the Title bar, as shown in figure 8.10. The original is unchanged.

Figure 8.10. *A converted drawing.*

While you can always copy and paste information from one ClarisWorks file to another, you also can insert an entire document into a ClarisWorks document.

To insert a document, follow these steps:

1. Open or create the document into which the document will be inserted.

2. Place the cursor where the document should be inserted.

3. Open the File menu and select the Insert command. The Insert dialog box displays.

4. Choose the document you want to insert, as shown in figure 8.11.

Tip

To make it easier to import other files, use the Save As command in the original program and save the document as a file type that will be readable by ClarisWorks. For example, choose Text for word processing, PICT for a painting image, or SYLK for a spreadsheet.

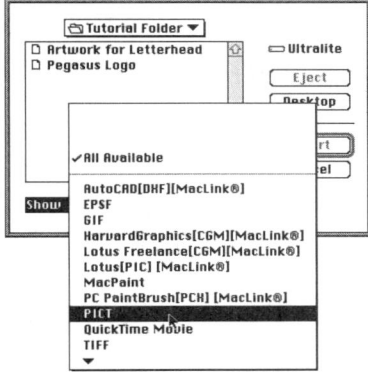

Figure 8.11. *Choosing a document in the Insert dialog box.*

5. Click on the Insert button or press the Enter or Return key. The contents of the file are inserted into your ClarisWorks document, in the frame you indicated.

Automating Custom Printed Output

One of the common reasons why people buy a computer is to create form letters and mailing labels. Users rightly assume that these repetitive tasks are best done by a computer, but users often get confused by the process.

ClarisWorks' integrated environments make it an excellent choice for combining the information in a database with the text and formatting created in a word processing document or frame.

When you create customized form letters or labels, you are combining a source document (the one with the information) with a template (the document or frame which contains the formatting) to create new printed documents that have the style and substance of both parent environments. The concept, called a *mail merge* or *print merge,* is illustrated in figure 8.12.

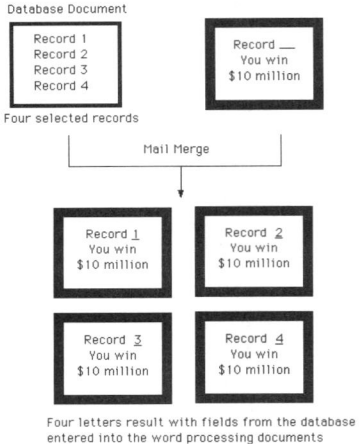

Figure 8.12. *The mail or print merge concept.*

About Mail Merge

To do a mail merge, you must first open a database with the fields that contain your source data. Then from within a word processing document or a text frame, you use the Mail Merge command and dialog box to put field place holders where the data is to appear. Finally, the Print Merge button launches your mail merge and prints your documents.

To set up a word processing document or frame:

1. Open or create a database document that contains the information needed. Select the records you want to use to be merged. Each record generates one form, letter, or label.
2. Open or create the word processing document or frame that contains formatting and the rest of the text.
3. Open the File menu and select the Mail Merge command. The Select Data dialog box, which lists the names of open database files, displays, as shown in figure 8.13.

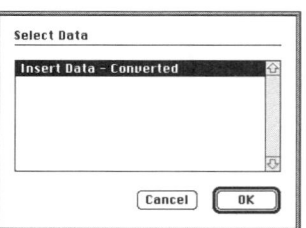

Figure 8.13. *The Select Data dialog box.*

Shortcut
Press Command-Shift M as a shortcut for selecting the Mail Merge command from the File menu.

4. Select the name of the database file and click on the OK button or press the Return or the Enter key. ClarisWorks displays the Mail Merge dialog box, as shown in figure 8.14.

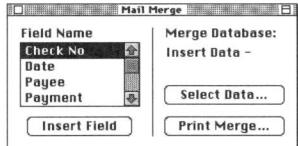

Figure 8.14. *The Mail Merge dialog box.*

5. As you type your letter, insert the field names that appear in the Mail Merge dialog box by scrolling through the list and clicking on the Insert button. ClarisWorks puts a field place holder "«fieldname»" to the left of your insertion point.

   Insert field place holders where needed. Be sure to use any punctuation required by your document. Look your document over carefully and correct any punctuation or spelling errors.

6. Turn on your printer and insert any special stationery or labels.
7. Click on the Print Merge button in the Mail Merge dialog box to merge the records with your form letter. The merged documents are automatically printed.

Shortcut
You also can use Option-\ and Shift-Option-\ to create the bracket symbols, or chevrons («, ») which are used for mail merges.

When you finish inserting the field names, you need to check through both the database and the word processing documents for any spelling or punctuation errors. In ClarisWorks, it is not possible to preview a merged document onscreen; the merge goes directly to the printer. For this reason, it's best first to experiment with a small sample of names on inexpensive paper. It's rather frustrating to print 50 or so letters on your highest-quality paper, only to find the same error repeated on each page.

Printing Envelopes

To print merged information to an envelope, you need to create a layout in a word processing document that determines the positioning of the Return and Sending addresses. The following procedure was developed for printing on a standard #10 business envelope.

1. Create a new word processing document.
2. Pull down the File menu and choose Page Setup. The Page Setup dialog box displays, as shown in figure 8.15

Caution
If you mistype the name of a field, ClarisWorks prints out a blank sheet of paper. Field names are case-sensitive. Be careful to select only the records in the database for which you want documents to be printed.

232   Chapter 8 • Making It All Work Together

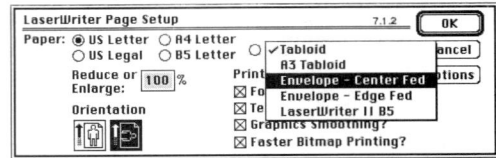

Figure 8.15. *The Page Setup dialog box.*

3. Click on one of the landscape icons to change the orientation of the paper.
4. Click on the drop down menu for paper size and select Envelope-Center Fed or Envelope-Edge Fed for a laser printer, or No. 10 Envelope for a StyleWriter printer.
5. Click on the OK button (or press the Return or the Enter key) to close the Page Setup dialog box.
6. Open the Format menu and select the Rulers command. The Rulers dialog box displays, as shown in figure 8.16.

Caution
Experiment with several types of envelopes. My laser printer consistently eschews Southworth envelopes but prints beautifully on Strathmore envelopes.

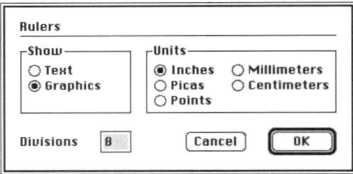

Figure 8.16. *The Rulers dialog box.*

7. Select the Graphics ruler option and click on the OK button to close the Rulers dialog box. Your page will display with 6.5-inch by 9-inch margins, as shown in figure 8.17.
8. For a printer that feeds envelopes from the center of the paper tray, type the return address at 1.5 inches. You may have to adjust this for left-feeding printers.
9. Bring the text cursor down to 3.5 inches and use the Tab key or the left-margin control to indent the sending address.
10. Format the envelope with fonts, clip art, and so on.
11. Save your document as a stationery template. Use the procedure for merging files and inserting the field names that form the sending address.

Tip
Before you print out your first set of labels, print out a page on your regular paper. Then hold the printout and a sheet of computer labels up to a light, and check that the text is properly positioned on the page. After you have made any tweaks necessary, you're ready to use the labels.

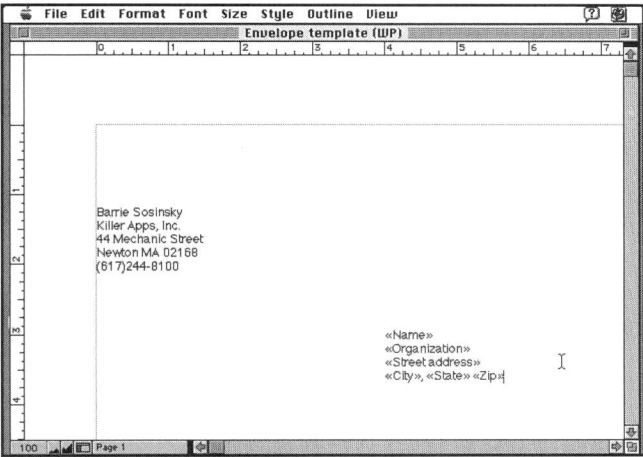

Figure 8.17. *The Word processing document with margins for a #10 envelope.*

Printing Mailing Labels

To create mailing labels or other types of labels, you work exclusively in the database environment. ClarisWorks comes with more than 50 templates for standard Avery labels.

When you shop for labels, take careful note of the number and size of labels per page. It's also important that you buy the type of label appropriate for your printer. If you are not sure, consult your printer's documentation.

Laser printers require labels specially made for laser printers because of the heat involved in the printing process. Normal labels can come off the label sheet as they feed through the printer, literally gumming up the works.

To select a mailing label format, follow these steps:

1. In the database environment, open the Layout menu and choose New Layout. The New Layout dialog box displays.
2. Click on the Labels button.
3. Open the Custom pop-up menu and select the label template you want to use.
4. Click on the OK button, or press the Return or Enter key. The Set Field Order dialog box displays, as shown in figure 8.18.

Tip
Automate envelope printing by creating a macro.

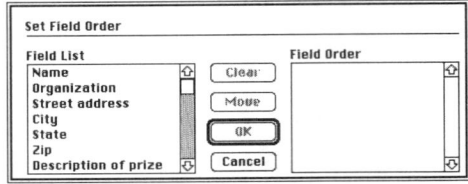

Figure 8.18. *The Set Field Order dialog box.*

5. From the Field List, select the fields that are to compose the information on the labels. You must select the fields in the order in which they are to print.
6. Click on the Move button after selecting each field.
7. When finished, click on the OK button or press the Return or Enter key. The label layout displays, as shown in figure 8.19.

Figure 8.19. *The label layout.*

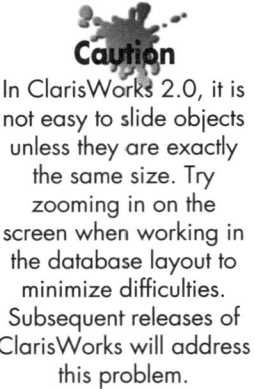

In ClarisWorks 2.0, it is not easy to slide objects unless they are exactly the same size. Try zooming in on the screen when working in the database layout to minimize difficulties. Subsequent releases of ClarisWorks will address this problem.

8. Pull down the Layout menu and choose Browse to preview how the labels will look when printed. ClarisWorks closes up the gaps that appear onscreen when the labels are printed.

For more information on the database environment and working with layouts, refer to chapter 5, "Databases."

In many instances you want to have parts of your documents close up when there is blank space. On a label it looks much more attractive when lines of an address move up to close the gap caused by a blank address field line. When printing a list of records you can have a more attractive report when parts are closed up to eliminate blank space. This feature, called slide object, allows you to eliminate blank spaces by moving objects either left or up when a blank field exists. The enclosing part also can be reduced in size, a feature that you want to turn off for a label layout.

Remember, for sliding objects left to work properly, fields need to be the same size in the direction of sliding. That is, to slide left the field heights must be identical; to slide up, field widths must be identical. Refer to chapter 5, "Removing Unwanted Space."

Selective Merges and Sequenced Labels and Letters

Whether you are creating form letters or labels, you may want to print only selected parts of your database or print them in a specific sequence. You can modify or use a selected portion of your database records in the database environment.

- ❖ Use the Sort command in the database environment and sort the database by a particular field such as ZIP code to create a mailing that is in ZIP code order.
- ❖ Use the Find or the Match Records command to find records that have certain elements in common, such as a common billing date.

You need to modify the database records before you merge them. For more information on the database environment and working with layouts, refer to chapter 5 of this book.

Summary

In this chapter, you've learned how to create compound documents by using several kinds of frames in various types of documents. You learned that you cannot incorporate frames in drawing or communications documents. You also learned to use care when inserting a frame into a painting document, since when the frame is closed, its contents are saved as a bitmapped object and become uneditable. While the database environment supports frames, you only can work with them while you are in the Layout mode.

The Spreadsheet and the Word Processing environments provide the most flexibility when in comes to creating compound documents. You can incorporate spreadsheet, word processing, and painting frames in both of these environments.

Since frames can provide windows into complete documents of the same environment type, they are ideal for displaying charted results. Double-clicking on a frame opens it, and in the case of a chart, reveals the

Tip
When using the Slide Objects option, always preview your pages by using the Page View mode before printing.

Caution
After using the Find or the Match Records command to limit the amount of records printed, be sure to use the Find All command so you have access to the entire database.

information on which the chart is based. This capability to share both the results of your analysis and the reasoning behind it can make presentations created in ClarisWorks very powerful.

Another method of bring together various types of information is by merging records. When you merge records, you combine records from a database file with formatted text in a word processing document or frame. To specify where the database information will be inserted into a merged document, you need to insert the field names in the form letter. These fields are enclosed by special brackets («, »), which are also called chevrons. When you merge a document, the final product does not display onscreen or create a document that you can save. Instead, the results come directly out of your printer. For this reason, it's always a good idea to print a few samples before you print the entire batch.

In the next chapter, you'll learn other ways of incorporating information into your ClarisWorks documents by using the Publish and Subscribe function, available to System 7 users. You also will learn how to speed up your productivity by creating macros for common tasks.

Chapter 9
Advanced Topics

ClarisWorks supports a number of advanced technologies that will "wow" your friends and relatives, save you time, and make you the master of all you survey. Its extensive set of preferences enables you to change the way you work with text, graphics (mostly drawn objects), palettes, and communications documents. A recorder macro system enables you to capture a set of steps in a small program that you later can playback when you choose, by using a keystroke equivalent you name—a major savings of time. Those seconds mount up! Macros can be assigned to the Shortcuts palette you learned about in chapter 2. Shortcuts also can be single-step commands: Point, click, and voilà.

Below are some of the how-to topics covered in this chapter:

Topic	Page
How to set preferences within ClarisWorks	238
How to create a macro	242
How to assign a macro to the Shortcuts palette	246
How to create a publisher	250
How to create a subscriber	252
How to update your subscriber	252
How to place a QuickTime movie in a document	254
How to play a movie	256
How to create slides	259
How to create a slide show	260
How to create layered slides	261
How to run a slide show	262

Some of System 7's advanced features are supported by ClarisWorks. For example, Publish & Subscribe enables you to create live copy and pastes, so that data can appear in one document and also be updated automatically in its source document. You also can choose to have published or subscribed data objects updated manually at a time of your choosing. QuickTime video movies can be played in ClarisWorks documents. Finally, you can create slide shows in ClarisWorks that rival the creations of presentation programs that cost hundreds of dollars.

Setting Preferences Within ClarisWorks

ClarisWorks enables you to tailor your working environments through the use of the Preferences command on the Edit menu. The Preferences dialog box changes, depending upon which set of preferences you choose from the scrolling list. Your choices are: Text, Graphics, Palettes, and Communications. The Preferences dialog boxes for each of these choices are shown in figures 9.1, 9.2, 9.3, and 9.4, respectively. Text, graphics, and communications preferences were discussed in chapters 3, 6, and 7, respectively. You may want to refer back to those chapters for a fuller explanation of the options available to you.

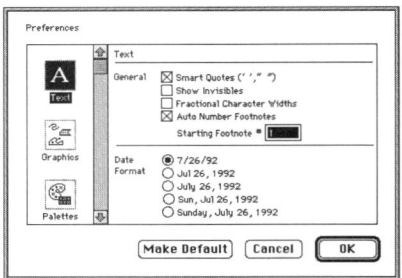

Figure 9.1. *Text preferences.*

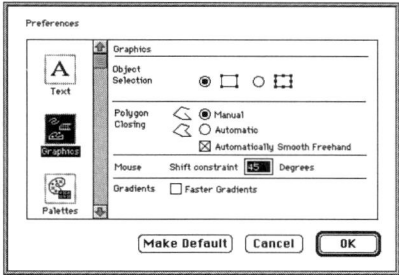

Figure 9.2. *Graphics preferences.*

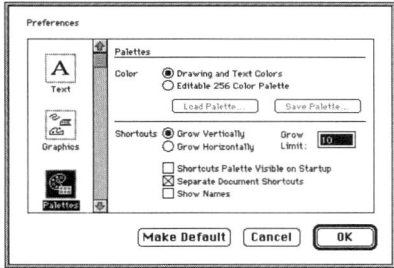

Figure 9.3. *Palettes preferences.*

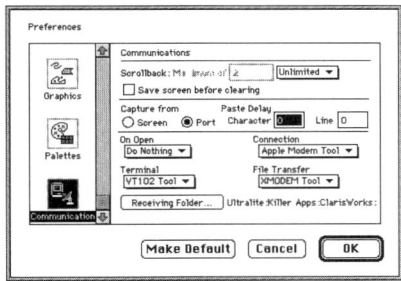

Figure 9.4. *Communications preferences.*

When you set preferences within a given document, those preferences apply to that document only. To have preferences apply to any document, click on the Make Default button in the Preferences dialog box.

Obviously some preferences have no effect on some documents. If you set a communications preference within a word processing document, you won't observe an effect unless you make it a default choice. Then, you'll see that preference take effect in your communications documents.

Using Macros to Automate Repetitive Tasks

Many tasks that you do repetitively can be captured and saved to a macro file that you can play back later. You also can work with the Shortcuts palette to perform commands with your mouse. ClarisWorks enables you to assign a Shortcuts button to a macro with an icon of your choosing and then to initiate your macro when appropriate.

What Is a Macro?

A *macro* is a small program or set of actions that you record, and that you can play at a later time by using a menu command or a keystroke. Essentially, macros automate tasks. If there's a task that you repeat over and over, always the same, it's probably worth recording that task as a macro. ClarisWorks has a tape-recorder macro that watches what you do and writes down each step. You do not need to know anything about programming to use the macro recorder, only how to turn the recorder on and off. (An example of a log-on macro was created in chapter 7, "Communications.")

You record macros by using the Shortcuts submenu found on the File menu, shown in figure 9.5. The macro recorder can record clicks, keystrokes, and menu commands, some click-and-drags, and, if you desire, waits or pauses. When a click-and-drag is recorded, only the starting and ending positions of the drag are recorded. Waits and pauses are a separate step that must be selected by the Macro Waits command. A macro can be recorded as a set of steps to be played back at the maximum possible speed, or in real time at the speed you recorded it.

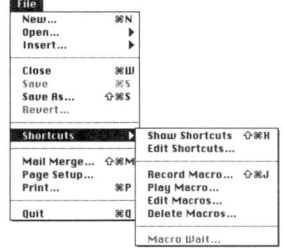

Figure 9.5. *The Shortcuts submenu.*

To play a macro, select the Play Macro command from the Shortcuts submenu on the File menu. The Play Macro dialog box appears, as shown in figure 9.6. Double-click on the macro you want to play, or click once to highlight a macro name, and press the Play button.

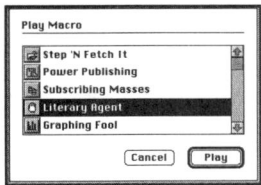

Figure 9.6. *The Play Macro dialog box.*

Keep in mind that macros work only for the situations for which they were created. A macro presupposes that all of the conditions exist that enable its operation. If a macro cannot complete a step, then an error message is posted and the macro is aborted. For this reason, macros are recorded for specific document types, or even for specific documents.

You also can assign your macro to a shortcut icon in the Shortcuts palette. Then that macro is available by clicking on it with your mouse. See "Assigning Macros to the Shortcuts Palette," later in this chapter.

Shortcut
If you have assigned a keystroke to the macro, you do not have to select that macro from the Play Macro dialog box. Just press the keystroke instead.

Recording and Editing a Macro

To create a macro:

1. Select the Record Macro command from the Shortcuts submenu under the File menu (see figure 9.5) or press the Command-Shift-J keystroke. The Record Macro dialog box appears, as shown in figure 9.7.

> **Shortcut**
> Press Command-Shift-J to begin defining a macro. Press Command-Shift-J again to give the Stop Macro command and terminate your recording.

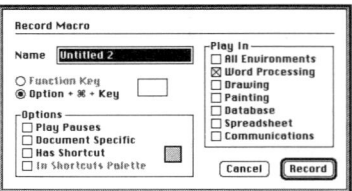

Figure 9.7. *The Record Macro dialog box.*

2. Enter the name of your macro into the Name text box and assign a Function key or a Command-Option key letter in the text box.

3. Select the document types in the Play In section appropriate to your macro.

4. Make additional choices for the attributes of the macro in the Options section:

    ❖ Play Pauses plays back your macros at the speed you record them (real time). This option is particularly useful for communications documents where you are waiting for the host computer to complete an action.

    ❖ Document Specific plays this macro only in active documents.

    ❖ Has Shortcut assigns a button in the Shortcuts palette to the macro.

    ❖ In Shortcuts Palette installs the button into the Shortcuts palette.

    To assign an icon (picture) to the button, click the gray box next to the In Shortcuts Palette checkbox; the icon editor shown in figure 9.8 appears. Use the color picker and the cursor to change the icon's pixels in the Working grid. The Button image appears in the upper-right of the dialog box.

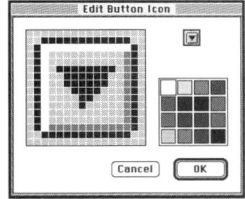

Figure 9.8. *The Edit Button Icon dialog box.*

5. Click the Record button or press the Return or Enter key. A flashing microphone appears in place of the Apple icon in the menu bar, as shown in figure 9.9.

Figure 9.9. *The Record Macro menu bar indicator.*

6. Perform the actions that you want to record.

7. Terminate your recording by selecting the Stop Recording command from the Shortcuts submenu of the File menu, or by giving the Command-Shift-J keystroke.

    Sometimes, you want to end the macro when a dialog box is onscreen. The problem is that the menus are unavailable while the dialog box is onscreen, so you can't select the Stop Recording command. In this case, your only alternative is to use the Command-Shift-J keystroke.

Communications macros often need pauses. Many sequences in communications require a pause for a condition (such as a modem connection) to be established, for a text string to be returned, or for user input (for example, to let the user enter a required text string or action). Create a pause in the Menu Wait dialog box (see figure 9.10) by using the Macro Wait command from the Shortcuts submenu. Pauses can occur in a macro for a timed interval or until at text string is returned.

> **Tip**
> To quickly create a picture icon, copy an icon picture to the Clipboard and paste it into the Edit Button Icon dialog box. You can create a screen capture (press Command-Shift-3), edit it in a ClarisWorks picture document, and copy it to your Clipboard. See chapter 6, "Capturing and Editing a Screen" for details.

> **Note**
> ClarisWorks records mouse clicks, some click-drags (for objects, tools, palettes, and menu commands, but not for window elements), keystrokes, and menu commands. Window actions such as scrolling or dragging objects are not recorded.

> **Tip**
> Always record keystrokes when possible, as they are more accurate than clicks or selecting menu commands. For instance, if a window isn't in quite the same position as when you recorded the macro, your clicks won't fall in the right place.

244   Chapter 9 • Advanced Topics

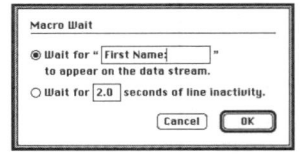

Figure 9.10. *The Macro Wait dialog box.*

To edit a macro, do the following:

Note
You can only record Macro Wait commands in a macro for a communications document.

1. Select the Edit Macros command from the Shortcuts submenu of the file menu. The Edit Macro dialog box appears, as shown in figure 9.11. This dialog box is similar to the Record Macro dialog box shown in figure 9.7.

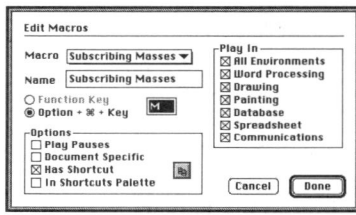

Figure 9.11. *The Edit Macros dialog box.*

2. Select the macro you want to edit from the Macro pop-up menu, and change your keystroke, options, and the type of documents the macro can play in.
3. Press the Done button or the Return key to store your changes.

You are limited in the changes you can make to a pre-existing macro. If you want to change any of the steps of a macro, you will need to re-record it. ClarisWorks 2.0 has no macro editor.

Caution
You cannot undo the deletion of a macro; once it's gone, it's gone forever.

To delete a macro, select the Delete Macros command from the Shortcuts submenu found on the File menu. The Delete Macros dialog box appears. Double-click on the macro name you want to delete, or click on the macro once and press the Done button.

Assigning Macros to the Shortcuts Palette

The Shortcuts palette was described previously in chapter 2, "Some Basics." A shortcut is a single command or action, whereas a macro is a set of commands or actions. If you want to record a single command or action, check the Shortcuts palette to see if one exists and has been or can be installed into the palette. Use the Show Shortcuts command on the Shortcuts submenu of the File menu, or the Command-Shift-X keystroke to display the Shortcuts palette. Apply the keystroke again to use the Hide Shortcuts command to remove the palette. A sample Shortcuts palette for a word processing document is shown in figure 9.12.

Figure 9.12. *A word processing Shortcuts palette.*

Each document type can have its own shortcuts, if you choose that option in the Palettes preferences (see figure 9.3). Unfortunately, you cannot use Balloon Help to determine what a shortcut icon does; nor is the ClarisWorks Help system of use in this regard either. The ClarisWorks User's Guide has an extensive list on pages 8.41 to 8.45. To view the Shortcuts palette in its name rather than picture mode, open the Preferences dialog box (from the Edit menu), select the Palettes section, and click the Show Names checkbox as was described in "Setting Preferences in ClarisWorks" at the beginning of this chapter. Figure 9.13 shows the Shortcuts palette in its name mode. Click once on a shortcut name to initiate the action.

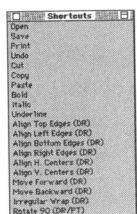

Figure 9.13. *The Shortcuts palette in its name mode.*

Tip: You may want to record a macro that enables you to switch back and forth between displaying the Shortcuts palette as icons and as names.

To assign a macro to the Shortcuts palette:

1. When the Record Macro dialog box is open (shown in figure 9.7), click the Has Shortcut checkbox to create the shortcut, and click the In Shortcut Palette checkbox to add the icon to the palette.

2. If you have finished recording your macro, use the Edit Macro command and the Edit Macro dialog box (shown in figure 9.11) to make the selections in step 1.

You also can use the Edit Shortcuts dialog box shown in figure 9.14 to assign it a purpose and to add or delete a macro shortcut icon to or from the palette. Display this dialog box by selecting the Edit Shortcuts command from the Shortcuts submenu.

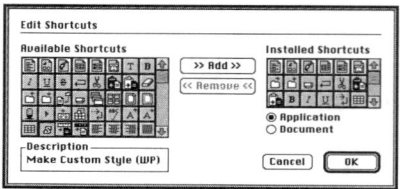

Figure 9.14. *The Edit Shortcuts dialog box.*

Testing Your Macro

There is no better time to test your macro than right after you create it. The conditions are ripe, so to speak. There are any number of reasons that a macro can fail, so it's better to test it immediately. In fact, you should not consider your macro complete until you've seen it run correctly. Since you are intimate (or "at one") with your macro at the time of creation, that is also a good time to vary the conditions under which it is used to see how broadly the action applies.

Macro Ideas

You can create global macros that work in all environments, macros specific to a particular environment, or macros that are specific to a particular purpose. Some suggestions to get you going are:

- Global macros (all environments).
- Keystrokes for commands that have none assigned.
- Tool and environment selection in the Tool panel.
- Combining commands and dialog boxes into sequences.
- Creating and placing frames.
- Page setup and document setup sequences.
- Word Processing macros.
- Glossary entries for phrases and boilerplate.
- Text attributes.
- Header and footer creation.
- Automated finds and replaces.
- Window setup.
- Drawing and Painting.
- Setting up your window.
- Changing tools and setting line and fill attributes.
- Creating objects or painted elements. Remember that only the starting and ending point of a click-drag is recorded. Irregular shapes such as freehand curves are recorded as straight lines.
- Changing painting modes or applying transformations.
- Spreadsheet and database macros.
- Repetitive data entry.
- Formatting internal field or cell data for display.
- Capturing and remembering search, find, and match operations.
- Actions that navigate your spreadsheet or database, taking you to a specific cell, field, or record.
- Automatic charting or report generation for your database or spreadsheet, respectively.
- Communications macros.

Note
The Play Macros command is (surprisingly) one that cries out for a keystroke, but you can't assign one—you can't issue that command when you are recording a macro in ClarisWorks.

- ❖ Automated log-on and log-off procedures (see chapter 7).
- ❖ Navigating to a section of an online service or bulletin board service.
- ❖ Automating a file transfer sequence.

Linking Information With Publish & Subscribe

> **Tip**
> If you find yourself needing a more complete macro or automation environment, check out CE Software's QuicKeys, Infinity Microsystem's Tempo II Plus, or Apple's AppleScript. They provide considerably more tools and capabilities. QuicKeys is the easiest to use; Tempo and AppleScript are procedural scripting (programming) environments, which enable you to include repeat loops and conditional control of scripts.

System 7 contains a feature called *Publish & Subscribe* that enables you to place information in the document of an application, and to retain a link back to the creator document and the creator application. The source document is the *publisher*, and the destination document is the *subscriber*. An intermediate data file, called the *Edition* file, is created first; the Edition file contains the objects you published. You then place the data into a subscriber for viewing. Publish & Subscribe is a two-step process. Figure 9.15 illustrates the concept.

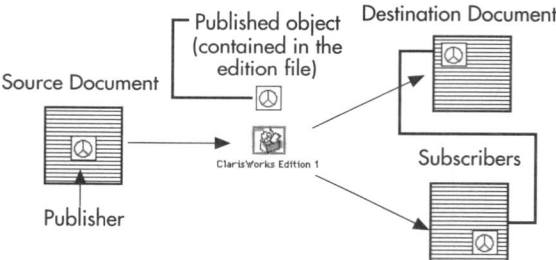

Figure 9.15. *Publish & Subscribe.*

Some people refer to the creator application as the server, and the subscriber's application (or more loosely the subscriber itself) as the client. The client/server naming convention is most often applied to Microsoft's version of Publish & Subscribe for the Microsoft Windows operating system, called Object Linking and Embedding, or OLE.

An edition can contain objects supported by the Clipboard. Published and subscribed objects are denoted by a heavy gray border in both document types, as shown in figure 9.16. This scheme, which some have labeled "live copy and paste," enables the one-to-many relationship of one publisher to multiple subscribers through the edition file. You can use documents with published objects in them in System 6; however, only System 7 has the Edition Manager for updating work or for creating an edition. The Edition Manager is a System 7 toolbox, which at its heart is a database, noting all of the interested parties for each linkage. The Edition Manager ensures that when a published document is updated, the changes are sent to the Edition file, and thence to all subscribers.

Quarter	Sales	Profits
1st	$40.0	$23.0
2nd	$60.0	$29.0
3rd	$75.0	$42.4
4th	$110.0	$66.4

Figure 9.16. *A published or subscribed object with its border showing.*

Two types of Publish & Subscribe are permitted—the so-called hot and cold links. Hot links update automatically whenever the subscriber opens. Cold links require that you command an update whenever you desire it.

You can publish and subscribe to most ClarisWorks documents, with the exception of the painting and communications documents, and the Browse and the Find modes of the database environment. You can even publish and subscribe between two ClarisWorks documents themselves, or even between different parts of the same document.

You are, of course, limited to subscribing to data types that the documents support. Spreadsheet data is saved to tab-delimited tables in the edition file so that it can be subscribed into text, drawing, painting, or other non-spreadsheet documents. Tab-delimited tables opened in a spreadsheet document or a spreadsheet frame return to cell-based formatting.

Few Macintosh users currently apply System 7's Publish & Subscribe feature in their daily work. That's too bad, because the feature cuts down on redundant data, reduces data entry time, and improves accuracy. Publish & Subscribe is pretty close to the top of David Letterman's "Top 10 List of Great System Software Nobody Uses."

How to Publish a Document

The Publish & Subscribe feature is easier to use than it sounds. If you can copy and paste, you can publish and subscribe. All of the Publish & Subscribe commands are on the Publishing submenu of the Edit menu (see figure 9.17).

Note
While Publish & Subscribe is a powerful tool, it is not the be-all and end-all of linked documents. Be wary of creating a complicated, tangled web of publishers, Edition files, and subscribers. As things get more complex, it becomes more difficult to ensure that all the links work correctly.

Chapter 9 • Advanced Topics

Figure 9.17. *The Publishing submenu.*

To create a publisher:

1. Open the document that contains the data object you want to publish and select that object. (Your choices of data types are text, drawn objects, and spreadsheet cells or charts.)

2. Select the Create Publisher command from the Publishing submenu of the Edit menu. The Publisher dialog box appears, as shown in figure 9.18.

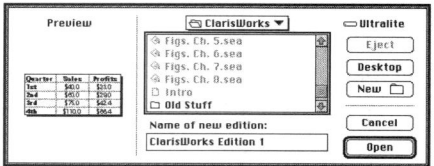

Figure 9.18. *The Publisher dialog box.*

3. Name your edition file, or accept ClarisWorks's default file name, "ClarisWorks Edition _." The icon is shown in figure 9.15. (Think about giving your Edition a relevant name—a named file is much easier to manage.)

4. Navigate the file structure to place your edition file in the location you want.

5. Press the Publish button to create the edition file. Notice that the published object is surrounded by a heavy gray border, indicating that an Edition has been defined for this object.

After you publish an object, you work with the publisher document normally. Make any changes you want to any part of the document, even the published object itself. Changes to the published object modify the Edition file the next time that file is updated (unless the changes are made while working in System 6.) In a spreadsheet, deleted cells are left blank in the edition—they are not removed from the edition.

You define whether you want a hot link or a cold link by first selecting the object, and then choosing the Publisher Options command from the Publisher submenu. The Publisher Options dialog box (shown in figure 9.19) contains all of the controls for determining when an edition gets updated.

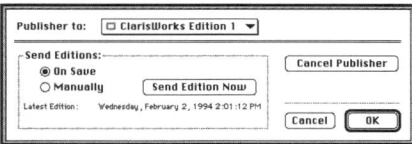

Figure 9.19. *The Publisher Options dialog box.*

The default choice is to have your edition file update whenever you save the file. You do not have to open the Publisher Options dialog box to have this happen automatically. If you only want to save changes to the edition file when you choose, click on the Manually radio button. You update the edition whenever you click on the Send Edition Now button. Your most recent update date and time is shown below the Send Edition Now button.

Cancel a publisher by first selecting the published object, then opening the Publishing Options dialog box shown in figure 9.19, and finally clicking the Cancel Publisher button. When you cancel a publisher, you delete the link to the edition file. Only the link is severed—the edition file is intact, as are all of the links from the edition file to any subscribers. When you cancel a publisher, you no longer have the capablity to update the edition file. The gray border surrounding the published object disappears. When canceling a selection of multiple publishers, the link of the initially published object is broken first. This can be confusing, so it's better to cancel publishers one at a time.

How to Subscribe to a Document

Subscribing to an edition file places the object contained in the edition file into the subscriber at the position of your insertion point. The object is surrounded by the same dark gray border you saw for it in the publisher.

Note

Canceling a publisher is final when you save the document. Up to that point you can either close the document without saving changes or use the Revert command on the File menu to re-establish the link by reverting to the last saved copy.

To delete an edition, drag its file to the Trash in the Finder.

Tip

If you don't want to see the borders for a publisher or a subscriber, turn them off by using the Hide Borders command on the Publishing submenu. Display them by selecting the Show Borders command.

To create a subscriber:

1. Open your destination document, and place your insertion point where you want the subscriber object to appear. You can select text, spreadsheet cells, or drawn frames or documents. Also, you can select any area of a database layout.

2. Select the Subscribe To command from the Publishing submenu of the Edit menu. The Subscriber dialog box appears, as shown in figure 9.20. This dialog box is functionally identical to the Publisher dialog box discussed previously.

Figure 9.20. *The Subscriber dialog box.*

3. Find and select the edition file that contains the object to which you want to subscribe. A Preview of the object appears in the Subscribe To dialog box.

4. Click on the Subscribe button to create the subscriber, or double-click on the edition file name. The subscriber object appears at your location. If you haven't selected a location, the subscriber object appears in the center of the page.

In System 7, subscribers can change automatically when your edition file changes, or when you select the option to have updates be made manually. In System 6 subscribers do not change; subscribed objects can only be handled as normal objects (that is, moved, resized, copied, or deleted). You cannot edit part of a subscriber within the document in which it appears, unless you set that capability as an option.

If you want your subscriber to be updated automatically, you do not need to set any additional options. To change a subscriber so that it is manually updated at a time of your choosing, select the subscriber, choose the Subscriber Options command from the Publishing submenu of the Edit menu, and make some changes to the Subscriber Options dialog box, shown in figure 9.21. The Subscriber Options command replaces the Publisher Options command on the Publishing submenu when a subscriber is selected.

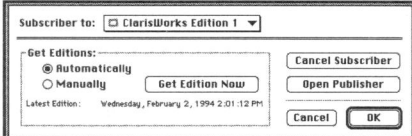

Figure 9.21. *The Subscriber Options dialog box.*

Click on the Manually radio button in the Subscriber Options dialog box to change the subscriber to a cold link, and click on the Get Edition Now button to update the subscriber when you choose. Note the date and the time of the last update below the Get Edition Now button. You can sever the link to the Edition file by clicking on the Cancel Subscriber button, and view the original data by clicking the Open Publisher button. If you choose to edit a subscriber (change the object to data you can work with), click the Allow Modification checkbox.

> **Note**
> Canceling a subscriber becomes final when you save the document. Up to that point you can close the document without saving changes or use the Revert command on the File menu to re-establish the link by reverting to the last saved copy.

Using QuickTime Movies in Your Documents

With Apple's QuickTime extension, a part of System 7 software, you can put moving pictures inside your ClarisWorks documents. QuickTime stores video as a set of frames inside a document called a Movie file. Movies are objects that you can cut, copy, and paste into your ClarisWorks documents. You also can move and resize movies, as you would any object. Movies resemble pictures in your ClarisWorks document, but have additional controls to allow you to play their contents (see figure 9.22).

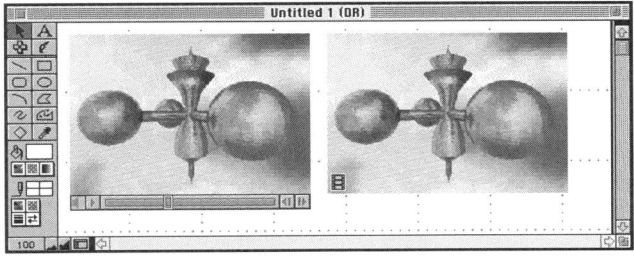

Figure 9.22. *A movie with and without its controls showing.*

> **Note**
> You can obtain QuickTime from most online services or user group BBSes. If you want to purchase QuickTime with documentation, Apple sells the QuickTime Starter Kit. The current version is 1.6, although version 2.0 is supposed to arrive soon.

Not all versions of system software ship with the QuickTime extension; only System 6.0.7 and later versions are compatible with it. If you are running ClarisWorks, then your system software is compatible. To see if your Macintosh has QuickTime installed, check the Extensions folder, found in the System folder. You should see the icon for QuickTime; it will also appear when you start up your Macintosh, when icons for other extensions and control panels appear. Without QuickTime installed, ClarisWorks cannot read the Movie file.

When you see the picture for a movie object, what you are seeing is called the *movie poster*. The poster is a predefined frame from the movie (often the first frame); it helps you determine the contents of the movie. The actual QuickTime movie is stored in the original file; what you open, insert, or paste into ClarisWorks is the poster and a pointer to the movie file. If your movie file is stored on another disk, that disk must be mounted and available or the movie won't play.

There are three ways to add a movie to a ClarisWorks document: (1) by importing (opening) the movie as a drawing document; (2) by inserting the movie into a document; and (3) pasting the movie from the Clipboard into a document. When you view the movie in a painting document or in a frame, you see a static poster. In a database document, movies can be played in the Layout mode only. In the Browse mode, you also see only a poster. Since the Browse mode is where data is manipulated, and a QuickTime movie is data, this limitation is a design defect that probably will be corrected in the next version of ClarisWorks.

You can change various aspects of a movie's playback. These options (for a selected movie) are contained in the Movie Info dialog box shown in figure 9.23. Open this dialog box by using the Movie Info command from the Options menu. A movie pasted into a text frame or a word processing document as an inline character cannot be modified.

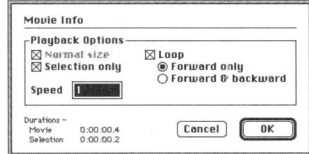

Figure 9.23. *The Movie Info dialog box.*

You can make the following changes to a movie:

- ❖ Normal Size. Normal size changes a resized movie so that it plays back at its original size. If a movie was not resized, this option is checked, but dimmed.
- ❖ Selection Only. You can select part of a movie, and this option enables you to play back only that part. See "Playing Movies" to learn how to select a part of a movie.
- ❖ Speed. Enter 1 to play back at normal speed. From 0 to 1 plays back at slower speeds, and greater than 1 at faster speeds in the forward direction. To play your movie in reverse, use negative numbers.
- ❖ Loop. The movie plays continuously. Forward Only starts the movie over from the beginning when its end is reached. Forward & Backward plays to the end of the movie, and then plays in reverse to the beginning.

Creating a QuickTime Movie

Creating QuickTime movies falls outside of the scope of this book. However, creating QuickTime movies isn't difficult, and it needn't be particularly expensive. Two pieces of hardware are required: an external source and a digitizing board. External video sources can be raw videotape, a video camera, or a television.

Note
The Durations section tells you the length of the movie, and identifies the length of your particular movie selection. Times are described as hours:minutes:seconds.tenths of a second.

> **Note**
> QuickTime is an immature technology with great promise. Future Apple PowerPC Macintoshes should have the necessary horsepower to increase picture sizes and frame rates to make the technology more useful.

Digitizing boards or video capture boards come with software that enables you to record QuickTime movies by using VCR-like controls, and to select the kind of compression-decompression routines you want to use. Apple Video and Compact Video are your best choices. Compact Video gives smaller file sizes and smoother playback. Each compression method takes a long time to save to disk.

Videotape and TV signals are normally recorded in NTSC (National Television Society Committee) format, one that is not read directly by your Macintosh. Those signals require translation to an RGB (red, green, blue) format that can be stored as a Macintosh file format using a converter device. Video capture is often in RGB format, and requires only a camera and video capture board for direct video recording. One video capture board, SuperMac Technology's VideoSpigot digitizing board is both low-cost and high-quality.

To edit video files, consider purchasing Adobe Systems's Premiere or DiVA Corporation's VideoShop. Premiere has become something of a standard, and is highly recommended. You also may want to purchase Adobe Press's excellent book on Abode Premiere from its classroom-in-a-book series, published by Hayden Books.

Playing Movies

Working with a movie is similar to using a tape recorder or a videocassette recorder. The play, pause, fast forward, and rewind buttons in the Play bar control will be familiar to you. View the play bar shown in figure 9.24 by clicking on the movie control badge.

Figure 9.24. *A movie play bar.*

The elements of the play bar are:

❖ The volume control. Click to open and drag the volume slider, up for louder, down for quieter, as shown in figure 9.25

Figure 9.25. *The volume control.*

- ❖ The Start/Stop button. Click once to play the movie, and once again to stop it.
- ❖ Forward/Reverse slider. Shows the current position of your movie frame. Click and drag to a position where you want your playback to begin for fast forward or fast reverse.
- ❖ The Step Forward/Step Backward control. The Step Forward/Step Backward controls are the equivalent of a frame stepper. These controls move the movie one frame at a time in either direction, one frame for each mouse click.

You can change the rate of speed at which a movie plays by holding the Control key, clicking on a step button, and then moving the slider in the resulting speed bar, as shown in figure 9.26.

Figure 9.26. *A speed bar showing as part of the play bar.*

To play back a movie, click on the movie badge to display the play bar, then click on the Start button. Alternately, double-click on the movie. (This method even works for movies which have been pasted or inserted into a text frame, or inserted as an inline character in a word processing document.)

To play back part of a movie:

1. Move to the frame at which you want the selection to begin. Use the Start button, the slider, or the step buttons to position the movie, then click on the Stop button.
2. Hold down the Shift key, then use the step buttons, the slider, or the play button to advance the movie to the last frame of your selection. Your selection is indicated by a black bar in the play bar, as shown in figure 9.27.

Shortcut
Use the following keystrokes to control the playback for a QuickTime movie: the Return or the Spacebar key for the Start/Stop button, the Period key to stop playback, the Up Arrow key for increased volume, the Down Arrow key for decreased volume, the Right Arrow key to step forward, and the Left Arrow key to step backward.

Figure 9.27. *A selected part of a movie.*

3. Extend a selection by holding down the Shift key and dragging the slider, by clicking on the step buttons, or by clicking the play button.

4. Deselect the movie selection by clicking once on the play bar without holding down the Shift key.

You can delete, cut, copy, and paste a movie selection. The Delete key or the Cut command remove all selected frames from the movie. The Copy command places the selection in the Clipboard. When you paste a movie into a document, it becomes a movie object containing only the selected frames. You also can paste your selection permanently into the Scrapbook. You can add your selection to another movie by pasting it into the selected movie. It adds your selection to the movie appearing after the active frame.

QuickTime is memory-, processor-, and hard disk-intensive. Consider using a RAM disk for improved performance, turning off virtual memory, and using a faster Macintosh. Consult your Macintosh documentation for details on these procedures.

Setting Up a Slide Show

One of the nicest features of ClarisWorks is its slide-presentation capability. Presentation software is usually an expensive category of software. ClarisWorks shows the pages of a document as your slides, one after the other on your main computer monitor. For any purpose for which you use visual aids, you now can use ClarisWorks, with quite effective results.

Consider using a slide presentation for:

❖ A speech, a talk, or a lesson.

❖ A self-running demo for a show or store.

❖ A presentation of a product or service.

Any document that supports multiple pages can be used for a presentation. Communications documents are the only type that can't be used. Drawing documents are perhaps the best because they support master pages, as described in chapter 8. With a master page, you only need to create the new elements of each slide. In drawing documents, you can also use spreadsheet frames and charts, text frames, and painting frames.

Ordering and Slides

The number of pages in a document determines the maximum number of slides in your presentation. Since each page is a slide, it's best to work in the Page View mode when creating slides so that you can see what each slide looks like. Word processing documents automatically create pages as you add content, and you can specify where each page ends by using a page break. Use the Insert Break command in the word processor for this purpose.

Drawing, painting, and spreadsheet documents require that you specify the number of pages from within the Document dialog box (Format menu). Insert a page break into a spreadsheet by using the Add Page Break command after the active cell. In a database document, your number of records selected and the layout determine the number of pages you see.

Do not worry about the order of your pages; you can change the order they are viewed in from within the Show Slide dialog box. You also can add and delete pages later, should you choose.

Master pages offer a particular advantage because you can store repeating elements such as borders, background colors, logos, and titles that appear on every slide. If you use a layered presentation, adding one bullet at a time to a slide, then master pages are particularly effective. This advanced presentation technique is described in the next section.

You set up the slide show in the Slide Show dialog box, as shown in figure 9.28. The default order is the page order, but you can click and drag each page to wherever you like in the Order area of the Slide Show dialog box.

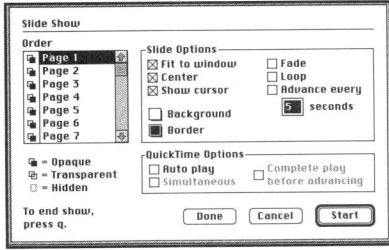

Figure 9.28. *The Slide Show dialog box.*

Display Options

Slides can be opaque (the default), transparent, or hidden. Opaque slides show one page only, transparent slides are a slide layer, and hidden slides are omitted from the slide order. To switch a slide type, click on the page, then on the icon for the page type.

The Slide Options available to you are:

- ❖ Fit to Window. The slide is resized to your monitor, but the aspect ratio is preserved.
- ❖ Center. The slide appears in the middle of your display. When deselected, the slide appears at the top left of your display.
- ❖ Show Cursor. With the cursor showing, you can point to places onscreen.

  The Fit to Window, Center, and Show Cursor options are on by default.
- ❖ Fade. As one slide disappears, it is replaced by the next.
- ❖ Loop. The last slide in a sequence goes next to the first slide until you halt the show.
- ❖ Advance Every…Seconds. This auto-advance option creates a self-running demo. Slides advance every number of seconds entered into the Advance text box. Use this option with the looping option to create a self-running demo.

With QuickTime installed in your system, you can choose to include QuickTime movies in your slides. To play a movie on your slide, you need to set some of the QuickTime Options in the Slide Show dialog box. Your three options are:

- ❖ Auto Play. This option plays any QuickTime movie when the slide appears, and plays more than one movie on a slide in the order of the object layers from back to front.
- ❖ Simultaneously. All movies on a slide play regardless of their layer order.
- ❖ Complete Play Before Advancing. All movies on a slide must finish playing, even if they take longer than the interval set in the auto-advance feature.

You pause a movie during playback in a slide show by holding down the Command or the Option key and clicking anywhere onscreen. When you restart a movie, it continues playing. Movie selections cannot be played, only an entire movie. You can, however, create a movie by using a selection of another movie.

Slide Layers

Layering slides gets your audience to concentrate on your points, one at a time. This is a very professional effect. You layer slides by making the first layer or slide opaque, and all subsequent slide layers transparent. Only colored objects like text will appear on that layer. Use no background on transparent layers so that you can see the opaque slide as background. Or, if you are using master pages, the same elements of the background or opaque slide appear superimposed on all layers.

To layer slides:

1. Make the first slide of a layered set opaque, if it isn't already so, by clicking on the opaque icon and then clicking on the page number. Refer to figure 9.29 to see how a layered set looks in the slide Order.
2. Move the next slide in the layered effect below the opaque slide by clicking on the transparent icon first, then on the page number.
3. Make that second slide transparent by clicking the transparent icon, and then its page number.
4. Continue adding transparent slides below each layer until you have completely positioned the set.

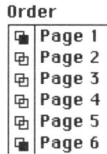

Figure 9.29. *A layered set of slides.*

To omit a slide, click on the Blank or the Hidden icon, then on the page number for that slide.

Omitted slides are ignored in any layered effect, just as they are in your slide show.

Running a Slide Show

To run your slide show:

1. Select Slide Show from the View menu to open the Slide Show dialog box (figure 9.28).
2. Select your options, if necessary, and click the Start button.
3. Alternately, to start a slide show with your current settings: hold down the Option key while selecting the Slide Show command.
4. To work with your slide show, refer to the actions in Table 9.1.
5. Stop the slide show by pressing the Q key, or the Clear or the Escape keys, or the Command-period keystroke.

   The Slide Show dialog box appears again. If you used the Option key to bypass that dialog box you are returned to your document, and step 5 is unnecessary.
6. Click the Done button to end the show.

Tip
Holding down the Option key as you choose a menu command is a standard Macintosh trick for initiating the command and bypassing its associated dialog box.

Table 9.1. *Slide Show controls.*

To...	Do This...
Go to the next slide	Click the mouse, or press the Right or the Down Arrow, the Page Down, the Return, or the Tab keys or the Space bar.
Go to the previous slide	Press the Left or the Up Arrows, the Page Up, keys or the Shift-Return, the Shift-Tab, or the Shift-Spacebar keystrokes.
Go to the end of the show	Press the End key.

To...	Do This...
Go to the beginning of the show	Press the Home key.
Play a movie	Click on it. Movies can be played automatically as an option.
Pause or resume a move	Command-click or Option-click on that movie.
Stop playing the movie	Click on the movie a second time.
End the Slide show.	Press the Q key, the Command-Period keystroke, or the Clear or Escape key.

Summary

In this chapter you have learned how to set preferences for text, graphics (mostly drawn objects), palettes, and communications documents. You also learned how to use the recorder macro system to capture a set of steps into a small program for later playback. This is great for automating repetitive actions. You saw how macros were assigned to the Shortcuts palette.

Some advanced features of System 7 were described in this chapter. With the Publish & Subscribe feature you linked data in one document to a copy in another so that the copies could be updated automatically from the source document. You also saw how to manually update published and subscribed objects. Additionally, you placed QuickTime video movies in your ClarisWorks documents. Finally, you created, set up, and ran a slide show within ClarisWorks.

Chapter 9, as well as all of the previous chapters, illustrates the richness of ClarisWorks. There is almost no end to the types of projects you can undertake in ClarisWorks, and it should serve you well for a long time to come—even long after you have advanced from novice, to intermediate, to power user, and beyond. Working with ClarisWorks and its integrated environments offers you a view of what computing will become in the future.

Index

A

absolute cell references, 98
Add Page Break command (Options menu), 122
Align Objects command (Arrange menu), 181
alignment, 65-66
    cells, 95
    objects (drawn), 181
Alignment command (Format menu), 95
Apple Modem Tool, 204-205
applications, copying graphics between, 72-73
Apply Ruler command (Edit menu), 67
    Arc tool, 173

area charts, 113-114
Arrange menu commands
    Align Objects, 181
    Flip Horizontal, 182
    Flip Vertical, 182
    Group, 181
    Lock, 182
Arrows tool, 186
assigning macros to Shortcuts palette, 245-246
Autogrid, 180
automating communications sessions, 209-212
axes (charts), 117-118
    tick marks, 113

Index

B

Backspace key, 47
Balloon Help, 41-42
bar charts, 113-114
BBSs (bulletin board systems), 199
   connections, 201-202
   disconnecting, 203
Bezigon tool, 174
bezigons, 178-179
blank space in databases, 161
body in database layout, 155
bold text, 57
Bookmarks, 146
borders
   spreadsheets, 94-95
      frames, 80
   tables, 79-81
Borders command (Format menu), 94
bps (bits per second), 199
Browse mode (databases), 129-130
browsing databases, 141-143
Brush tool, 190
bulleted lists, 63-64
bulletin board systems, *see* BBSs
business and financial functions, 101-102

C

Calculate menu commands
   Delete Cells, 110
   Insert Cells, 109
   Sort, 110
calculation fields (databases), 134-136, 140
calculations, 100
capturing screens, 195
cell references, 98
cells (spreadsheets)
   alignment, 95
   contents, 89
      editing, 88-89
      sorting, 110-111
   deleting, 110
   formatting, 93-94, 108
   inserting, 109
   ranges, *see* ranges
center tab, 62
character formatting
   fonts, 56-57
   WP documents, 55-56
characters, invisible, 55
chart types, 113-116
charts, 112
   axes, 113, 117-118
   creating, 112-113
   data ranges, 119
   series, 118-119
   titles, 117
Check Document command (Edit menu), 49
check register, 119-120
checking spelling, *see* Spelling Checker
ClarisImpact drawing software, 3
Clear command (Edit menu), 176
Clipboard, 25-26
Close Connection command (Session menu), 203
closing files, 24-25

CM (communications) documents, 5
  creating, 200-203
  frames, 220
color (paintings), 188, 193-195
column breaks, 76
Column Width command (Format menu), 92
columnar report layout, 152
columns, 75-76
  databases, 160
  deleting, 109
  inserting, 109
  linking text frames, 222
  resizing, 75
  tables, 77-79
  transposing, 111-112
Columns command (Format menu), 75
commands
  Arrange menu
    Align Objects, 181
    Flip Horizontal, 182
    Flip Vertical, 182
    Group, 181
    Lock, 182
  Calculate menu
    Delete Cells, 110
    Insert Cells, 109
    Sort, 110
  Edit menu
    Apply Ruler, 67
    Check Document, 49
    Clear, 176
    Copy, 25
    Copy Format, 108
    Cut, 25
    Fill Down, 98
    Fill Right, 98
    Find/Change, 53
    Insert #, 83
    Insert Date, 83
    Insert Time, 83
    Install Dictionaries, 49
    Paste, 26
    Paste Function, 100
    Preferences, 65
    Reshape, 178
    Show Clipboard, 26
    Undo, 47
  File menu
    Mail Merge, 230
    New, 21
    Open, 20, 24
    Page Setup, 90
    Print, 38
    Save, 24
    Save As, 22, 24
  Format menu
    Alignment, 95
    Borders, 94
    Column Width, 92
    Columns, 75
    Copy Ruler, 67
    Document, 67
    Insert Break, 76
    Insert Footer, 83
    Insert Footnote, 68
    Insert Header, 83
    Number, 96
    Paragraph, 60
    Resolution & Depth, 188
    Row Height, 92
    Rulers, 66, 179
  Layout menu
    Find, 130, 145
    Insert Field, 158
    Layout, 150
    New Layout, 150
    Tab Order, 143

Index

Options menu
  Add Page Break, 122
  Display, 106
  Edit Master Page, 226
  Frame Links, 223
  Make Chart, 112
  Object Size, 36
  Painting Mode, 188
  Print Range, 121
  Protect Cells, 107
  Scale Frame, 36
Organize menu
  Go To Record, 142
  Sort Records, 148
Outline menu (New Topic command), 70
Session menu (Close Connection command), 203
Settings menu
  Connection, 202
  Phone Book, 209
Shortcuts menu
  Edit Macros, 244
  Record Macro, 242
Style menu (Define Styles command), 58
Transformation menu, 193-194
View menu
  Show Tools, 32
  Stack Windows, 28
  Tile Windows, 28
communications, 197-200
  Apple Modem Tool, 204, 205
  downloading files, 212-214
  macros, 243
  preferences, 203-206
  receiving calls, 208-209
  settings, 203-206
  terminal emulation, 216-217
  uploading files, 212-214
  see also modems

communications (CM) documents, *see* **CM (communications) documents**
communications environment, 11
communications sessions
  automating, 209-212
  capturing text, 207-208
composing pages, 74-83
compound documents, 12, 220-227
Connection command (Settings menu), 202
connections
  BBSs, 201-202
  null-modem, 214-215
  online services, 201-202
  phone book, 210
Copy command (Edit menu), 25
Copy Format commands (Edit menu), 108
Copy Ruler command (Format menu), 67
copying, 25-26
  cell formatting, 108
  formulas, 98
    results, 108
  graphics, 72-73
  Ruler, 67
  spreadsheet data, 108-109
  text in WP documents, 47
correcting spelling (Spelling Checker), 49
Currency format (spreadsheets), 96
custom installation, 15
customizing Ruler, 66
Cut command (Edit menu), 25
cutting, 25-26
  spreadsheet data, 108-109
  text in WP documents, 47

Index

D

data entry, 88-89
  databases, 136-139, 143-144
data ranges (charts), 119
databases, 8, 125-132
  Browse mode, 129-130
  browsing, 141-143
  columns, 160
  data entry, 136-139, 143-144
  fields, 128
    defining, 132-140
    deleting, 140
    inserting, 132-133, 139
    names, 139
  Find mode, 130-131
  formatting, 128
  Layout mode, 129
  layouts, 149-161
    blank space, 161
    body, 155
    columnar reports, 152
    columns, 160
    creating, 150-155
    deleting, 150-155
    fields, 157-160
    footers, 156
    grand summary, 156
    header, 155
    label layout, 153
    resizing parts, 157
    subsummary, 155
  Page View mode, 131-132
  query by example, 130
  records, 127-128
    duplicating, 144
    inserting, 144
    moving between, 141
    searches, 144-148
    viewing as list, 141
  sorting, 148-149
  tab order, 143
  views, 128-132
date and time functions, 102
date format, 97
dates, 83
date fields (databases), 135
DB (databases) documents, 5
  frames, 220
decimal tab, 62
default fonts, 59-60, 94
Define Styles command (Style menu), 58
defining
  styles, 58-59
  fields (databases), 128, 132-140
Delete Cells commands (Calculate menu), 110
Delete key, 47
deleting
  cells, 110
  columns, 109
  fields (databases), 140
  frames, 176
  layouts (databases), 150-155
  macros, 244
  objects (drawn), 176
  ranges, 110
  rows, 109
  tabs, 63
  text frames, 224
deselecting
  frames, 176
  objects (drawn), 176
  paintings, 191
dialog boxes
  Find/Change, 53
  Rulers, 66
  Save As, 22
  WordFinder, 53

Index

dictionaries (Spelling Checker), 48-49
  adding words, 51
  removing words, 51
  User dictionary, 50
Display command (Options menu), 106
displaying
  columns/rows in tables, 78
  slides, 260-261
  spreadsheets, 106
division, 99-100
Document command (Format menu), 67
document formatting, 67
  WP documents, 55-56
documents
  CM (communications), 5
  compound documents, 12
  DB (databases), 5
  DR (drawing), 5
  graphics, copying between, 72-73
  inserting in documents, 227-229
  PT (painting), 5
  publishing, 249-251
  SS (spreadsheet), 5
  subscribing to, 251-253
  untitled, 22
  WP (word processing), 5, 44-45
  see also individual document listings (e.g. WP documents)
downloading files, 212-214
DR (drawing) documents, 5, 166, 168
  adding pages, 187
  frames, 220
  multipage spreads, 187

drawing environment, 9, 168-186
Drawing Tools, 171-175
drawn objects, see objects (drawn)
duplicating
  objects, 175
  records (databases), 144

E

Easy installation, 14
Edit Macros command (Shortcuts menu), 244
Edit Master Page command (Options menu), 226
Edit menu commands
  Apply Ruler, 67
  Check Document, 49
  Clear, 176
  Copy, 25
  Copy Format, 108
  Cut, 25
  Fill Down, 98
  Fill Right, 98
  Find/Change, 53
  Insert #, 83
  Insert Date, 83
  Insert Time, 83
  Install Dictionaries, 49
  Paste, 26
  Paste Function, 100
  Preferences, 65
  Reshape, 178
  Show Clipboard, 26
  Undo, 47
editing
  cell contents (spreadsheets), 88-89
  macros, 242-244
  objects in frames, 221

Index

paintings, 191-193
WP documents, 47
entering data, *see* **data entry**
entities (object-oriented graphics), 167
envelopes, 231-236
environment tools, 171
environments, 5-12
   communications, 11
   databases, 8
   drawing, 9
   painting, 10
   spreadsheet, 6, 7
   word processing, 6
Eraser tool, 191
errors in formulas, 104-105
exporting database data, 161-163
extensions, turning off, 13
Eyedropper tool, 174

F

faxes, 37
fields (databases), 128
   calculation fields, 134-136, 140
   dates, 135
   defining, 128, 132-140
   deleting, 140
      from layout, 157-160
   inserting, 132-133, 139
   names, 139
   numbers, 135
   summary fields, 134-136
   text fields, 135, 158
   time, 135
File menu commands
   Mail Merge, 230
   New, 21
   Open, 20, 24
   Page Setup, 90
   Print, 38
   Save, 24
   Save As, 22, 24
FileMaker Pro database software, 3
files
   closing, 24-25
   creating, 20-22
   frames, 35
   importing, 227-229
   opening, 24-25
   saving, 22-24
   viewing multiple, 28
Fill Color tool, 184
Fill Down command (Edit menu), 98
Fill Indicator tool, 175, 183
Fill palette, 184
Fill Palettes tool, 175
Fill Right command (Edit menu), 98
Fill tools, 183, 185
Find command (Layout menu), 130, 145
Find mode (databases), 130-131
Find/Change command (Edit menu), 53
Find/Change dialog box, 53
Fixed format (spreadsheets), 96
Flip Horizontal command (Arrange menu), 182
Flip Vertical command (Arrange menu), 182
fonts, 56-57
   default, 59-60
   spreadsheets, 93-94

Index

footers, 82-83, 156
footnotes, 67-69
Format menu commands
    Alignment, 95
    Borders, 94
    Column Width, 92
    Columns, 75
    Copy Ruler, 67
    Document, 67
    Insert Break, 76
    Insert Footer, 83
    Insert Footnote, 68
    Insert Header, 83
    Number, 96
    Paragraph, 60
    Resolution & Depth, 188
    Row Height, 92
    Rulers, 66, 179
formats
    copying, 108
    mailing labels, 233-234
    outlines, 71
formatting
    character formatting, 55-57
    databases, 128
    document formatting, 55-56, 67
    paragraph formatting, 55-56, 60-62
    spreadsheets, 93-97
    SS documents, 90-97
    WP documents, 55-56, 60-62
formulas (spreadsheets), 97-107
    copying, 98
        results, 108
    errors, 104-105
    functions, 100-101
    totalling ranges, 98-99
    variables, 106

Frame Links command (Options menu), 223
frames, 35-37, 75
    compound documents, 220-227
    creating in open files, 35
    databases, 220
    deleting, 176
    deselecting, 176
    editing objects, 221
    graphics frames, 73-74, 224-225
    linking, 226
    moving, 35, 176
    objects, 221
    resizing, 177, 222
    scaling, 36
    spreadsheets
        borders, 80
        creating, 87
        creating tables, 76
        frames, 225-226
        text entry, 81-82
    text frames, 45-46, 221-222
Freehand tool, 174
functions
    business and financial, 101-102
    date and time, 102
    information, 102
    inserting in formulas, 100-101
    logical, 102-103
    numeric, 103
    statistical, 103
    text, 103
    trigonometric, 104

G

General format (spreadsheets), 96
Go To Record command (Organize menu), 142
Gradient palette, 184
gradients (paintings), 193-195
grand summary (database layout), 156
graphics, 72-74
    copying, 72-73
    frames, 73-74, 224-225
    logos, 186
    object-oriented graphics, 166
Graphics Grid, 180
grids, 180
Group command (Arrange menu), 181
grouping objects (drawn), 181

H

handshaking (modems), 199
hard disks, 13, 15
headers, 82-83
    database layout, 155
headings (tables), 78-79
Help, 39-42
high-low charts, 115
horizontal bar chart, 114

I

image resolution (paintings), 188
importing
    database data, 161-163
    files, 227-229
indents, 61-62
information functions, 102
Insert # command (Edit menu), 83
Insert Break command (Format menu), 76
Insert Cells command (Calculate menu), 109
Insert Date command (Edit menu), 83
Insert Field command (Layout menu), 158
Insert Footer command (Format menu), 83
Insert Footnote command (Format menu), 68
Insert Header command (Format menu), 83
Insert Time command (Edit menu), 83
inserting
    cells, 109
    columns, 109
    documents in documents, 227-229
    fields (databases), 132-133, 139
    footnotes, 68
    functions in formulas, 100-101
    pages in DR documents, 187
    ranges, 109
    records in databases, 144
    rows, 109
Install Dictionaries command (Edit menu), 49
installation, 13-17
    custom, 15
    dictionaries (Spelling Checker), 49
    Easy installation, 14
    master disks, 14
    on hard disk, 15
    software registration, 16

Index

integrated software, 2-5
invisible characters, 55
italic text, 57

J–K

keyboard
    Backspace key, 47
    Delete key, 47
    navigating spreadsheets, 90

L

label layout (databases), 153
labels
    mailing labels, 233-235
    outline topics, 71
laptop computers, 3
Lasso tool, 189
layers
    objects, 170
    slides, 261-262
Layout command (Layout menu), 150
Layout menu commands
    Find, 130, 145
    Insert Field, 158
    Layout, 150
    New Layout, 150
    Tab Order, 143
Layout mode (databases), 129
layouts (databases), 149-161
    blank space, 161
    body, 155
    columnar reports, 152
    columns, 160
    creating, 150-155
    deleting, 150-155
    fields, 157-160
    footers, 156
    grand summary, 156
    header, 155
    label layout, 153
    parts creation, 156
    resizing parts, 157
    subsummary, 155
left tab, 62
line charts, 114
Line tool, 172
line tools, 185-186
lines
    spreadsheets, 94-95
    tables, 79-81
linking
    frames, 226
    text frames, 222-224
listing synonyms (thesaurus), 52
Lock command (Arrange menu), 182
locking objects (drawn), 182
logging on/off, 200
logical functions, 102, 103
logos, 186

M

MacDraw Pro painting software, 3
macros, 240-248
    assigning to Shortcuts palette, 245-246
    deleting, 244
    editing, 242-244
    logons, 211-212
    recording, 242-244
    testing, 246
MacWrite Pro word processing software, 3
Magic Wand tool, 190
Mail Merge, 230-233
    selective merges, 235

Index

Mail Merge command (File menu), 230
mailing labels, 233-235
Make Chart command (Options menu), 112
margins, 60-61
   indents, 61, 62
   SS documents, 90-91
   text frames, 221
master disks (installation), 14
master pages, 226-227
memory, 3
menus, 6
minimizing
   palettes, 185
   Shortcuts palette, 34
modems, 198
   Apple Modem Tool, 204-205
   bps (bits per second), 199
   handshaking, 199
   receiving calls, 208-209
modifying
   bezigons, 178-179
   Shortcuts palette, 34
   styles, 59
moving, 25-26
   frames, 35, 176
   objects (drawn), 176
   paintings, 192
   text in WP documents, 46-47
multiplication, 99-100

N

names of fields (databases), 139
navigating
   screen, 26-37
   spreadsheets, 89-90

New command (File menu), 21
New Layout command (Layout menu), 150
New Topic command (Outline menu), 70
newsletters, 222-224
nudging objects, 177
null-modem connections, 214-215
Number command (Format menu), 96
numbered footnotes, 68
numbered lists, 63-64
numbers fields (databases), 135
numeric formats, 95-97
   databases, 159
numeric functions, 103

O

Object Size command (Option menu), 36
object tools (Tool panel), 172-173
object-oriented graphics, 166
objects
   frames, 221
   layers, 170
objects (drawn), 169
   alignment, 181
   deleting, 176
   deselecting, 176
   duplicating, 175
   filling, 183, 185
   flipping, 182
   grouping, 181
   layers, 170
   locking, 182

Index

moving, 176
nudging, 177
resizing, 177
scaling, 177
selecting, 176
stacking order, 170
transforming, 169
online services, 217-218
connections, 201-202
disconnecting, 203
Opaque painting mode, 189
Open command (File menu), 20, 24
opening files, 24-25
Option menu commands (Object Size), 36
Options menu commands
Add Page Break, 122
Display, 106
Edit Master Page, 226
Frame Links, 223
Make Chart, 112
Painting Mode, 188
Print Range, 121
Protect Cells, 107
Scale Frame, 36
ordering slides, 259
Organize menu commands
Go To Record, 142
Sort Records, 148
orientation (SS documents), 90
Outline menu commands (New Topic), 70
outlines, 69-72
Oval tool, 172

P

page breaks, 76, 122
page numbers, 83
Page Setup command (File menu), 90
Page View mode (databases), 131-132
pages, inserting in DR documents, 187
Paint Bucket tool, 190
painting
brush size/shape, 190
editing images, 191-193
frames, 226
Tool panel, 189-191
painting (PT) documents, *see* **PT documents**
painting environment, 10, 188-195
Painting Mode command (Options menu), 188
painting modes, 188-189
Painting tool, 171
paintings
color, 193-195
color depth, 188
deselecting, 191
gradients, 193-195
image resolution, 188
moving, 192
patterns, 193-195
selecting, 191
Pane controls (windows), 31
Paragraph command (Format menu), 60
paragraph formatting
indents, 61, 62
margins, 60
WP documents, 55-56, 60-62

Index

passwords, 202
Paste command (Edit menu), 26
Paste Function command (Edit menu), 100
pasting, 25-26
   spreadsheet data, 108-109
   text
      frames, 222
      WP documents, 47
patterns in paintings, 193-195
Pen Indicator tool, 175, 185
Pen Palettes tool, 175
Pen Width tool, 185
Pencil tool, 190
Percent format (spreadsheets), 96
phone book, 210
Phone Book command (Settings menu), 209
pictogram charts, 116
pie charts, 115
pixels, 166
playing macros, 241
playing movies (QuickTime), 256-258
Pointer tool, 171
Polygon tool, 173
PowerBook, 3
preferences, 203-206, 238-240
Preferences command (Edit menu), 65
previewing master page, 227
Print command (File menu), 38
Print Range command (Options menu), 121
printing, 37-39
   envelopes, 231-236
   mailing labels, 233-235
   options, 39

page breaks, 122
ranges, 121-122
selecting printer, 37-38
spreadsheets, 121-122
Protect Cells command (Options menu), 107
protecting spreadsheets, 107
PT (painting) documents, 5, 166
   frames, 220
Publish & Subscribe, 248-253

Q–R

query by example (databases), 130
QuickTime movies, 253-258
quitting ClarisWorks, 26

RAM (random-access memory), 3, 22
ranges
   deleting, 110
   inserting, 109
   printing, 121-122
   selecting, 92
   sorting contents, 110-111
   totalling with formulas, 98-99
rearranging spreadsheets, 107-112
rearranging outlines, 70-71
receiving calls, 208-209
Record Macro command (Shortcuts menu), 242
recording macros, 240, 242-244
records (databases), 126-128
   creating for data entry, 143-144
   duplicating, 144

Index

inserting, 144
modifying for data entry, 143-144
moving between, 141
searches, 144-148
viewing as list, 141
Rectangle tool, 172
registering software, 16
Regular Polygon tool, 174
relative cell references, 98
replacing text, 54-55
   see also search and replace
requirements for installation, 13
Reshape command (Edit menu), 178
Resize box, 27
resizing
   columns, 75
   frames, 177
   layout parts, 157
   objects (drawn), 177
   text frames, 222, 224
Resolution & Depth command (Format menu), 188
Resolve spreadsheet software, 3
restoring windows, 31
right tab, 62
Rounded Rectangle tool, 172
Row Height command (Format menu), 92
rows
   deleting, 109
   inserting, 109
   tables, 77-79
   transposing, 111-112
Ruler
   copying, 67
   customizing, 66
   margins, 60
   tabs, 62-63
   units of measurement, 179
Ruler command (Format menu), 66, 179
Rulers dialog box, 66

S

Save As command (File menu), 22, 24
Save command (File menu), 24
saving files, 22-24
Scale Frame command (Options menu), 36
scaling
   frames, 36
   objects (drawn), 177
scatter charts, 115
Scientific format (spreadsheets), 96
screen, navigating, 26-37
screen captures, 195
search and replace in WP documents, 53-55
searching for records in databases, 144-148
security (spreadsheets), 107
selecting
   objects (drawn), 176
   paintings, 191
   printers, 37-38
   records (database), 142
   text in WP documents, 46-47
   windows, 29
Selection Rectangle tool, 189
selective merges, 235
series (charts), 118-119
Session menu commands (Close Connection), 203

Index

Settings menu commands
   Connection, 202
   Phone Book, 209
Shortcuts menu commands
   Edit Macros, 244
   Record Macro, 242
Shortcuts palette, 32-35
   macros, 245-246
Show Clipboard command (Edit menu), 26
Show Tools command (View menu), 32
sizing windows, 27
slide shows, 258-263
smoothing objects (drawn), 183
snaking columns, 75
software
   ClarisImpact (drawing), 3
   FileMaker Pro (database), 3
   installation, 16
   integrated software, 2-5
   MacDraw Pro (painting), 3
   MacWrite Pro (word processor), 3
   registration, 16
   Resolve (spreadsheet), 3
Sort command (Calculate menu), 110
Sort Records command (Organize menu), 148
sorting
   databases, 148-149
   spreadsheets, 110-111
spacebar, 62-63
Spelling Checker, 48-51
   correcting spelling, 49
   dictionaries, 48-49
      adding words, 51
      removing words, 51
      User dictionary, 50

splitting windows, 31-32
Spray Can tool, 191
spreadsheet (SS) documents, see **SS documents**
spreadsheet environment, 6-7
Spreadsheet tool, 171
spreadsheets, 86
   borders, 94-95
   cells
      alignment, 95
      contents, 89
      editing contents, 88-89
      formatting, 93-94
   creating, 87
   data entry, 88-89
   design, 104-105
   displaying, 106
   fonts, 94
   formatting numeric entries, 95-97
   formulas, 97-107
   frames, 225-226
      borders, 80
      creating, 87
      creating tables, 76
      text entry, 81-82
   lines, 94-95
   navigating, 89-90
   printing, 121-122
   protecting, 107
   ranges, 92
   rearranging, 107-112
   security, 107
   sorting, 110-111
SS (spreadsheet) documents, 5
   formatting, 90-97
   frames, 220
   margins, 90, 91
   orientation, 90
Stack Windows command (View menu), 28

Index

stacked area charts, 114
stacked bar charts, 113
stacking windows, 28
stacking order (objects), 170
statistical functions, 103
Style menu commands (Define Styles), 58
styles
   creating, 58, 59
   defining, 58-59
   fonts, 59-60
   modifying, 59
   text, 55
   WP documents, 57
subscribing to documents, 251-253
subsummary (database layout), 155
subtraction, 99-100
summary fields (databases), 134-135, 136
System 7 Balloon Help, 41-42

T

tab order (databases), 143
Tab Order command (Layout menu), 143
tables, 76-77
   borders, 79-81
   columns, 77-79
   lines, 79-81
   rows, 77-79
tabs, 62-63
terminal emulation, 216-217
testing macros, 246
text
   capturing (communications), 207-208
   communications settings, 207
   fields (databases), 158
   frames, 81-82, 222
   spreadsheets, 81-82, 93
   viewing outlines as, 72
   WP documents
      copying, 47
      cutting, 47
      editing, 47
      formatting, 55
      moving, 46-47
      pasting, 47
      selecting, 46-47
      styles, 55
text fields (databases), 135
text frames, 45-46, 221-222
   deleting, 224
   linking, 226
      newsletters, 222-224
      resizing, 224
   margins, 221
   pasting text, 222
text function, 103
Text tool, 171
text wrap, 44
thesaurus, 52-53
tick marks (axes), 113
Tile Windows command (View menu), 28
tiling windows, 28
time, 83
time fields (databases), 135
time format, 97
Tint painting mode, 189
titles (charts), 117
Tool panel, 32, 172-173
tools
   Drawing Tools, 171-175
   line tools, 185-186
   painting, 189-191
topics (outlines), 70-71

Index

totalling ranges in formulas, 98-99
Transformation menu commands, 193-194
transforming objects, 169
Transparent painting mode, 189
transposing rows/columns, 111-112
trigonometric functions, 104

U

underline text, 57
Undo command (Edit menu), 47
undoing, 47
units of measurement (Ruler), 179
untitled documents, 22
updating footnotes, 68
uploading files, 212-214
User dictionary (Spelling Checker), 50

V

values (databases), 137-139
variables in formulas, 106
View menu commands
   Show Tools, 32
   Stack Windows, 28
   Tile Windows, 28
viewing
   Clipboard contents, 26
   databases, 128-132
   files, 28
   outlines as text, 72
   records (databases), 141
volatile memory, 22

W

windows
   Pane controls, 31
   restoring, 31
   selecting, 29
   sizing, 27
   splitting, 31-32
   stacking, 28
   tiling, 28
word processing (WP) documents, *see* WP documents
word processing environment, 6
word processor, 44-69
word wrap, 44
WordFinder dialog box, 53
worksheets, *see* spreadsheets
WP (word processing) documents, 5
   creating, 44-45
   editing, 47
   fonts, 56-57
   formatting, 55-56
   frames, 221
   moving text, 46-47
   paragraph formatting, 60-62
   search and replace, 53-55
   selecting text, 46-47
   styles, 55, 57-59
wrapping text, 44

X–Y–Z

X-axis, 113

Y-axis, 113

Zoom box, 27
zooming, 29-31